T0223109

Lecture Notes in Computer Science 1312

Edited by G. Goos, J. Hartmanis and J. van Leeuwen

Advisory Board: W. Brauer   D. Gries   J. Stoer

Springer
Berlin
Heidelberg
New York
Barcelona
Budapest
Hong Kong
London
Milan
Paris
Santa Clara
Singapore
Tokyo

Andreas Geppert   Mikael Berndtsson (Eds.)

Rules in
Database Systems

Third International Workshop, RIDS '97
Skövde, Sweden, June 26-28, 1997
Proceedings

 Springer

Series Editors

Gerhard Goos, Karlsruhe University, Germany

Juris Hartmanis, Cornell University, NY, USA

Jan van Leeuwen, Utrecht University, The Netherlands

Volume Editors

Andreas Geppert
University of Zurich, Department of Computer Science
Winterthurerstr. 190, CH-8057 Zurich, Switzerland
E-mail: geppert@ifi.unizh.ch

Mikael Berndtsson
University of Skövde, Department of Computer Science
Box 408, S-541 28 Skövde, Sweden
E-mail: mikael.berndtsson@ida.his.se

Cataloging-in-Publication data applied for

Die Deutsche Bibliothek - CIP-Einheitsaufnahme

Rules in database systems : third international workshop ;
proceedings / RIDS '97, Skövde, Sweden, June 26 - 28, 1997.
Andreas Geppert ; Mikael Berndtsson (ed.). - Berlin ; Heidelberg ;
New York ; Barcelona ; Budapest ; Hong Kong ; London ; Milan ;
Paris ; Santa Clara ; Singapore ; Tokyo : Springer, 1997
    (Lecture notes in computer science ; Vol. 1312)
    ISBN 3-540-63516-5

CR Subject Classification (1991): H.2

ISSN 0302-9743
ISBN 3-540-63516-5 Springer-Verlag Berlin Heidelberg New York

© Springer-Verlag Berlin Heidelberg 1997
Printed in Germany

Typesetting: Camera-ready by author
SPIN 10545858   06/3142 – 5 4 3 2 1 0   Printed on acid-free paper

Preface

This book is the proceedings of the Third International Workshop on Rules in Database Systems (RIDS '97). This workshop was organized by the database groups at University of Skövde (Sweden) and at the University of Zurich (Switzerland) and was held at the University of Skövde in June 1997.

Following the success of RIDS '93 (First International Workshop on Rules in Database Systems), and RIDS '95, the aim of the successor RIDS '97 was to bring together researchers working on both theoretical and practical aspects of rules in database systems. Although extensive work has been carried out on supporting active rules and deductive rules in database systems, many questions must still be answered in order to turn these kinds of database systems into a practical technology. The RIDS '97 workshop examined the current state of the art, presented novel and innovative approaches to rule systems, discussed experiences with operational systems and real-life applications, and identified future trends and developments.

In response to the call for papers for RIDS '97, the program committee received 33 submissions. Each of them was reviewed by 3 members of the program committee, and comments were returned to the authors. Papers submitted by one of the organizing groups were reviewed by a sub-committee headed by Peter C. Lockemann. 13 papers were selected for inclusion in the workshop proceedings and presentation at the workshop. The papers covered the following aspects:

- Deductive databases
- Active database system architecture
- Events in workflow management
- Rule modelling and simulation
- Rule confluence
- Rule termination analysis
- Rule testing and validation
- Active database system design

In addition, there was one industrial presentation by USoft and one panel discussion. The industrial presentation covered recent experiences with developing real-life applications. The panel discussion addressed the future of rules in database management systems.

June 1997   Andreas Geppert
                                                             Mikael Berndtsson

Acknowledgements

We are indebted to the program committee for carefully reviewing the 33 submissions received. The program committee consisted of:

M. Bouzeghoub, University of Versailles, France
A. Buchmann, TU Darmstadt, Germany
S. Ceri, Politecnico di Milano, Italy
S. Chakravarthy, University of Florida, USA
U. Dayal, HP Laboratories, USA
O. Diaz, University of the Basque Country, Spain
K.R. Dittrich, University of Zurich, Switzerland
S. Embury, University of Aberdeen, UK
N. Gehani, Bell Laboratories, USA
A. Geppert, University of Zurich, Switzerland
M. Kersten, CWI, The Netherlands
B. Lings, University of Exeter, UK
P.C. Lockemann, University of Karlsruhe, Germany
N.W. Paton, University of Manchester, UK
T. Risch, Linköping University, Sweden
T. Sellis, National Technical University of Athens, Greece
E. Simon, INRIA, France
H. Williams, Heriot-Watt University, UK

We are also grateful to the following who helped with the reviews:
M.L. Barja (UBILAB, Switzerland), A. Behm (Univ. of Zurich, Switzerland), H. Fritschi (Univ. of Zurich, Switzerland), S. Gatziu (Univ. of Zurich, Switzerland), B. Koenig-Ries (Univ. of Karlsruhe, Germany), D. Lieuwen (Bell Laboratories, USA), D. Tombros (Univ. of Zurich, Switzerland), and A. Vaduva (Univ. of Zurich, Switzerland)

Special thanks to the following people who helped us with the local arrangements: Charlotte Rapp, Åsa Björk, Henrik Gustavsson, Per Burman, Björn Lundell, and Henrik Engström.

Finally, we would like to express our gratitude to the University of Skövde for providing financial support to the workshop.

Contents

Deductive Object-Oriented Database Systems: A Survey

Pedro R. Falcone Sampaio and Norman W. Paton
Department of Computer Science, University of Manchester
Oxford Road, Manchester, M13 9PL, United Kingdom
Fax: +44 161 275 6236 Phone: +44 161 275 6124
E-mail: [sampaiop,norm]@cs.man.ac.uk

Abstract. Deductive object-oriented databases (DOODs) seek to combine the complementary benefits of the deductive and the object-oriented paradigms in the context of databases. Research into DOODs has now been taking place for almost ten years, and a significant number of designs and implementations have been developed. This paper categorises proposals for DOODs, based on the language design strategy pursued, and compares the resulting systems in terms of the support provided for specific deductive and object-oriented features. It is shown how comprehensive proposals have emerged from significantly different design strategies, and it is argued that research on DOODs is now quite mature, in that consensus is emerging on the capabilities that it is appropriate for DOODs to support.

1 Introduction

The observation that object-oriented and deductive database systems generally have complementary strengths and weaknesses gave rise to interest in the integration of the two paradigms in the late 80s. Initial proposals involved the extension of deductive languages with limited facilities for modelling complex values [AG88], and the view was sometimes expressed that DOODs could not be developed without detracting substantially from the benefits of at least one of the component paradigms [Ull91]. However, although there has never been a flood of proposals for DOODs, there has been a steady flow of new ideas, techniques and systems throughout the 90s, so that there are now more than ten working prototypes and one product [FLV96]. It seems suitable, therefore, to review the work carried out to date, to identify the approaches that have been taken, the achievements that have been made, and to assess the quality of the current state-of-the-art.

This survey provides an overview of DOOD systems and an evaluation of language proposals. The survey is organised according to the language design strategy adopted, which highlights how new proposals for DOODs build upon earlier work on deductive systems, programming languages, or logic theory. The systems that result from the different approaches are then compared according to two orthogonal language criteria: *declarative support:* language features that support the declarative programming style; and *object-orientation support:*

language features that support the object-oriented programming style. The following proposals are reviewed in this work: Chimera, ConceptBase, Coral++, ESQL2, FLORID, Gulog, Logidata+, Logres, Noodle, Orlog, Peplom^d, Quixote, ROCK & ROLL, ROL and Validity. The choice of systems was based on the availability to the authors of an implemented prototype and/or suitable papers describing the language. There is evidence that at least a partial prototype exists for every language in the survey except Gulog, and versions of ConceptBase, FLORID, ROCK & ROLL, ROL and Quixote are available in the Internet.

The paper is organised as follows. Section 2 presents an overview of the different design strategies for DOODs from the deductive language perspective. In section 3 the proposals derived using the strategies of section 2 are compared in terms of the functionalities they support. Section 4 presents some conclusions. Throughout the paper, some familiarity with deductive database concepts, as described in [CGT90], is assumed.

2   Design Strategies

In this section, DOODs are classified according to the language design strategy exploited during their development. There is more variety in the approaches taken to the development of DOODs than was the case with deductive relational databases (DRDBs), as in the latter case an agreed data model gave rise to the development of Datalog as a widely accepted starting point for the development of practical DRDBs.

The following strategies, which are illustrated in figure 1, have been adopted in the design of DOOD systems:

Language Extension: an existing deductive language model is extended with object-oriented features. This approach is familiar from work on DRDBs such as LDL [NT89] or CORAL [RSS92], in which the syntax and semantics of Datalog were extended incrementally with negation, set terms, built in predicates, etc. In the language extension approach to DOODs, Datalog is generally an ancestor of the DOOD language, which is extended to support identity, inheritance, etc. Note that this strategy does not imply the existence of an earlier deductive database implementation or syntactic conformity with existing languages.

Language Integration: a deductive language is integrated with an imperative programming language in the context of an object model or type system. In this strategy, the resulting system supports a range of standard object-oriented mechanisms for structuring both data and programs, while allowing different and complementary programming paradigms to be used for different tasks, or for different parts of the same task. The idea of integrating deductive and imperative language constructions for different parts of a task was pioneered in the Glue-Nail DRDB [DM93], and is now adapted for object-oriented databases. The success of this strategy depends on the seamlessness of the integration of the deductive language and the imperative language.

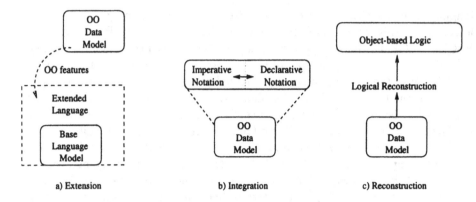

Fig. 1. Language design strategies for DOODs

Language Reconstruction: an object model is reconstructed following the rationale of Reiter [Rei84], creating a new logic language that includes object-oriented features. In this strategy, the goal is to develop an object logic that captures the essentials of the object-oriented paradigm and that can also be used as a deductive programming language in DOODs. This is a revolutionary approach in the sense that much of the associated implementation technology may have to be conceived from scratch. The driving force behind the language reconstruction strategy is an argument that language extensions fail to combine object-orientation and logic successfully [KLW95], by losing declarativeness through the introduction of extra-logical features, or by failing to capture all aspects of the object-oriented model. The major drawbacks of reconstruction are the difficulty of providing efficient implementations of all the features of the object logic and the lack of agreement on the target model to be formalised.

Within the strategies described, different approaches can be adopted, depending on the choice of the base language to be extended, the the nature of interaction between the integrated languages, or the object model reconstructed by the logic. The main approaches, examples of which are given in table 1, are:

1. Extend a Datalog-based language with object-oriented features.

2. Extend a Prolog-based language with object-oriented features.

3. Extend a SQL-based language with deduction and object-orientation.

4. Integrate a declarative rule language with an object-oriented programming language, allowing one of the languages to borrow programming constructs from the other (unilateral integration).

5. Integrate a declarative rule language with an object-oriented programming language, allowing each of the integrated languages to borrow programming constructs from the other (bilateral integration).

6. Reconstruct a data model from the database community.

7. Reconstruct a data model from the knowledge representation community.

Strategy	Approach	Proposals
Extension	1	ConceptBase[JGJS94] Logres[CCF+93] Logidata+[NST93] ROL[Liu96b]
	2	Quixote[YTM93]
	3	ESQL2[GV92b]
Integration	4	Chimera[CM94] Peplom^d[DR94] Coral++[SRSS93] Validity[FGVLV95]
	5	Noodle[MR93] ROCK & ROLL[BPF+94]
Reconstruction	6	Gulog[Dob96] Orlog[JL92]
	7	FLORID[FHKS96]

Table 1. Strategies and approaches to DOOD language design

The different strategies and approaches reflect general disagreement on how to combine object-orientation and deduction. An interesting issue is the expectations towards the delineation of an *Oblog*: the equivalent of Datalog for the object-oriented world [FPWB92]. Three lines of thinking seem to emerge from the literature: that *Oblog* is Datalog extended with object-oriented features, that *Oblog* is a reconstructed language, or that *Oblog* will never exist.

2.1 Language Extension Strategy

Language extension proposals aim to enhance the modelling power and programming style of declarative languages by supporting object-oriented features within the data models associated with such languages. The critical issues in this strategy relate to the choice of declarative language model that underlies the extension (logic programming, relational programming) and to the technique used to map features like objects, classes, object sharing, inheritance, methods and encapsulation into the declarative language.

Datalog and Prolog Extensions Extension-based DOODs have been derived incrementally from Datalog or Prolog by adding structural and behavioural features from the object-oriented model. Theoretical languages [CG88, AK89, BM92, ACM93] were proposed to provide a foundation to the strategy, with IQL [AK89] being the first theoretical language extension proposal to support the structural complexity of the main object model features (classes, identity, complex objects and inheritance). IQL had a major impact on many later DOOD languages.

There is also a substantial amount of work on concepts and techniques for extending logic programming with object-oriented features – for a comprehensive overview see [McC92, Mos94]. A brief summary of how the main object-oriented concepts can be mapped into the logic programming world is shown in Table 2.

Logic Programming	Object-Orientation
complex terms	complex values
object theories or predicate extensions	classes
OIDs in predicate extensions labels in object theories	object identity
ground instances of predicate extensions labelled object theory	objects
OID-based references label-based references	object sharing
unification through generalisations	inheritance

Table 2. Support for object-orientation within logic programming

Two alternatives to mapping structural object-oriented concepts into logic programming have been identified [CT93]: *predicate extensions* define an object as an identity-based ground instance of an extended predicate and *logical theories* define an object as a set of facts and rules defining properties of an object.

Predicate extensions

In implementations based on predicate extensions, identity is represented in the predicate by a special argument that stands for the object identifier (OID), providing an identity-based data model on top of a value-based system implementation. The creation and manipulation of OIDs is under the control of the system, which provides special methods for object creation (e.g. a *new* operator or OID invention). The management of *is-a* relationships can be done by adding clauses to each program, that enforce the *is-a* relationships defined over the corresponding schema. The following rules show the definition of system generated clauses added for managing the relationship C_1 *is-a* C_2 in Logres and Logidata+, where facts for the satisfaction of containment constraints are generated, propagating OIDs along *is-a* relationships, assuring that instances of the subclass C_1 are included in the extension of the superclass C_2.

$C_2(OID : x_0, A_1 : x_1, \ldots, A_k : x_k) \leftarrow C_1(OID : x_0, A1 : x_1, \ldots, A_k : x_k, \ldots, A_{k+h} : x_{k+h})$

$TYPE(C_2) = (A_1 : \tau_1, \ldots, A_k : \tau_k) \ TYPE(C_1) = (A_1 : \tau_1, \ldots, A_k : \tau_k, \ldots, A_{k+h} : \tau_k)$
and $x_i \in$ Attribute Names, $\tau_i \in$ Attribute Types.

Logical theories

Within the implementation based on logical theories, a set of facts and rules defines each object or class. Class hierarchies are represented by specialisation rules and OIDs can be supported by a user-defined label attached to the theory defining an object or by a built-in predicate *new* that generates the OIDs. The example in figure 2 specified in the syntax proposed in [BM92], shows two classes (stop, train_arrival) defined as theories, with declarative database updates expressed as a side-effect of the deductive process by applying the operators minus and plus to denote deletion and insertion, respectively.

```
stop:(NM,CD)
      { name(NM).
        code(CD).
        CN:change_name(N,NewN) <- -name(N), +name(NewN).
      }
train_arrival:(TC,T,PS,OC)
      {
        train_code(TC).
        time_at_stop(T).
        place_of_stop(PS) <- stop:code(PS).
        origin_code(OC) <- stop:code(OC).
      }

?- new(stop,euston,lon_e,Oid).
?- new(stop,manchester_picadilly,mcr_p,Oid).
?- new(train_arrival,t42,16:55,mcr_p,lon_e,Oid).
```

Fig. 2. Object theories

In the example, goals are used to create objects using the built-in *new* predicate. When the predicate receives as parameters the class name and the values of the properties of the object to be created, the predicate succeeds and an OID is generated for the object.

Example systems

ConceptBase is a multi-user DOOD adopting a client-server architecture that provides a CORBA compliant interface. ConceptBase supports a wide range of deductive and object-oriented features that are accompanied by graphical tools for browsing and manipulating the system. ConceptBase's language O-TELOS can be seen as an amalgamation of a declarative rule language and an object-oriented data model, where the object structure is mapped as facts, rules and integrity constraints within Datalog with negation.

Logres and Logidata+ provide a deductive language to query an object-relational data model. Logres introduces the notion of *application* as an abstraction unit for grouping rule definitions and goals relating to a specific task.

Transitions between database states in Logres are controlled by the execution of *applications* that can update the database as a side effect of the deductive process.

Quixote is a persistent constraint logic programming language with top-down evaluation extended with identity-based objects represented as labels in object theories. Methods define properties of objects, and inheritance is supported through subsumption constraints. Quixote supports a concept of module that provides encapsulation and a modular programming style, and also provides support to updates as a side effect of the query process.

ROL is a typed extension to Datalog that supports the widest range of deductive and object-oriented features within the surveyed prototypes (see tables 3 and 4). ROL provides a mechanism for representing both partial and complete information on sets and avoids procedural extensions.

The example in figure 3 in Logres illustrates the language extension strategy. In the example, the database describes a graph representing train and flight connections between stops. The flights and trains connect stops that can be airports or train stations. Classes STOP, TRAIN-STOP and FLIGHT-STOP are declared in the database schema and rules are provided to recursively compute paths among cities and the total duration of the travel. A set of intermediate nodes is computed to avoid cyclic paths of infinite duration.

```
DOMAINS SECTION
    NAME = STRING; CODE = INTEGER; TIME = INTEGER;
CLASSES SECTION
    STOP = (NM:NAME, CD:CODE);
    TRAIN-STOP = (ST:STOP, ORIGIN:STOP, DEST:STOP, T:TIME);
    FLIGHT-STOP = (ST:STOP, ORIGIN:STOP, DEST:STOP, T:TIME);
    TRAIN-STOP isa STOP;
    FLIGHT-STOP isa STOP;
ASSOCIATIONS SECTION
    PATH = (ORIGIN:STOP, DEST:STOP, INT:{S}, T:TIME);

path(origin:X,dest:Y,int:I,t:Z) <- train-stop(st:S,origin:X,dest:Y,t:Z),I=0.
path(origin:X,dest:Y,int:I,t:Z) <- flight-stop(st:S,origin:X,dest:Y,t:Z),I=0.
path(origin:X,dest:Y,int:I,t:Z) <- path(origin:X,dest:X1,int:I1,t:Z1),
                                   train-stop(st:S,origin:X1,dest:Y,t:Z2),
                                   Z=Z1+Z2,append(X1,I1,I),
                                   not member(Y,I1).
path(origin:X,dest:Y,int:I,t:Z) <- path(origin:X,dest:X1,int:I1,t:Z1),
                                   flight-stop(st:S,origin:X1,dest:Y,t:Z2),
                                   Z=Z1+Z2,append(X1,I1,I),
                                   not member(Y,I1).
```

Fig. 3. Example rules in Logres

Language extension proposals based on predicate extensions solve the problems of infinite set generation summarised in [Ull91] by supporting value-based as well as identity-based entities. In the Logres example, path is modelled as an association (unnormalised relation), and thus individual paths are not represented as objects with distinct identities.

SQL extensions ESQL2 is a language extension proposal that extends the relational model of SQL2 with deductive and object-oriented capabilities. Classes are implemented as relations extended with a system controlled attribute that stands for the OID. A rich set of generic abstract data types are supported, which can be specialised, providing a tool for building complex types based on sets, lists, bags and vector constructs. Updates are provided as an extension of the SQL2 syntax and deduction is implemented as an extension of the view mechanism of SQL2.

2.2 Language Integration Strategy

The rationale behind language integration is expressed by the following argument stated in [UZ90]:

> A declarative formulation cannot compete with the cogency and optimality of textbook algorithms for specific problems. These situations call for a mixed mode, and for the harmonious cooperation between the two modes at the language and system levels.

DOODs with integrated languages are designed to support the synergy of the different components: the logic language can be used to support those parts of an application that are suitable for declarative rule-based expression, and the imperative language can be used to support updates, input/output, and the expression of algorithms normally written in a procedural manner. Both languages operate in the context of an OO data model or type system.

A significant strength of language integration is the conventionality of its individual components. Most of the integration can be carried out without altering the defining principles of the component paradigms or introducing complex new concepts in order to achieve integration. Originality exhibited in the enactment of this strategy is found in the methodology adopted to achieve integration, rather than in the individual components that have been integrated.

The critical issues in this strategy are related to the flexibility of the integration approach (unilateral or bilateral), the choice of the source languages, and the selection of object model or type system underlying the integration.

Example systems

Chimera integrates sub-languages supporting active, imperative and declarative constructs in the context of the Chimera object model. Together with Validity and unlike other language integration proposals, it provides support for declarative integrity constraints, and with ROCK & ROLL [DPWF96], is unusual among DOODs in supporting Event-Condition-Action rules. Chimera is classified as an unilateral language integration approach, as there are limitations on the bilateral embedding of the deductive and imperative sub-languages.

Coral++ integrates the Coral rule language with the C++ type system. Arbitrary C++ objects are allowed in database facts and C++ expressions are allowed in rules (unilateral integration). An advantage of Coral++ in relation to other integrated proposals is the access provided to the popular and powerful language C++, whereas other DOODs generally exploit their own data models and languages. However, Coral++ manifests impedance mismatch problems.

Noodle provides a declarative query language for the SWORD object-oriented database system [MR92]. Noodle is integrated with the O++ language of the Ode DBMS [AG89] following a bilateral approach to integration. Noodle defines a powerful declarative query language supporting higher order features, OID-based and value-based elements in collections, and collections as first-class objects. It is the only language integration proposal to support schema browsing.

Peplom^d integrates a deductive notation with the Peplom database programming language, which is superficially similar to C. The deductive language is a significantly extended Datalog.

In ROCK & ROLL the starting point for the development of the subsequently integrated languages is an object-oriented semantic data model. The deductive language ROLL and the imperative language ROCK are then derived from this model, and integrated with minimal impedance mismatches. Type inference in ROLL prevents runtime type errors occurring across the language interface, and later work has added active [DPWF96] and spatial [FDPW97] facilities.

Validity is the first DOOD to become a product. The system integrates declarative and imperative constructs in the DEL language. Validity is classified as an unilateral language integration approach as there are limitations on the bilateral embedding of the deductive and imperative sub-languages (methods can only be implemented by the imperative component).

To illustrate language integration ideas, the example in figure 4 shows the definition of a type *stop* in ROCK & ROLL, combining imperative object-oriented and declarative styles of programming— the type definition indicates that stop is an association of other adjacent stops (defining stops that are directly linked to a stop, denoted by the set brackets symbol) and that it has properties *name*, *code* and three public methods *print*, *adjacent* and *reachable*. The *print* method displays the properties of a stop and is implemented in the imperative language ROCK. The *adjacent* method indicates if a stop is directly linked to another and *reachable* indicates if a stop is reachable from another stop. Both *adjacent* and *reachable* are implemented in the ROLL language. All methods are statically type checked, can be inherited or overridden, and can be invoked from the same program or interactively. Methods starting with the prefix *get* are system generated and are used to retrieve properties and to access members of collections.

```
type stop:
  properties:code:integer,
            name:string;
            public: {stop};
  interface: ROCK: public: print();
            ROLL: public: adjacent(stop):bool, reachable(stop):bool;
end-type;

class stop
      public:
         print()
         begin
          write "name=", get_name()@self, ",code=",get_code()@self, nl;
         end
         adjacent(stop)
         begin
          adjacent(OtherStop)@ThisStop
                              :- OtherStop == get_member@ThisStop;
         end
         reachable(stop)
         begin
           reachable(OtherStop)@ThisStop
                              :- adjacent(IntermediateStop)@ThisStop,
                                 reachable(OtherStop)@IntermediateStop;
         end
end-class
```

Fig. 4. Imperative and declarative methods in ROCK & ROLL

2.3 Language Reconstruction Strategy

The language reconstruction strategy is based on the formal description of data model concepts in a mathematical framework with the aim of formalising the notions underlying implemented systems. In the database field, logic foundations are useful for defining a declarative semantics for the data model, for underpinning query optimisation, for providing concise specifications of implemented systems, and for adding deductive capabilities.

The critical decision in this strategy relates to the nature of the object model to be reconstructed. The expressiveness, tractability and programming style of the logic will be affected by this decision.

Example systems

FLORID is a partial implementation of the features and syntax defined by F-logic [KLW95]. FLORID supports a powerful logic, departing from a frame-based knowledge representation scheme, adopting a style of programming that mixes intensional and extensional definitions and supporting higher order syntactic constructs. The notion of schema is formed by the definition of class signatures and class hierarchies, and no distinction is made between data and schema declarations.

Gulog tries to provide a more database-oriented formal foundation than F-logic, by reconstructing a more conventional object-oriented data model and supporting only first-order syntactic constructs. Gulog distinguishes between schema and instance level constructs.

Orlog departs from an object-relational data model, and supports the notions of schema and integrity constraints. Schema definitions are separated from data declarations and higher order syntactic constructs are supported.

Another difference between reconstruction proposals stems from the way that ambiguously defined object-oriented features like multiple inheritance and over-riding are dealt with: conflicts due to multiple inheritance in FLORID are solved by a non-deterministic choice of the inherited property (one of the definitions is inherited). Gulog prohibits programs with ambiguities due to multiple inheritance and Orlog does not address the issue.

Overriding is the redefinition of methods and attributes in subtypes. The combination of overriding and inheritance can cause non-monotonic behaviour. This can be noticed in the following example in FLORID:

```
person[believes_in*->god].
employee::person.
john:employee.
?- john[believes_in->X].
X/god
```

In the example, every person believes in god, employee is a subclass of person and john is an employee. With non-monotonic inheritance, if the fact john[believes_in]-> ghosts] is added to the database, the answer to the previous query is X/ghosts. Monotonic inheritance is inheritance without over-riding. In the example, after the new clause is added with monotonic inheritance, both values for X could be derived. It is interesting to note that in this example, overriding occurs at the instance level.

Overriding can be static or dynamic. With static overriding, overriding definitions replace the definition in the parent regardless of the validity of the body of the overriding definition. In dynamic overriding, a definition is overridden only if the body of the overriding clause is true. FLORID and Gulog adopt dynamic overriding while Orlog adopts static overriding.

The distinction between objects and classes also differentiates the proposals. FLORID gives full object status to all elements in the language, while Orlog and Gulog distinguish between the two concepts. Giving full object status to all elements in the language allows FLORID to perform schema browsing operations (query schema elements like classes and attributes) and also to attach properties (e.g. attributes) to schema elements.

Figure 5 shows a program in FLORID that illustrates the mix of data declarations and schema definitions, and gives an overall idea of the F-logic programming style:

```
/* class signatures ---------------------------------------------*/
/* 1 */ stop[name=>string].
/* 2 */ stop[departure@(train)=>>time;arrival@(train)=>>time].
/* 3 */ stop[adjacent=>>stop;reachable=>>stop].
/* 4 */ train[destiny=>stop;origin=>stop].
/* subclass relationship -----------------------------------------*/
/* 5 */ cargo_train::train.
/* 6 */ passenger_train::train.
/* data declarations ---------------------------------------------*/
/* 7 */ london_euston:string.
/* 8 */ stockport:string.
/* 9 */ mcr_piccadilly:string.
/*10 */ mcr_victoria:string.
/*11 */ lon_e:stop[name->london_euston].
/*12 */ stc_1:stop[name->stockport;adjacent->>{lon_e}].
/*13 */ mcr_v:stop[name->mcr_victoria].
/*14 */ mcr_p:stop[name->mcr_piccadilly;adjacent->>{mcr_v,stc_1}].
/* Rules ---------------------------------------------------------*/
/*15 */ X[reachable->>{Y}] :- X:stop[adjacent->>Y].
/*16 */ X[reachable->>{Y}] :- X:stop,X[adjacent->>Z],Z[reachable->>Y].
```

Fig. 5. Train program in FLORID

Lines 1-4 define signatures for single-valued methods(name,destiny,origin) and multi-valued methods (adjacent,departure, arrival, reachable) applicable to instances of the classes *stop* and *train* respectively. Lines 5 and 6 define the subclass relationship between classes (*cargo_train, passenger_train*) and *train*. Lines 7-14 declare instances and their properties, and lines 15 and 16 define deductive rules.

3 Comparison Criteria

In this section, general criteria are defined and used to compare the different proposals. Two main groups of criteria are used: *declarative support* and *object-orientation support*.

3.1 Declarative Support

This subsection outlines a range of declarative language features that can be used to distinguish between DOOD proposals, whatever strategy has been adopted in the design of the DOOD. It can be taken that all proposals support standard deductive features like recursive rules and negation.

Declarative Database Updates: the capability to update the database as a side-effect of the deductive process using the rule language, instead of separating query and update functions as is traditionally done in database languages. This feature is implemented in DRDBs like LDL [NT89], and is supported by extending the set of predicates that can occur in a rule, allowing predicates of the form $\alpha p(t_1, t_2, \ldots, t_n)$. The intuitive meaning of $+p(t_1, t_2, \ldots, t_n)$ is to insert the tuple or object $p(t_1, t_2, \ldots, t_n)$ into the corresponding relation or class p and the intuitive meaning of $-p(t_1, t_2, \ldots, t_n)$ is to delete the tuple or object $p(t_1, t_2, \ldots, t_n)$ from the corresponding relation or class p.

Schema Browsing: the capability to express queries on metadata contained in the schema without explicit reference to the database catalog (e.g 'Find all classes or subclasses of the *Vehicle* class that have an attribute engine_capacity'). This feature is supported in deductive languages by allowing variables to range over schema elements.

Higher Order Syntax: the capability to express rules that are not syntactically first-order logic (e.g. to quantify over predicates).

Integrity Constraints: the capability to directly support logical rules that define conditions that cannot be violated by the data, in addition to defining intensional predicates.

Formal Semantics: this criterion relates to the formal definition of the semantics of the deductive language. The semantics can be defined directly (D) or by an indirect approach of translating to a language that has a well-defined semantics (I).

The declarative support provided by the DOOD proposals from table 1 is summarised in table 3.

3.2 Object-Orientation Support

This subsection outlines a range of object-oriented features that can be used to distinguish between DOOD proposals, whatever strategy has been adopted in the design of the DOOD. It can be taken that all proposals support standard object-oriented features such as some notion of identity, some form of inheritance (in fact, all the systems reviewed here support multiple inheritance), and some form of overriding.

Object-Relational: the capability to support relations in addition to classes as elements in the data model.

Modularity: the capability to organise a complex program in terms of abstraction units. Units can be abstract data types implemented as classes that define the structure and behaviour of objects, or modules that group rules relating to a specific subpart of a task.

Encapsulation: the capability to control access to software components (rules, data, methods) defined in the abstraction units.

DOOD	Criteria				
	Declarative Database Updates	Schema Browsing	Higher Order Syntax	Integrity Constraints	Formal Semantics
Chimera	No	No	No	Yes	No
ConceptBase	No	Yes	No	Yes	[JGJS94] (I)
Coral++	No	No	No	No	No
ESQL2	No	No	No	Yes	[GV92a] (I)
FLORID	No	Yes	Yes	No	[KLW95] (D)
Gulog	No	No	No	No	[DT95] (D)
Logidata+	No	No	No	Yes	[ACMT93] (D)
Logres	Yes	No	No	Yes	[CCCR+90] (D)
Noodle	No	Yes	Yes	No	No
Orlog	No	No	Yes	Yes	[JL92] (D)
Peplom^d	No	No	No	No	No
Quixote	Yes	No	No	No	No
ROCK & ROLL	No	No	No	No	[FBPHW97] (D)
ROL	No	Yes	Yes	Yes	[Liu96a] (D)
Validity	No	No	No	Yes	No

Table 3. Declarative support criteria

Collections as 1st Class Citizens: the capability of attaching properties to collections (e.g., set attributes or class attributes) and querying the properties within the rule language.

Method Implementation: the capability to implement methods declaratively and/or procedurally. The implementation can be done using an integrated imperative language (language integration), or through functions or adorned predicates in the rule language.

The support for object-orientation provided by the DOOD proposals from table 1 is summarised in table 3.

3.3 Summary of Comparison

The comparison provided by this section has to be interpreted with some care – it is not necessarily the case that systems that have more features than others in tables 4 and 3 are the best. In many cases, it depends upon the emphasis taken by the developers. For example, declarative database updates are considered

DOOD	Criteria				
	Object-Relational	Modularity	Encapsulation	Collections as 1st Class	Method Implement.
Chimera	No	Class	Yes	Yes	Dec + Imp
ConceptBase	No	Class	Yes	Yes	Dec
Coral++	Yes	Class + Module	Yes	No	Imp
ESQL2	Yes	Class	Yes	No	Imp
FLORID	No	Class	No	Yes	Dec
Gulog	Yes	Class	No	No	Dec
Logidata+	Yes	Class	No	No	Dec
Logres	Yes	Class + Module	Yes	No	Dec
Noodle	Yes	Class	Yes	Yes	Dec + Imp
Orlog	Yes	Class	Yes	Yes	Dec
Peplom[d]	No	Class + Module	Yes	No	Dec + Imp
Quixote	No	Module	Yes	No	Dec
ROCK & ROLL	No	Class + Module	Yes	No	Dec + Imp
ROL	Yes	Class	No	Yes	Dec
Validity	No	Class	No	No	Imp

Table 4. Object-orientation support criteria

beneficial by many as they allow updates as well as querying to take place within the logic language. However, supporting updates often complicates the semantics of the logic language, and proponents of the language integration approach claim that procedural issues such as updates and I/O should be addressed outside the logic language.

4 Conclusions and Future Work

In spite of the perceived difficulties involved in combining the deductive and object-oriented paradigms for use in database systems, considerable progress has been made in this area during the last ten years. It was at first felt by many that the paradigms were incompatible, or that combining them would lead to unacceptable compromises, but in fact a number of proposals have been made that support both comprehensive deductive inference and rich object-oriented modelling facilities.

Although different strategies have been adopted to the development of DOOD systems, as outlined in section 2, much of the challenge for researchers has involved reconciling a tension between: (1) the development of powerful but complex and inefficient languages; and (2) the development of efficient but semantically inexpressive languages. It might have been anticipated that research would move incrementally from less expressive systems towards more expressive systems, but this is not how things have worked out in practice. Early proposals fell at opposite ends of this spectrum. F-logic, which was first proposed in 1989, can be seen with hindsight as rather too expressive to yield practical implementations, whereas some of the other early proposals, such as COL, can be seen as not expressive enough. Various research projects have proceeded by following the reconstruction strategy of F-logic, but with rather less expressive models and languages, and others have sought to extend systems such as COL with additional modelling and programming features. This has led to something of a consensus among the more recent systems, such as ROL and Orlog, as to what facilities it is practical to support.

While DOOD researchers working on language extensions or language reconstruction were focusing on the expressiveness of logic languages for objects, language integration researchers were playing a different game altogether. The power of the logic language is not the principal concern in a system with integrated languages, as the effectiveness of the system derives from the capabilities provided by all its components and from the ease with which they can be used together. This has led some systems, such as ROCK & ROLL, to provide a logic language that is much less powerful (complex) than would be considered appropriate in a stand-along language, on the grounds that if a task cannot be carried out by the logic language, it can always be addressed by the closely associated imperative facilities. Thus, while three strategies have been identified for the development of DOOD systems, there are really only two competing camps – one based on single language systems and the other based on multiple (two) language systems.

How does the future look for DOOD systems? The basic technology for developing DOOD systems is now reasonably well understood, although there are not yet many systems that have proved their worth on large scale applications.

Some applications that have been reported in the literature relate to metadata management [JS93] (ConceptBase), GIS [PAHW96] (ROCK & ROLL), natural language processing [TTYY93] (Quixote) and data mining [FGVLV95] (Validity).

The current risk is probably that DOOD systems will go the way of their deductive relational predecessors, by providing facilities that may be desirable in packages that are not attractive to consumers. The near total commercial failure of DRDBs can be ascribed, at least in part, to the fact that such systems were poorly integrated with existing database systems or programming languages. A number of proposals for DOODs successfully combine the complementary features of their component paradigms, but if these benefits are to be widely exploited they will probably have to be made more readily available to existing users of object-relational or object-oriented database systems.

Acknowledgements: The first author is sponsored by Conselho Nacional de Desenvolvimento Científico e Tecnológico - CNPq (Brazil) – Grant 200372/96-3.

References

[ACM93]   P. Atzeni, L. Cabibbo, and G. Mecca. Isalog(¬): a deductive language with negation for complex-object databases with hierarchies. In *Proc. of the 3rd Intl. Conference on Deductive and Object-Oriented Databases,* 1993.

[ACMT93]   P. Atzeni, L. Cabbibo, G. Mecca, and L. Tanca. The logidata+ language and semantics. In *LOGIDATA+: Deductive Databases with Complex Objects,* number 701 in LNCS. Springer-Verlag, 1993.

[AG88]   Serge Abiteboul and Stéphane Grumbach. COL: A Logic-Based Language for Complex Objects. In Joachim W.Schmidt, Stefano Ceri, and Michele Missikoff, editors, *Advances in Database Technology - EDBT'88, International Conference on Extending Database Technology,* LNCS 303, pages 271–293, Venice, Italy, March 1988. Springer-Verlag.

[AG89]   R. Agrawal and N. Gehani. Ode (object database and environment):the language and the data model. In *Proc. of ACM Sigmod Intl. Conference on Management of Data,* 1989.

[AK89]   S. Abiteboul and P. Kanellakis. Object identity as a query language primitive. In *Proc. of The ACM SIGMOD Intl. Conference on Management of Data,* 1989.

[BM92]   E. Bertino and M. Montesi. Towards a logical object-oriented programming language for databases. In *Proc. Intl. Conference on Extending Database Technology EDBT,* number 580 in LNCS, pages 168–183, 1992.

[BPF+94]   M. L. Barja, N. W. Paton, A. A. Fernandes, M. Howard Williams, and Andrew Dinn. An effective deductive object-oriented database through language integration. In *Proc. of the 20th VLDB Conference,* 1994.

[CCCR+90]   F. Cacace, S. Ceri, S. Crespi-Reghizzi, L. Tanca, and R. Zicari. Integrating object-oriented data modeling with a rule-based programming paradigm. In *Proc. of the ACM SIGMOD Intl. Conference on Management of Data,* 1990.

[CCF+93]   F. Cacace, S. Ceri, P. Fraternali, S. Paraboschi, and L. Tanca. An overview of the logres system. In I. S. Mumick, editor, *Proc. of the Workshop on Combining Declarative and Object-Oriented Databases,* 1993.

[CG88]   Q. Chen and G. Gardarin. An implementation model for reasoning with complex objects. In *ACM-SIGMOD International Conference on Management of Data,* 1988.

[CGT90]   S. Ceri, G. Gottlob, and L. Tanca. *Logic Programming and Databases.* Springer-Verlag, Berlin, 1990.

[CM94]   S. Ceri and R. Manthey. Chimera: A model and language for active dood systems. In *Proc. of the East/West Database Workshop,* pages 3–16, 1994.

[CT93]   S. Ceri and L. Tanca. Bridging objects with logical rules: Towards object-oriented deductive databases. In *Logidata+: Deductive Databases with Complex Objects (LNCS 701).* Springer-Verlag, 1993.

[DM93]   M. A. Derr and S. Morishita. Design and implementation of the glue-nail database system. In *Proc. of the ACM SIGMOD Intl. Conference on Management of Data,* 1993.

[Dob96]   G. Dobbie. *Foundations of Deductive Object-Oriented Database Systems.* PhD thesis, Victoria University Of Wellington, Comp. Science Dept., 1996.

[DPWF96]   A. Dinn, N.W. Paton, M.H. Williams, and A.A.A. Fernandes. An Active Rule Language for ROCK & ROLL. In R. Morrison and J. Kennedy, editors, *Proc. 14th British National Conference on Databases*, pages 36–55. Springer-Verlag, 1996.

[DR94]   P. Dechamboux and C. Roncancio. Integrating deductive capabilities into an object-oriented database programming language. In *Proc. of 10 Journées Bases de Données Avancées*, 1994.

[DT95]   G. Dobbie and R. Topor. On the declarative and procedural semantics of deductive object-oriented systems. *Journal of Intelligent Information Systems*, 4:193–219, 1995.

[FBPHW97]   A. A. A. Fernandes, M. L. Barja, N. W. Paton, and M. Howard-Williams. The formalisation of rock & roll: A deductive object-oriented database system. *to appear in Information and Software Technology*, 1997.

[FDPW97]   A.A.A. Fernandes, A. Dinn, N.W. Paton, and M.H. Williams. Extending a Deductive Object-Oriented Database System with Spatial Data Handling Facilities. 1997. submitted for publication.

[FGVLV95]   O. Friesen, G. Gauthier-Villars, A. Lefebvre, and L. Vieille. Applications of deductive object-oriented databases using del. In Raghu Ramakrishnan, editor, *Applications of Logic Databases*, chapter 1, pages 1–22. Kluwer Academic Publishers, 1995.

[FHKS96]   J. Frohn, R. Himmeroder, P. Kandzia, and C. Schlepphorst. *How to Write F-Logic Programs in FLORID: A Tutorial for the Database Language F-Logic*. Institut Fur Informatik, Universitat Freiburg, Germany, version 1.0 edition, September 1996.

[FLV96]   O. Friesen, A. Lefebvre, and L. Vieille. VALIDITY: Applications of a DOOD System. In *Proc. EDBT*, pages 131–134. Springer-Verlag, 1996.

[FPWB92]   A. A. Fernandes, N. W. Paton, M. H. Williams, and A. Bowles. Approaches to deductive object-oriented databases. *Information Systems*, 34(12):787–803, 1992.

[GV92a]   G. Gardarin and P. Valduriez. Esql: An object-oriented sql with f-logic semantics. In *Proc. Intl. Conference on Data Engineering*, 1992.

[GV92b]   G. Gardarin and P. Valduriez. Esql2 - extending sql2 to support object-oriented and deductive databases. Technical report, INRIA, 1992.

[JGJS94]   M. Jarke, R. Gallerrsdorfer, M. Jeusfeld, and M. Staudt. Conceptbase - a deductive object base for meta data management. *Journal of Intelligent Information Systems*, 3:167–192, 1994.

[JL92]   H. M. Jamil and L. V. S. Lakshmanan. Orlog: A logic for semantic object-oriented models. In *Proc. of the ACM Conference in Knowledge Management - CIKM*, 1992.

[JS93]   M. Jarke and M. Staudt. An application perspective to deductive object bases. In *Workshop on Combining Declarative and Object-Oriented Databases*, 1993.

[KLW95]   M. Kifer, G. Lausen, and J. Wu. Logical foundations of object-oriented and frame-based languages. *Journal of the ACM*, May 1995.

[Liu96a]   M. Liu. Rol: A deductive object base language. *Information Systems*, 21(5):431–457, 1996.

[Liu96b]   M. Liu. The rol deductive object base language. In *Proc. of 7th Intl.*

Workshop on Databases and Expert Systems Applications (DEXA). IEEE-CS Press, 1996.

[McC92]   F. G. McCabe. *Logic and Objects*. Prentice-Hall International, 1992.

[Mos94]   C. Moss. *Prolog++ The Power of Object-Oriented and Logic Programming*. Addison-Wesley, 1994.

[MR92]   I. S. Mumick and K. A. Ross. Sword: A declarative object-oriented database architecture. Technical report, AT&T Bell Labs., 1992.

[MR93]   I. S. Mumick and K. A. Ross. Noodle: A language for declarative querying in an object-oriented database. In *Proc. of the Third Intl. Conference on Deductive and Object-Oriented Databases*, volume 760 of *LNCS*. Springer-Verlag, 1993.

[NST93]   U. Nanni, S. Salza, and M. Terranova. The logidata+ prototype system. In *Logidata+: Deductive Databases and Complex Objects*, number 701 in Lecture Notes in Computer Science. Springer-Verlag, 1993.

[NT89]   S.A. Naqvi and S. Tsur. *A Logical Language for Data and Knowledge Bases*. Computer Science Press, Rockville, MD, 1989.

[PAHW96]   N. Paton, A. Abdelmoty, and M. Howard-Williams. Programming spatial databases: A deductive object-oriented approach. In Taylor & Francis, editor, *Innovations in GIS 3*, 1996.

[Rei84]   R. Reiter. Towards a logical reconstruction of relational database theory. In M. L. Brodie, J. Mylopoulos, and J. Schmidt, editors, *On Conceptual Modelling: Perspectives from Artificial Intelligence, Databases and Programming Languages*. Springer-Verlag, 1984.

[RSS92]   R. Ramakrishnan, D. Srivastava, and S. Sudarshan. CORAL-Control, Relations and Logic. In *Proc. of the 18th Intl. Conference on Very Large Databases*, pages 239–250. Morgan Kaufman, 1992.

[SRSS93]   D. Srivastava, R. Ramakrishnan, P. Seshadri, and S. Sudarshan. Coral++: Adding object-orientation to a logic database language. In *Proc. of the 19th VLDB Conference, Dublin, Ireland*, 1993.

[TTYY93]   S. Tojo, H. Tsuda, H. Yasukawa, and K. Yokota. Quixote as a tool for natural language processing. Technical Report TM-1282, ICOT Research Center - Japan, 1993.

[Ull91]   J. Ullman. A comparision between deductive and object-oriented database systems. In *Proceedings of the 2nd Intl. Conference on Deductive and Object-Oriented Databases*, 1991.

[UZ90]   J. Ullman and C. Zaniolo. Deductive databases: Achievements and future directions. *ACM - SIGMOD Records*, 19(4), December 1990.

[YTM93]   K. Yokota, H. Tsuda, and Y. Morita. Specific features of a deductive object-oriented database language quixote. Technical report, Institute for New Generation Computer Technology (ICOT), 1993.

Integrating Dynamic Aspects into Deductive Object-Oriented Databases

Wolfgang May*   Christian Schlepphorst**   Georg Lausen

Institut für Informatik, Universität Freiburg, Germany
{may,schlepph,lausen}@informatik.uni-freiburg.de

Abstract. We show how the dynamics of database systems can be modeled by making states first-class citizens in an object-oriented deductive database language. With states at the same time acting as objects, methods, or classes, several concepts of dynamic entities can be implemented, allowing an intuitive, declarative modeling of the application domain. Exploiting the natural stratification induced by the state sequence, the approach also provides an implementable operational semantics.

The method is applicable to arbitrary object-oriented deductive database languages which provide a sufficiently flexible syntax and semantics. Provided an implementation of the underlying database language, any specification in the presented framework is directly executable, thus unifying specification, implementation, and metalanguage for proving properties of a system.

The concept is applied to F-Logic. Besides the declarative semantics given by the rules of a State-F-Logic program, the use of F-Logic's inheritance semantics for modeling states provides an effective operational semantics exploiting the naturally given state-stratification. State-F-Logic programs can be executed using the FLORID implementation.

1 Introduction

Rules in database systems appear twofold: *Deductive* rules are used to express knowledge within states, and, orthogonally, *active* rules derive and express actions to be performed in transitions between states. In general, for modeling a temporally changing application domain, a more or less explicit notion of state is needed. Especially in deductive frameworks, integrating states explicitly into a database language provides additional flexibility and clarity in modeling, also supplying a model-theoretic base for reasoning about the database behavior. From the theory defined by the program specifying and implementing the deductive *and* dynamic behavior, correctness and liveness properties can be stated and verified using standard formal methods, such as temporal logics. Thus, for example, workflow systems can be defined, implemented, and validated from the same given specification/implementation.

In this paper, we present an abstract concept for modeling dynamic behavior by integrating explicit states into deductive, object-oriented frameworks. State

---

* Supported by grant no. GRK 184/1-97 of the Deutsche Forschungsgemeinschaft.
** Supported by the Deutsche Forschungsgemeinschaft, La 598/3-2.

changes can be reflected by dynamic objects, dynamic methods, or dynamic classes, allowing an intuitive modeling of the application domain.

The concept is applied to F-Logic [KLW95], which by providing the required semantic and syntactic flexibility allows for a comprehensive treatment of state-changes and updates in databases. Providing as well a model-theoretic, declarative semantics as an operational semantics which is implemented by the FLORID system, State-F-Logic acts at the same time as specification language, implementation language, and metalanguage for proving properties of a system.

The paper is structured as follows: the introduction is completed with a review of related work. In Section 2, the roles of states in an object-oriented model are investigated. In Section 3, semantical aspects of state changes are analyzed, leading to a classification of rules wrt. their temporal scope and a class of programs suitable for specification and implementation of database systems. In Section 4, the approach is instantiated for F-Logic. Section 5 illustrates the concept and its application by examples. Section 6 closes with some concluding remarks.

Related Work. The temporal, dynamic aspect of databases can be regarded as orthogonal to the static, data-oriented aspect: A single-state framework can be transferred into a multi-state framework by *versioning* (e.g. [TCG$^+$93]), i.e. attaching an additional dimension by duplicating and indexing the single-state framework. Versioning can be employed with different granularity, e.g. the whole database, relations, objects, etc. In relational database languages, explicit states are introduced via *reification*, i.e., by adding an additional argument to each relation, corresponding to versioning of relations. Following this way, in [BCW93] (*Datalog$_{1S}$*) and [Zan93] (*XY-Datalog*), *Datalog* has been extended to explicit states. *Templog* [AM89] is another extension of Datalog, using temporal logic operators. Datalog$_{1S}$, XY-Datalog, and Templog have been proven to be equivalent. A similar concept with explicit states in Datalog, *Statelog*, has been presented in [LML96]. There, every atom $R(\bar{x})$ is augmented by a state term S to $[S]R(\bar{x})$. Thus, Statelog amounts to versioning the whole database. Since complex state terms are allowed, Statelog is not bound to linear time, but also allows branching or hierarchical state spaces. Versioning in object-oriented databases is dealt with in [CJ90]. There, the granularity of versioning is by objects, each database version consists of a version of each object stored in the system. Updates and versioning of objects in F-Logic has been presented in [KLS92]. There, updates are restricted to the form *ins*, *mod*, and *del* of method applications. Transaction Logic [BK94] is a deductive language focussing on the dynamic acspects of processes, supporting an abstract notion of states as theories. In [FWP97], an active rule language is incorporated into an object-oriented deductive database concept by introducing explicit states into the sublanguages concerned with events, conditions, and actions. Summarizing, in these approaches, the temporal aspect is not actually *integrated* into the modeling.

Notation. Object-oriented models can be represented by three types of atoms, i.e. method applications, class membership, and the subclass relation. In order to obtain a uniform notation, we will use F-Logic syntax (cf. Section 4) throughout this paper: o[m→v] denotes that application of method m to object o results in the value v. Parameterized methods are written as o[m@(x$_1$,...,x$_n$)→v]. Furthermore, o:c denotes that o is a member of class c; and c::d denotes that c is a subclass of d. We will use capital letters for variables.

2 The Roles of States in an Object-Oriented Model

As mentioned in the previous paragraph, every object-oriented structure can be encoded into a relational schema, using atoms meth_appl(o,m,v), isa(o,c), and subcl(c,d). In this modeling, states can be introduced in the same way as in relational systems, via reification/versioning, i.e. augmenting every relation by an additional argument, denoting the state. Beyond the fact that the relational encoding impairs the intuitive modeling capabilities provided by the object-oriented paradigm, with this approach, states are not really integrated as first-order citizens into the modeling.

In an object-oriented modeling, providing a rich variety of concepts to cover different roles, such as objects, class hierarchy, and methods, there are several possibilities how states can interfere with entities of the application domain. Moreover, for every entity, it can be chosen individually how to model this interference. An important point when modeling large systems is that in every state transition, only some objects, classes, and methods will be affected. To take care of this, *abstract objects*, the "objects" of the application domain (e.g. the persons x, y), are distinguished from *object instances* which represent x and y at certain time point(s). Thus, if in state s, x is married to y, e.g. in x[married@(s)→y], x and y refer to the abstract objects, whereas, detailed state-dependent information about x in state s is provided by the *instance* of x in state s. The same applies to classes.

States as objects: If the focus is on the computation sequence represented by a specification, it is preferable to regard states s as objects. Abstract objects o act on them as methods, addressing the instance i corresponding to object o in this state. Then, state changing is simply modeled by changing the interpretation of methods from state to state.

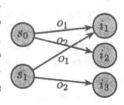

Dynamic objects: Objects changing their behavior only from time to time can be modeled by the concept of dynamic objects, i.e., for an abstract object o, a state s is a method, giving the instance of o corresponding to state s. In this case, the result of applying some method m to an object o in state s is derived as the result of the application of m to the corresponding instance.

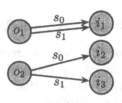

Dynamic classes: Dynamic classes are closely related with dynamic objects since classes and objects can be seen as two roles of the same entities (cf. F-Logic): For an abstract class c, a state s is a method, giving the instance of the class c_s in this state. Dynamic classes are suitable if over a computation, classes change their extension or some (default) properties inherited to all their members:

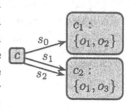

If an object instance i is a member of class c in state s, $i : c_s$ s.t. $c[s \to c_s]$, it inherits some properties from the instance of the class in this state (in general, these are dynamic methods; cf. Example 5).

Dynamic methods: If for some object, only parts of its behavior are changing, those can be modeled by dynamic methods (cf. Example 6). For an object o, a state s is an additional argument of a method m, $o[m@(s) \to X]$, giving the value of the method in this state. The concept of dynamic methods is in some sense complementary to dynamic objects.

States as classes: A state can be regarded as a class, being able to have other states as subclasses and/or members, $s' :: s$ resp. $s' : s$ and to inherit properties to them.

A dynamic *EDB* entity is an instance whose behavior in some state is derived from its behavior in the predecessor state, i.e., by frame rules, whereas the behavior of a dynamic *IDB* entity is derived from the behavior of other entities in the same state.

For providing this semantical flexibility when choosing an optimal way for modeling changing properties, the object-oriented facet of the framework to be used must allow entities to act simultaneously as objects, classes, and methods. Additionally, the deductive facet should also support this flexibility by allowing variables to occur at arbitrary positions of rules, standing for arbitrary entities.

Especially, "states as objects", "dynamic objects", and "dynamic classes" require variables to appear at method positions: In "states as objects", the objects are methods to states, thus, variables at object positions become variables at method positions. In "dynamic objects" and "dynamic classes", states appear as methods, thus state variables appear as variables at method positions. Both approaches also require object creation, anonymous objects, and anonymous classes.

"Dynamic methods" corresponds directly to reification in relational frameworks, but must be complemented by one of the other approaches to cover also a state-dependent class-membership and class hierarchy.

3   States and Rules

For the abstract treatment, assume a deductive, object-oriented framework, called $\mathfrak{X}$, providing the facilities mentioned in the previous section. $\mathfrak{X}$ defines the syntactic notions of terms, atoms, literals, rules, and programs (recall that a logical rule is of the form $h \leftarrow b$ where h is an $\mathfrak{X}$-atom, and b is a conjunction of $\mathfrak{X}$-literals), and the semantic notions of an $\mathfrak{X}$-structure and a truth relation $\models$ between $\mathfrak{X}$-structures and $\mathfrak{X}$-formulas. As usual, for an $\mathfrak{X}$-structure $\mathfrak{I}$ and a ground instance of an $\mathfrak{X}$-rule $r := h \leftarrow b$, $\mathfrak{I} \models r$ iff $\mathfrak{I} \models b \rightarrow h$, and $\mathfrak{I}$ is a model of an $\mathfrak{X}$-program P iff $\mathfrak{I} \models r$ for all ground instances of rules r of P. Let $\mathfrak{D}(P)$ denote $\mathfrak{X}$'s notion of declarative semantics, assigning an $\mathfrak{X}$-structure to every $\mathfrak{X}$-program P (for instance, if $\mathfrak{X}$ is first-order logic, $\mathfrak{D}_{FO}(P)$ could be the well-founded model of P).

Definition 1 (State-$\mathfrak{X}$-Structure) A *State-$\mathfrak{X}$-structure* $\mathfrak{I}$ is an $\mathfrak{X}$-structure where the universe $\mathfrak{U} = \mathfrak{U}' \,\dot\cup\, \mathfrak{S}$ consists of a classical universe $\mathfrak{U}'$ and a distinguished universe $\mathfrak{S}$, the state space. □

For modeling database behavior, some acyclic ordering on the state space $\mathfrak{S}$ is required. In this paper, we assume $\mathfrak{S} = (\mathbb{N}, <)$. In general, arbitrary state spaces can be modeled, for instance branching models, hierarchical models (as presented for Statelog in [LML96]), or even a possible-worlds semantics can be specified. For states, the notions of "next" state(s), "earlier", and "later", expressed by atoms $S > T$ or $S = T+n$ (occurring in the bodies of rules) play an important role.

Definition 2 For a linear state space $\mathfrak{S}$, a state $s \in \mathfrak{S}$, and a State-$\mathfrak{X}$-structure $\mathfrak{I}$ with a universe $\mathfrak{U}' \cup \mathfrak{S}$, the part which is *known in state s*, denoted by $\mathfrak{I}|_{\leq s}$ is obtained by restricting $\mathfrak{I}$ to the universe $\mathfrak{U}' \cup \{s' \in \mathfrak{S} \mid s' \leq s\}$. □

Given an $\mathfrak{X}$-program P, the database evolution is determined by an initial database D and a sequence $E_0, E_1, \ldots$, where each E_i is the set of events occurring in state i, leading to the transition to state $i+1$. For simplicity, assume a mapping which maps every set E_i to a E_i' of ground $\mathfrak{X}$-atoms, representing the events in state i.

Example 1 For instance, an event *move x to y* occurring in state s is encoded as x[moveTo@(s)→y]. □

Definition 3 A State-$\mathfrak{X}$-structure is a model of P, D, and $E_0, E_1, \ldots, E_n$ (as above) if $\mathfrak{X} \models P \cup D \cup E_0' \cup \ldots \cup E_n'$. The *declarative semantics* of a State-$\mathfrak{X}$-program P wrt. D and $E_0, \ldots, E_n$ as above is defined as $\mathfrak{D}(P \cup D \cup E_0' \cup \ldots \cup E_n')$. □

When describing database *evolution* by a State-$\mathfrak{X}$-program, a model $\mathfrak{I}$ is generated by successively computing its restrictions $\mathfrak{I}|_{\leq 0}, \mathfrak{I}|_{\leq 1}, \ldots$. To ensure a proper sequence, if some state is reached, *no* atoms must be derived which contribute to the interpretation relevant to a previous state. Also, as long as there are no events in a state s, no facts about state $s+1$ are derived.

Definition 4 A State-$\mathfrak{X}$-program P is *incremental* if for every D, $E_0, \ldots, E_n$ as above, with $\mathfrak{I} := \mathfrak{D}(P \cup D \cup E_0' \cup \ldots \cup E_n')$, for every $s \in \mathbb{N}$, the following holds:

$$\mathfrak{I}_{\leq s+1} = \mathfrak{D}(P \cup \mathfrak{I}_{\leq s} \cup E_s') \,.$$

□

Obviously, incremental programs do not only give a declarative specification, but provided an implementation of $\mathfrak{D}$, can also serve as an implementation of the database system. In the sequel, a sufficient *syntactical* criterion for an $\mathfrak{X}$-program to be incremental is developed based on considering *state terms*: Presume that in every rule, every term s denoting a state also occurs in an atom s:state in the body[3]. Then, s is called a state term.

Definition 5 A *state-ground* instance of an $\mathfrak{X}$-rule is obtained by replacing all state variables of the rule by some elements of $\mathfrak{S}$ (e.g. natural numbers). A state ground instance can be given as an assignment $\beta := \{s_1/n_1, \dots, s_k/n_k\}$ of elements of $\mathfrak{S}$ to state terms.

A *state-ground model* of an $\mathfrak{X}$-rule is a state-ground instance such that all elements of $\mathfrak{S}$ which are replaced for state terms satisfy the requirements imposed by the rule for states/natural numbers. □

Example 2 For a rule $h(t) \leftarrow \dots$, s:state, t: state, $t > s$, $\dots$, every $\beta \colon (s, t) \to \mathbb{N}^2$ is a state-ground instance, but only those $\beta \colon (s, t) \to \{(n, m) \in \mathbb{N}^2 \mid m > n\}$ are state-ground models. □

State-$\mathfrak{X}$-rules can be classified wrt. their temporal scope (cf. [LML96]):

Definition 6 (Rule Types for Linear State Spaces)
A State-$\mathfrak{X}$ rule $r = h \leftarrow b$ is

- *global* if there occurs no state term in it.
- *local* if there is at least one state term S occurring in h, and for every state-ground model β of $h \wedge b$, for all state terms S_i, S_j occurring in r, $\beta(S_i) = \beta(S_j)$.
- *progressive* if for every state-ground model β of $h \wedge b$, there is a state term S occurring in h s.t. $\beta(S) \geq \beta(T_i)$ for all other state terms T_i occurring in r.
- *definite progressive* if there is a state term S occurring in h such that for all other state terms T_i occurring in r, there is a $k_i \in \mathbb{N}$ s.t. for every state-ground model β of $h \wedge b$, $\beta(S) = \beta(T_i) + k_i$.
  (*strictly definite progressive*, if each $k_i > 0$ and S does not occur in the body except in an atoms comparing S to other state terms).
  For a definite progressive rule, its *temporal scope* is defined to be the maximum of the above k_i.
- *1-progressive* if it is definite progressive with $k_i = 1$ for all i (analogous *strong 1-progressive*).
- *collective* if h contains no state term, but b contains one or more state terms.
- *backwards* a state-ground model β s.t. there is a state term S occurring in b such that for every state term T occuring in h, $\beta(T) < \beta(S)$.

Note, that local rules are also definite progressive rules with $k_i = 0$ for all i. □

Since the above criteria refer only to elements of S, the above properties can be decided without regarding any object-oriented features, solely by reasoning about the set S and its partial ordering.

---

[3] or s:x for some subclass x of state

Example 3 The rules

O.T[M→X] ← S:state, T:state, O.S[M→X], T= S + 1, not O.change@(S,M)[ ].
O.T[M→Q] ← S:state, T:state, T= S + 1, O[change@(S,M)→Q].

are 1-progressive: in every state-ground model, due to the literal T= S + 1, $\beta(T) = \beta(S)+1$. These rules act as frame rules for methods of dynamic objects, i.e., objects o which have an individual instance $o.s$ for every state s.
The rule

P[hasTalkedTo→→X] ← P[talksWith@(S)→X], S:state.

is collective: at the end of a workflow, for every person P, the method hasTalkedTo gives all persons, P has talked with. □

Obviously, for *specifying* database behavior reasonably, only global and progressive rules make sense (a past database state cannot be changed). Especially, the EDB is computed by 1-progressive rules, and the IDB is computed by local rules. Progressive rules with a scope > 1 are used mainly for transaction definitions, coupling modes etc.

Theorem 1 *Every program P containing only progressive rules and not deriving any facts about a state $s+1$ if there are no events in state s is incremental.* □

Clearly, backward rules impair the temporal stratification (and also the intuitive understanding of a running database system), they do not fit into the presented approach.
Note, that collective rules are problematic: For P[hasTalkedTo→→X], the answer set is different in every state s, although not directly visible from the rule. On the other hand, for reasoning *about* database behavior, collective and global rules can be quite useful. When modeling and reasoning about database behavior a distinguished set $\mathfrak{M}$ of ground atoms represents the knowledge *about* a process. Here, for instance, for every x,y of the active domain, the atom y[hasTalkedTo→→x] is in $\mathfrak{M}$ (for example, if a workflow should guarantee, that at the end, every person has talked to every other person).

Definition 7 A State-$\mathfrak{X}$-program P is *incremental modulo* a set $\mathfrak{M}$ *of ground atoms* if for every $D, E_0,\ldots,E_n$ as above, for $\mathfrak{I} := \mathfrak{D}(P \cup D \cup E_0' \cup \ldots \cup E_n')$, for every $s \in \mathbb{N}$, the following holds:

$$\mathfrak{I}_{\leq s+1}\backslash\mathfrak{M} = (\mathfrak{D}(P \cup \mathfrak{I}_{\leq s} \cup E_s'))\backslash\mathfrak{M}$$
$$= (\mathfrak{D}(P \cup \mathfrak{I}_{\leq s}\backslash\mathfrak{M} \cup E_s'))\backslash\mathfrak{M} .$$
□

Theorem 2 *Let P be a State-$\mathfrak{X}$-program containing only global, progressive, and collective rules and $\mathfrak{M}$ a set of ground atoms. Then, P is incremental modulo $\mathfrak{M}$ if $\mathfrak{M}$ contains all ground atoms unifying with heads of collective rules and no atom from $\mathfrak{M}$ is used to derive any state-dependent information.* □

This corresponds to the intuitive understanding: collective rules are not used to derive data of the application domain, but to derive information *about* the running process.

Definition 8 For a State-$\mathfrak{X}$-program P which is incremental modulo a set $\mathfrak{M}$ of ground atoms representing knowledge, a database D, sets $E_0, E_2, \ldots$ of events, and $\mathfrak{I} := \mathfrak{D}(P \cup D \cup E_0 \cup E_1 \cup \ldots)$, the *operational semantics* is defined as the sequence $\mathfrak{I}_{\leq 0} \backslash \mathfrak{M}, \mathfrak{I}_{\leq 1} \backslash \mathfrak{M}, \ldots$. □

Theorem 3 *For a State-$\mathfrak{X}$-program P which is incremental modulo a set $\mathfrak{M}$ of ground atoms, the database in state $s+1$ can be computed from the database D_s and a set of events E_s as $D_{s+1} = \mathfrak{D}(P \cup D_s \cup E_s)$.* □

Now, after identifying a class of programs suitable for specifying *and* implementing dynamic systems, the details of modeling an evolving system can be considered.

In general, each state consists of several stages $stage_1, stage_2, \ldots, stage_n$; for instance, computing the EDB, then computing the IDB, and then deriving the actions to be performed in the transition to the successor state. With this, the rules have to be associated to stages:

Definition 9 For every rule r, a state term S occurring in r is a *governing* state term if for every state-ground model of r, $\beta(S)$ is maximal among the set $\{\beta(T) \mid T \text{ is a state term in } r\}$. □

Note that for local or definite progressive rules, the head contains at least one governing state term. Assume that for every local or progressive rule, at least one governing state term S of the rule is associated to one of the stages via S:stage$_i$. The partitioning of rules into stages imposes a kind of application-semantic stratification along the temporal axis which corresponds to the execution of a database system: each state represents one (or several successive) fixpoint(s). Since in general, local stratification is undecidable [CB94], for providing an evaluation and implementation for state-$\mathfrak{X}$-programs according to the above ideas, some mechanism is needed which controls the application of rules dependent on the instantiation of their state variables, their association to stages, and the existence of events.

4 Applying the Concept to F-Logic

F-Logic [KLW95] is a deductive, object-oriented database language, combining the advantages of deductive databases with the rich modeling capabilities (objects, methods, class hierarchy, non-monotonic inheritance, signatures) of the object-oriented data model. The syntax and semantics satisfies the requirements stated in Section 2 for exploiting the conceptual flexibility of states in an object-oriented framework. For the full syntax and semantics in all details, the reader is referred to [KLW95, FHKS96]. Here, only the features which are relevant for handling explicit states are presented. The modeling directly exploits F-Logic's inheritance mechanism and dynamic class-membership; the other features – both the rich built-in semantical concepts and the syntactical opportunities – make an intuitive modeling of the application domain possible, which will show up in the examples. F-Logic has been implemented in FLORID (F-LOgic Reasoning In Databases) [FHK+97][4].

---

[4] available at http://www.informatik.uni-freiburg.de/~dbis/flogic-project.html.

For a short glance, the syntax and semantics can be described as follows:

- The alphabet of an F-Logic language consists of a set $\mathcal{F}$ of *object constructors*, playing the role of function symbols, a set $\mathcal{V}$ of variables, several auxiliary symbols, containing), (,], [, $\rightarrow$, $\leftrightarrow$, $\twoheadrightarrow$, $\leftrightarrow\!\!\!\rightarrow$, :, and the usual first-order logic connectives. For convention, object constructors start with lowercase letters whereas variables start with uppercase ones.
- *id-terms* are composed from object constructors and variables. Id-terms are interpreted as elements of the universe.

In the sequel, let O, C, D, M, Q_i, S, S_i, ScM, and MvM stand for id-terms.

- A *method application* is an expression $M@(Q_1, \ldots, Q_k)$.
- if $M@(Q_1, \ldots, Q_k)$ is a method application and O an id-term, the *path expression* $O.(M@(Q_1, \ldots, Q_k))$, denoting the object resulting from applying $M@(Q_1, \ldots, Q_k)$ to O, can occur instead of an id-term.
- An *is-a assertion* is an expression of the form $O : C$ (object O is a member of class C), or $C :: D$ (class C is a subclass of class D).
- The following are *object atoms*:
  - $O[ScM@(Q_1, \ldots, Q_k) \rightarrow S]$: applying the *scalar* method ScM with arguments $Q_1, \ldots, Q_k$ to O – as an object – results in S,
  - $O[ScM@(Q_1, \ldots, Q_k) \leftrightarrow S]$: O – as a class – provides the *inheritable scalar* method ScM to its members, which, if called with arguments $Q_1, \ldots, Q_k$ results in S,
  - $O[MvM@(Q_1, \ldots, Q_k) \twoheadrightarrow \{S_1, \ldots, S_n\}]$: applying the *multivalued* method MvM with arguments $Q_1, \ldots, Q_k$ to O results in some S_i.
  - $O[MvM@(Q_1, \ldots, Q_k) \leftrightarrow\!\!\!\rightarrow \{S_1, \ldots, S_n\}]$, analogous for an *inheritable multivalued* method.
- *Formulas* are built from is-a assertions and object atoms by first-order logic connectives and quantifiers.
- An F-Logic *rule* is a logic rule h $\leftarrow$ b over F-Logic's atoms, i.e. is-a assertions and object atoms.
- An F-Logic *program* is a set of rules.

The syntax shows that in F-Logic, entities, described via *id-terms*, act at the same time as classes, objects, and methods. Also, variables can occur at arbitrary positions of formulas. Thus, states can be integrated into F-Logic as first-class citizens like all other entities, and they can be replaced by state variables in all positions.

4.1 Programming Explicit States in F-Logic

In F-Logic, the state-by-state evaluation can be enforced using its trigger mechanism which allows insertion of atoms into the database after a deductive fixpoint has been reached. Originally, this mechanism is used to implement non-monotonic inheritance: Non-monotonic inheritance of a property from a class to an object takes place if a) it is inheritable, and b) no other property can be derived for the object. Thus, inheritance is done *after* pure deduction: fixpoint computation and inheriting one fact at a time alternate until an outer fixpoint is reached.

This mechanism can be utilized to define a sequence of deductive fixpoint computations: Every (abstract) state passes through several stages until it is computed completely. This is implemented using a distinguished class **state**, having subclasses $stage_1 \ldots stage_n$. Every stage corresponds to a fixpoint computation. When a stage is computed completely, a trigger inserts the facts which create the next stage resp. state. This is implemented via inheritable methods, defining suitable triggers.

The schema in Table 1 gives the rules for handling a four-stage state concept for an active database system, consisting of generating the EDB, calculating the IDB, receiving users' requests, and finally computing the changes to be executed in the transition to the next state:

(A) inheritable methods:	(B) the stage sequence:
stage1::state[ready_edb•↦true].	S:stage2 ← S.ready_edb[ ].
stage2::state[ready_idb•↦true].	S:stage3 ← S.ready_idb[ ].
stage3::state.	S:stage4 ← S:stage3, S.ready_user[ ].
stage4::state[ready_changes•↦true].	T:stage1 ← S.ready_changes[ ], T= S + 1.
0:stage1. % the initialization	

Table 1. Basic Schema for Implementing States

Every fact in (A) – for instance stage1::state[ready_edb•↦true] – defines an inheritable method of the subclass $stage_i$, e.g. every member s of class stage1 can inherit the property s[ready_edb→true]. Since deduction precedes inheritance, only when the computation of associated with stage 1 is completed, s[ready_edb→true] is inherited which enables the rule S:stage2 ← S.ready_edb[ ] (B.1), deriving that s also becomes a member of stage2, and the next deductive fixpoint is computed by the rules associated with stage 2. After stage 2 which computes the IDB, stage2::state[ready_idb•↦true] (A.2) and S:stage3 ← S.ready_idb[ ] (B.2) define the transition to stage 3. Then, the user interaction takes place, finished by s.ready_user[ ]. This leads to stage 4, where the changes to be executed in the transition to the next state are derived. Finally, s[ready_changes→true] is inherited by (A.3), and the next state $t = s+1$ is founded by (B.4).

Example 4 Together with the rules given in Table 1, the following program maintains the invariant that in state s, the method r gives exactly the value s if $s < 10$, then, in state 10, r returns no value, and the program stops. Here, states are objects, providing an EDB-method r and IDB-methods p, del_r and ins_r, representing the requested changes.

T[r↠X] ← S[r↠X], not S[del_r↠X], T:stage1, T=S+1.	% frame rules for r.
T[r↠X] ← S[ins_r↠X], T:stage1, T=S+1.	
S[q↠X] ← not S[r↠X], 0≤X<10, S:stage2.	% q is {1,...,9}\ r:
S[del_r↠X] ← S[r↠X, q↠Y], Y=X-1, S:stage3.	% derive changes.
S[ins_r↠X] ← S[q↠X, r↠Y], Y=X-1, S:stage3.	
S[ready_user→true] ← 0≤S<10, S:stage3.	% run for 10 states.
0[r↠0].	% initialization.

□

5 Applications and Examples

In this section, we show how different situations can be modeled by different concepts of change.[5] Also, *generic* frame rules are given which model different kinds of dynamic entities as introduced in Section 2.

5.1 Simple Updates to a Database

This example shows a scenario where State-F-Logic's ability of modeling state change by *dynamic classes* provides an elegant and intuitive specification. It reveals only a very simple active behavior by translating user requests into the internal representation and creating an object.

Example 5 Imagine a tram net, consisting of stations and sections. For repairs, some sections have to be closed for some time. For each day, the possible connections are computed. Additionally, for each section, it has to be determined whether it runs hourly or two-hourly at some day (as a default, at weekend days, trams go only two-hourly). But, for single sections (e.g. between the stadium and the railway station on saturdays) it should be possible to deviate from this default.

Here, *dynamic classes* are well-suited for modeling: each section is a static object, the set of open sections is a dynamic EDB class. By implementing the running frequency as an *inheritable* dynamic IDB method, the desired properties can easily be modeled. For dynamic EDB classes, the *generic* frame rules read as follows (insert(E,C,S) means to insert an object E in state S into a dynamic class C; analogous for delete(E,C,S)):

```
% Frame rules for dynamic classes:
E:(C.T) ← T:stage1, T = S + 1, C:edbclass, E:(C.S), not delete(E,C,S).
E:(C.T) ← T:stage1, T = S + 1, C:edbclass, insert(E,C,S).
```

The problem-specific part includes the specification of weekdays, weekend days (using multivalued methods), and the frequency of running the sections for every day. The frequency is implemented as an inheritable method of every class *sections.s*, which is overwritten in case of the section $(stadium, railwStat)$ on saturdays. The computation of the reflexive transitive closure is implemented by local rules.

```
% Problem specific rules:
sections:edbclass.
days[isWeekday→↠{0,1,2,3,4}].
days[isWeekend→↠{5,6}].
S[weekno→N] ← N = S / 7, S:stage2.          % Here, a state acts as an object.
S[weekday→D] ← D = S - N * 7, S[weekno→N], S:stage2.
sections.S[frequency@(S)•→hourly] ← days[isWeekday→↠S.weekday], S:stage2.
sections.S[frequency@(S)•→twohourly] ← days[isWeekend→↠S.weekday], S:stage2.
E[frequency@(S)→hourly] ←
          E:(sections.S)[start→stadium; end→railwStat], S[weekday→5], S:stage2.
```

---

[5] The examples are available at
   http://www.informatik.uni-freiburg.de/~dbis/flsys/moreexamples.html.

```
% Compute reflexive transitive closure
(sections.S)::(connections.S) ← S:stage2.
p(X,Y):(connections.S)[start→X; end→Y] ←
    E:(sections.S)[start→Y; end→X], S:stage2.
p(X,Z):(connections.S)[start→X; end→Z] ←
    E:(sections.S)[start→X; end→Y], P:(connections.S)[start→Y; end→Z], S:stage2.

% Actions
delete(E,sections,S) ← remove(X,Y,S), E:(sections.S)[start→X;end→Y], S:stage4.
insert(e(X,Y),sections,S), e(X,Y):sections[start→X;end→Y] ← add(X,Y,S), S:stage4.
```

The program uses the rules given in Table 1 for handling states which have to be inserted here.

The following interactive requests construct a small database:

state 0:	add(cathedral,zoo,0).	add(castle,stadium,0).
	add(stadium,railwStat,0).	0.ready_user[ ].
state 1:	add(airport,railwStat,1).	1.ready_user[ ].
state 2:	remove(castle,stadium,2).	2.ready_user[ ].

The following query outputs for every state all open sections with start and end point, and their frequency:

?- E:(sections.S), E[start→A, end→B, frequency@(S)→F].

As long as T is a state and its EDB is not yet computed, the frame rules are active, deriving T's EDB. When a fixpoint is reached, a trigger fires, setting $T.ready\_edb$ to true. Then, the IDB is computed, giving the set of connections and the frequencies. After this, the users give their update requests via add and remove. When the user has completed his requests, modeled by $T.ready\_user$, the change requests are processed, entering the next state.   □

5.2 Active Databases and Integrity Maintenance

Active database behavior, which is often utilized e.g. for integrity maintenance, can also be modeled in State-F-Logic: As in the first example, the user specifies update requests interactively, but now, from these updates and the current database state, the database system derives additional updates. Then, from both the user-requested and the internally derived updates, the next database state is computed.

Example 6 The scenario is as follows, modeling a part of a production planning system: An enterprise produces several types of items, from small screws up to automobiles. There are many compound products, consisting of several parts. The user can change the composition of compound products, say, removing the 145/75 wheels from the parts needed to built some car, instead adding 155/75 wheels. On the other hand, the production of parts can be stopped or started. Obviously, if the production of e.g. a 3"-screw is stopped, the production of all compound products needing 3"-screws also stops.

Here, dynamic multivalued methods are the best way of modeling. Both the production palette and the needs-part relation are represented by EDB-multivalued-methods.

% Frame rules for scalar methods:
O[M@(T)→Q] ← T:stage1, T = S + 1, apply(O,M):edbscalar,
                    O[M@(S)→Q], not O.change@(S,M)[ ].
O[M@(T)→Q] ← T:stage1, T = S + 1, apply(O,M):edbscalar, O[change@(S,M)→Q].
% Frame-rules for multi-valued methods:
O[M@(T)→→Q] ← T:stage1, T = S + 1, apply(O,M):edbmultivalued,
                    O[M@(S)→→Q], not delete(O,M,Q,S).
O[M@(T)→→Q] ← T:stage1, T = S + 1, apply(O,M):edbmultivalued, insert(O,M,Q,S).

The example shows the flexibility of our approach to deal with different kinds of changes: Since the set of products is assumed to change frequently, is it implemented as a multivalued method which changes with every state, thus it is propagated by a frame rule, considering current updates. On the other side, as the configuration of a certain product changes from time to time, a configuration is modeled as an object, addressed by the dynamic scalar method hasConfig of the product. Thus, for a sequence of states where the configuration does not change, only hasConfig has to be copied to the next state. If the configuration is changed, a new configuration object is introduced, and hasConfig is set to point to it.

% Problem Specific rules:
% Semantic Types:
apply(pps,produces):edbmultivalued.
apply(P,hasConfig):edbscalar ← pps[produces@(S)→→P], S:state.

% start or stop production of some part:
insert(pps,produces,P,S) ← start(P,S), S:stage4.
delete(pps,produces,P,S) ← stop(P,S), S:stage4.

% addTo and removeFrom: change Configurations:
change(O,S,hasConfig) ← addTo(O,P,S), S:stage4.
change(O,S,hasConfig) ← removeFrom(O,P,S), S:stage4.
O[change@(S,hasConfig)→newConfig(O,T)] ←
        T= S + 1, change(O,S,hasConfig), S:stage4.

% active behavior:
% if configuration changes, create new configuration object.
newConfig(O,T)[needsPart→→P] ← T= S + 1, change(O,S,hasConfig),
        O.hasConfig@(S)[needsPart→→P], not removeFrom(O,P,S), S:stage4.
newConfig(O,T)[needsPart→→P] ← T= S + 1, change(O,S,hasConfig),
        addTo(O,P,S), S:stage4.

% stop all products which need stopped parts.
stop(P,S) ← P.hasConfig@(S)[needsPart→→Q], stop(Q,S), S:stage4.

An example database and an example action sequence could be the following:

pps[produces@(0)→→{golf,passat,motor14,motor18,wheel145,screw}].
golf[hasConfig@(0)→newConfig(golf,0)].
passat[hasConfig@(0)→newConfig(passat,0)].
motor14[hasConfig@(0)→newConfig(motor14,0)].
newConfig(golf,0)[needsPart→→{motor14,wheel145}].
newConfig(passat,0)[needsPart→→{motor14,wheel145}].
newConfig(motor14,0)[needsPart→→{screw}].

```
removeFrom(passat,motor14,0).   addTo(passat,motor18,0).
   start(wheel155,0).            0.ready_user[ ].
   stop(screw,1).                removeFrom(golf,wheel145,1).
   addTo(golf,wheel155,1).       1.ready_user[ ].
```

With the following queries, for every state, all items which are currently produced and which parts they need are given:

?- pps[produces@(S)→→P].
?- P.hasConfig@(S)[needsPart→→Q].   □

5.3 Other Applications

In continuation of the above examples, the presented concept can be used for process modeling as a specification, implementation, and verification language. For instance, the Alternating-Bit-Protocol has been formulated as a transition system by State-F-Logic rules.

In the above examples, changes are only determined from the current database state. By using progressive rules with scope > 1, it is possible to specify and enforce transactions and dynamic constraints.

Additionally, the proposed extension by states can be employed for evaluating single-state programs wrt. complex logical semantics: Similar to relational databases and Datalog semantics, there is a hierarchy of differently expressive semantics for deductive object-oriented programs, including a well-founded style semantics. Analogous to well-founded Datalog semantics, it can be effectively computed as an alternating fixpoint by using explicit states.

An interesting aspect is the combination with Transaction Logic [BK94], a language dealing with transitions and transactions in a logic programming style. Transaction Logic makes no commitment which formalism to use for describing the interpretation of a state: Any kind of theory can be chosen. Then, the *transition oracle* must be instantiated accordingly. Here, for an arbitrary framework $\mathfrak{X}$ chosen as a state representation language, the transition oracle can be specified and implemented in State-$\mathfrak{X}$. The resulting language provides a powerful language for specification, implementation, and verification of databases and workflow-systems.

6 Conclusion

With its conceptional flexibility, i.e. allowing dynamic objects, dynamic classes, and dynamic methods, the presented approach allows a straightforward modeling of the application domain, thus relieving the user from the burden of encoding into some restrictive formalism. As shown in the examples, the frame rules can be given generically for each concept of object-oriented modeling. Thus, the user can concentrate on the application semantical aspects. With the given implementation scheme for a linear state space, provided an implementation of the underlying single-state framework $\mathfrak{X}$, State-$\mathfrak{X}$ can be used as an implementation language for an object-oriented interactive database system. Thus, a specification also provides an implementation, allowing rapid prototyping and testing. Due to the fact that the state sequence is isomorphic to the natural numbers, *temporal properties* can also be specified and verified by rules. Thus, meta-reasoning about the implemented specification can be done in the same language. Summarizing, the concept – and its instance State-F-Logic – provides an integrated framework for specification, implementation, validation, verification, and runtime checks in a single language.

Acknowledgements.
The authors thank BERTRAM LUDÄSCHER and RAINER HIMMERÖDER for many fruitful discussions.

References

[AM89] M. Abadi and Z. Manna. Temporal Logic Programming. *Journal of Symbolic Computation*, 8(3), September 1989.

[BCW93] M. Baudinet, J. Chomicki, and P. Wolper. Temporal Deductive Databases. In Tansel et al. [TCG$^+$93].

[BK94] A. J. Bonner and M. Kifer. An Overview of Transaction Logic. *Theoretical Computer Science*, 133(2):205–265, 1994.

[CB94] P. Cholak and H. A. Blair. The Complexity of Local Stratification. *Fundamenta Informaticae*, 21(4), 1994.

[CJ90] W. Cellary and G. Jomier. Consistency of Versions in Object-Oriented Databases. In *Proc. Intl. Conference on Very Large Data Bases*, pages 432–441, 1990.

[FHK$^+$97] J. Frohn, R. Himmeröder, P.-T. Kandzia, G. Lausen, and C. Schlepphorst. FLORID: A Prototype for F–Logic. In *Proc. Intl. Conference on Data Engineering*, 1997.

[FHKS96] J. Frohn, R. Himmeröder, P.-T. Kandzia, and C. Schlepphorst. How to Write F-Logic Programs in FLORID, 1996. Available from ftp://ftp.informatik.uni-freiburg.de/pub/florid/tutorial.ps.gz.

[FWP97] A. A. A. Fernandes, M. H. Williams, and N. W. Paton. A Logic-Based Integration of Active and Deductive Databases. *New Generation Computing*, 1997. to appear.

[KLS92] M. Kramer, G. Lausen, and G. Saake. Updates in a Rule-Based Language for Objects. In *Proc. Intl. Conference on Very Large Data Bases*, Vancouver, 1992.

[KLW95] M. Kifer, G. Lausen, and J. Wu. Logical Foundations of Object-Oriented and Frame-Based Languages. *Journal of the ACM*, 42(4):741–843, July 1995.

[LML96] B. Ludäscher, W. May, and G. Lausen. Nested Transactions in a Logical Language for Active Rules. In D. Pedreschi and C. Zaniolo, editors, *Proc. Intl. Workshop on Logic in Databases (LID)*, number 1154 in LNCS, pages 196–222, San Miniato, Italy, 1996. Springer.

[TCG$^+$93] A. U. Tansel, J. Clifford, S. Gadia, S. Jajodia, A. Segev, and R. Snodgrass, editors. *Temporal Databases*. Benjamin/Cummings, 1993.

[Zan93] C. Zaniolo. A Unified Semantics for Active and Deductive Databases. In N. W. Paton and M. H. Williams, editors, *Proc. of the 1st Intl. Workshop on Rules in Database Systems (RIDS)*, Workshops in Computing, Edinburgh, Scotland, 1993. Springer.

FOLRE: A Deductive Database System for the Integrated Treatment of Updates

E. Mayol, J. A. Pastor, E. Teniente, T. Urpí

Departament. de LSI (Universitat Politècnica de Catalunya)
Jordi Girona Salgado 1-3, Edifici C6
E-08034 Barcelona, Catalonia
{mayol I pastor I teniente I urpi }@lsi.upc.es

ABSTRACT

We present in this paper both a novel theoretically well-founded framework for integrating the treatment of advanced update and rule enforcement problems in deductive databases and the architecture of a new *deductive database management system* based upon such a framework. Our results extend the query-processing and basic updating functionalities provided by current deductive database systems with integrated view updating and materialization, integrity checking and maintenance, and condition monitoring; both for on-line updates and predefined transactions.

The distinguishing feature of our approach is the underlying integrative framework used to specify and combine update problems which facilitates their implementation. Our system bears an architecture consisting of a deductive front-end that takes care of any updating task, working on a pre-existing deductive back-end that handles all storage, retrieval and transaction management issues. Since the integrated treatment of advanced updating is an important issue both for deductive databases and for other database models, we hope that our approach helps to fill an important gap within current database technology.

1. Introduction

In the current times of "constant change", organisations need to master not just their data, but also the right *knowledge* that permits to convert this data into useful decisional information. This raises a general requirement for more "intelligence" within computer-based information systems, to be built on advanced technologies that go beyond efficient data handling towards effective knowledge management. For this purpose, several technologies will have to be combined, with interoperable, object-oriented, active and deductive capabilities [SSU96]. Among them, *deductive databases* are a theoretically well-founded technology around which to build the knowledge-intensive systems of the future.

Deductive databases, also known as *logic databases* or *knowledge bases*, result from decades of research in the areas of logic, databases, logic programming and artificial intelligence [Min96]. They extend relational databases by allowing for the representation and management of more general forms of "application semantics". Besides data stored in base relations, comprehensive *views* permit the handling of additional forms of derived data, while powerful *integrity constraints* can be used to care for overall data consistency. These features together with appropriate reasoning capabilities ease the sharing of common knowledge within complex application domains, facilitating program development and reuse on the way.

Results from the large amount of theoretical research devoted to deductive databases have both penetrated current relational DBMSs and inspired several extensions to the relational model. Furthermore, this research has recently materialised in some Deductive Database Management Systems (DDBMS), either prototypes or commercial products [RU95, Min96]. Among these developed systems, we have Aditi, CORAL, DECLARE, Glue-Nail, LDL (see [VLD94] for descriptions and references), EKS-V1 [VPK+90], and Validity [FLV96].

However, while [VLD94] presents deductive databases as the main effort to attack "one of the most fundamental uses of a computer, *i.e.* to *store* and *retrieve* information", it also identifies as some of the principal problems to be overcomed by current DDBMS the ones most closely related to the -also fundamental- task of *updating* information. Solving these problems is even more critical in deductive databases than in other models, since the view and integrity rules that these databases offer not only must be enforced when updating the database, but provide the means for expanding the possibilities for database updating. We consider in this paper as advanced database updating problems those of *view updating* and *materialization*, *integrity checking* and *maintenance*, and *trigger condition monitoring*.

Most of the research -and systems- have concentrated on providing theoretical foundations and efficient techniques for the storage and retrieval of large amounts of complex data. Thus, just a few current DDBMS provide some mechanism for advanced data updating, other than updates to base facts. To our fair knowledge, only EKS-V1 and Validity provide capabilities for integrity checking while EKS-V1 permits also view materialization. Rather than a lack of satisfactory theoretical results for most update problems, we believe the reason behind this situation to be the separate way in which they have been dealt with in the past.

Most of the methods have tackled their respective problem of interest in an isolated manner, without taking into account the strong interrelationships with other updating problems. This was also the case of our group's previous work on the subject, from which several competitive methods were produced for tasks such as integrity checking and maintenance, view updating and view materialization, and condition monitoring [Oli91, UO92, MT93, TO95, PO95].

However, a distinguishing feature of our methods is the common theoretical basis upon which they all were developed, which has facilitated their merging into a integrative framework [Oli91, UO92] for dealing with update problems in deductive databases as well as for their specification and combination [TU95]. Furthermore, by using these results, we have been able to develop the FOLRE DDBMS prototype, where FOLRE stands for "Facing On towards Logic database Rule Enforcement".

This paper is dedicated to the presentation of the integrative framework and of the architecture of our system. FOLRE bears a layered architecture where a deductive front-end takes care of any updating task, while a deductive back-end handles all storage, retrieval and transaction management issues. By considering the relationships between updating problems effectiveness and efficiency benefits are obtained. We have implemented FOLRE on a Sun OS environment, using ECLiPSe [ECL94] both as development environment and as deductive database back-end.

After this Introduction, next section reviews basic concepts of deductive databases. Section 3 presents the update capabilities provided by our system. Section 4 describes the underlying integrative framework. Section 5 covers the architecture of FOLRE while illustrating each of its components. Finally, section 6 presents some conclusions and comments on future research and development.

2. Deductive Databases

A *deductive database* D is a triple D = (EDB, DR, IC) where EDB is a set of facts, DR a set of deductive rules, and IC a set of integrity constraints. The *extensional* part of a deductive database is composed by the EDB facts. The *intensional* part contains deductive rules and integrity constraints. We assume that deductive database predicates are partitioned into base and derived (view) predicates. A base predicate appears only in the extensional part and (eventually) in the body of deductive rules. A derived predicate appears only in the intensional part.

A *deductive rule* is a formula of the form:

$$P(t_1, ..., t_m) \leftarrow L_1 \wedge ... \wedge L_n \text{ with } m = 0, n = 1$$

where $P(t_1, ..., t_m)$ is an atom and $L_1, ..., L_n$ are literals. Variables in P, $L_1, ..., L_n$ are assumed to be universally quantified over the whole formula. The definition of a predicate P is the set of all rules in the deductive database that have P in their head.

An *integrity constraint* is a formula that every state of the deductive database is required to satisfy. We deal with constraints in *denial* form:

$$\leftarrow L_1 \wedge ... \wedge L_n \text{ with } n = 1$$

where the L_i are literals and all variables are assumed to be universally quantified over the whole formula. Other constraints can be transformed into denials [LT84].

We associate to each constraint an inconsistency predicate Ic_n, with or without terms. Thus, denials are rewritten as $Ic_i \leftarrow L_1 \wedge ... \wedge L_n$, which we call *integrity rules*. We also define an auxiliary predicate Ic with rules: Ic $\leftarrow Ic_j$ with j=1...m. Hence, fact Ic would indicate that some constraint is not satisfied. We assume that each predicate has a vector of terms that form a *key* for that predicate.

3. Update Funcionalities Provided by FOLRE

Base predicates, deductive rules and integrity constraints, as defined in the previous section, are the basic components of a deductive database. The following are examples of these in the data definition language of FOLRE:

base predicate Emp (x: string)
key: x
description: x is an employee

integrity constraint
$Ic1(x) \leftarrow Emp(x) \wedge \neg Rr(x)$
description: Employees must be legal residents

derived predicate
$Cand(x) \leftarrow Int(x,y) \wedge Comp(y)$
key: x
description: Job candidates have interviews with companies

FOLRE allows the user to perform *updates of base facts* as well as *(view) updates of derived facts*. Basic update primitives of FOLRE allow to specify updates consisting of an *insertion*, a *deletion* or a *modification* of a base or of a derived fact. Given a base or derived predicate P, updates on P are specified in the following way:

$\iota P(K,X)$: insertion of fact P(K,X), where K and X are vectors of constants.
$\delta P(K,X)$: deletion of fact P(K,X), where K and X are vectors of constants.
$\mu P(K,X,Y)$: modification of fact P(K,X) to P(K,Y), where K, X and Y are vectors of constants and $X \neq Y$.

Additionally, the user can request the application of more *complex transactions* which consist of a set of update primitives. For instance, a complex transaction consisting of the deletion of derived fact Rr(Joan) together with the insertion of base fact App(Maria) would be expressed as { δRr(Joan), ιApp(Maria) }. Note that our notion of transaction extends the usual one by considering view updates in addition to updates of base facts. View update requests are automatically translated by our system into updates of the underlying base facts.

FOLRE also provides other advanced update capabilities the appropriate handling of which requires the database designer to specify additional knowledge about base predicates, derived predicates and integrity constraints. These capabilities are:

Integrity Constraints Enforcement: FOLRE allows two different integrity enforcement policies: *integrity checking* as well as *integrity maintenance*. Thus, in our system, the designer may distinguish between those constraints to be checked, so that any transaction that would violate them is to be simply rejected, and those to be maintained, which the system must try to automatically compensate by considering additional updates. The policy associated to a constraint is specified by either *type checking* or *type maintenance*.

Materialized view maintenance: the designer may specify for derived predicates that s/he wants to materialize them, that is, to explicitly store their extension in the database. This is useful, for instance, to minimize the time required to answer queries involving the materialized predicates. For this the definition of a derived predicate must include: *type materialized.*

Condition monitoring: the designer may express the kind of changes (insertions, deletions and/or modifications) to be monitored on a predicate. This may be useful to notify the user at execution time that a noteworthy change has been induced by the application of a given transaction. For instance, the system will monitor deletions on Cand if its definition includes: *monitor: deletions display x has been deleted as candidate.* A condition to monitor can be seen as a special case of trigger where the action to be performed is restricted to displaying information. We do not consider other more complex triggers in the present version of FOLRE.

Predefined transactions: the designer can specify predefined transactions which correspond to sets of parameterized update request that are automatically translated, at compile time, into update programs. At run time, these programs are ensured to satisfy the requested predefined transaction. This is useful when some update request will often be required and because the system may consider several optimizations when generating these programs.

In the following example (adapted from [SK88, QW91]) it is possible to see how to define a deductive database considering the above update funcionalities.

Example deductive database schema: Database for an "Employment Office" that arranges interviews between job applicants and companies, while keeping track of employees and, for legal reasons, of nationality status and criminal records. Described in our data definition language, the example is:

base predicate Emp (x: string)
key: x
description: x is an employee

base predicate App (x: string)
key: x
description: x is a job applicant

base predicate Comp (y: string)
key: y
description: y is a company

base predicate Int (x, y: string)
key: x
description: interview of x and y

base predicate Cit (x: string)
key: x
description: x is a citizen

base predicate Ra (x: string)
key: x
description: x is a registered alien

base predicate Cr (x: string)
key: x
description: x has criminal record

derived predicate
    Rr (x) $\leftarrow$ Ra (x) $\wedge \neg$ Cr (x)
    Rr (x) $\leftarrow$ Cit(x)
key: x
type: non-materialized
description: x is right-resident if
    s/he is a non-crimina registered
    alien or a citizen

derived predicate
    Cand (x) $\leftarrow$ Int(x,y)$\wedge$Comp (y)
key: x
type: materialized
monitor: deletions
display x deleted as candidate
description: job candidates have
    interviews with companies

integrity constraint
    Ic1 (x) $\leftarrow$ Emp (x) $\wedge \neg$ Rr (x)
type: maintenance
description: Employees must be
    legal residents

integrity constraint
    Ic2 (x) $\leftarrow$ Emp (x) $\wedge$ App (x)
type: checking
description: Employees cannot be
    applicants

integrity constraint
    Ic3 (x) $\leftarrow$ Cand (x) $\wedge \neg$ App (x)
type: maintenance
description: Candidates must be
    applicants

integrity constraint
    Ic4(x) $\leftarrow$ Int (x,y) $\wedge \neg$ Comp(y)
type: checking
description: Interviews must be
    scheduled with companies

predefined transaction
    Enter-employee (Per)
is { ιEmp(Per) }

4. The Underlying Integrative Framework

The general approach of the previous research related to database updating problems has been to provide specific methods for solving particular problems. However, most of these methods are explicitly or implicitly based on a set of rules that define the changes that occur in a transition from an old state of a database to a new one. In our case, we use the *Augmented Database* [Oli91, UO92], that contains a set of event rules that explicitly define the insertions, deletions and modifications induced by an update, for this purpose. These rules are used to integrate the treatment of view updating, materialized view maintenance, integrity checking and integrity maintenance, condition monitoring or predefined transaction generation.

Event rules can be interpreted in two different ways [TU95]. Their *upward interpretation* defines changes on derived predicates induced by changes on base predicates; their *downward interpretation* defines changes on base predicates needed to satisfy changes on derived predicates. As shown in [TU95], database updating problems can be specified in terms of these two interpretations.

In FOLRE, we have implemented two methods which are able to compute each of these interpretations: The upward method [UO92] computes the upward interpretation and it is able to incrementally handle integrity checking, materialized view maintenance and condition monitoring; the downward method [MT93, TO95] computes the downward interpretation and handles view updating and integrity maintenance appropriately. We integrate the treatment of updates by using these two methods, which take into account a unique set of event rules. The generation of predefined transactions is also based on taking into account the event rules and considering upward and downward aspects when generating transactions [Pas97].

Several effectiveness and efficiency advantages are obtained by dealing in an integrated way with update problems, since this allows to actively consider the close relationships among them. For example, if we consider different separate approaches for handling each individual problem isolately, then it is not clear how to perform the integration of the different problems nor of the different approaches. Moreover, if this integration was not performed appropriately, the effectiveness of the system could decrease. For instance, dealing with view updating and integrity maintenance separately hinders the obtention of solutions that may be generated when considering them together, while resulting less efficient than a combined approach.

The Augmented Database is based on the concept of *event*. For each predicate P of a deductive database D, *insertion event predicate* ιP, *deletion event predicate* δP, and *modification event predicate* μP are used to define the precise difference of deducible facts of consecutive database states. If P is a base predicate, ιP, δP and μP facts represent insertions, deletions and modifications of base facts, respectively. If P is a view predicate or a condition to monitor, ιP, δP and μP facts represent induced insertions, induced deletions and induced modifications, respectively. If P is an integrity constraint, ιP represents a violation of it.

The definition of ιP, δP and μP depends on the definition of P and is independent of any set of updates and of the extensional part of D. For each view predicate, integrity constraint and condition to monitor P, the Augmented Database contains rules about ιP, δP and μP, called *event rules*, defined as follows:

$$\forall k,x \ (\iota P(k,x) \leftrightarrow P^n(k,x) \wedge \neg \exists y P(k,y))$$
$$\forall k,x \ (\delta P(k,x) \leftrightarrow P(k,x) \wedge \neg \exists y P^n(k,y))$$
$$\forall k,x,x' (\mu P(k,x,x') \leftrightarrow P(k,x) \wedge P^n(k,x') \wedge x \neq x')$$

where P refers to predicate P evaluated in the old state of the database (before the application of the update), P^n refers to predicate P evaluated in the new state of the database and k, x, y and x' are vectors of variables.

The Augmented Database contains also a set of *transition rules* associated to each predicate P. These rules define the new state of predicate P (denoted by P^n) in terms of the old database state and the events occurring in the transition between the old and the new state. Given a deductive database D, the Augmented Database consists of D, its transition rules and its event rules. The procedure for automatically deriving an Augmented Database from a database can be found in [Oli91, UO92], where several important syntactical simplifications of these rules are also described.

5. Architecture of the FOLRE system

FOLRE consists of two parts clearly differentiated. First, a front-end that acts as an interface with the user or the database designer and whose main goal is to handle all issues related with defining, querying and updating a deductive database. Second, a deductive back-end platform that provides support for disk storage and full query and transaction management facilities. This architecture is illustrated in figure 1.

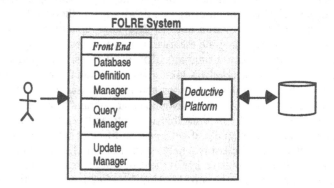

Figure 1 - System Architecture

The front-end is the core of our system and it is divided into three components: a Database Definition Manager, a Query Manager and an Update Manager, explained in detail in the rest of this section. FOLRE is independent of the deductive back-end platform chosen. In the current implementation of FOLRE we have used ECLiPSe [ECL94] as the back-end, since it perfectly suits our current needs and our previous experience with Megalog, a precursor of ECLiPSe.

5.1 Database Definition Manager

The Database Definition Manager allows the database designer to specify all the elements of a deductive database: base and view predicates, integrity constraints, information about the keys of base and view predicates, conditions to monitor and predefined transaction requests. The designer must also provide information about the views to be maintained, and s/he must distinguish between those constraints to be checked and those to be maintained. The modules comprised in the Database Definition Manager are shown in figure 2, where dotted lines represent flows of control and continuous lines represent flows of information.

The *Designer Interface* handles all input/output interaction and allows the designer to specify all the above database aspects. This specification is performed by means of the language illustrated in section 3. Once the database schema is defined, this module performs a lexical and syntactical analysis of the database schema and checks whether it is allowed and stratified.

The *Validator* is a tool for validating the deductive database schema definition. It allows the designer to ask questions about the accomplishment of certain properties of the schema, like schema satisfiability, predicate liveliness, reachability of partially-specified states or redundancy of constraints. These provide him/her with information on whether the schema correctly describes the users' intended needs.

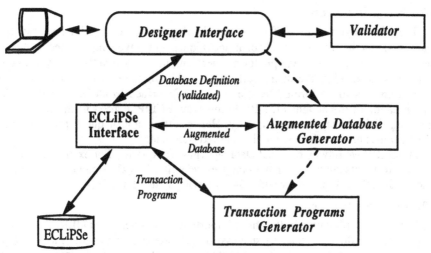

Figure 2 - Database Definition Manager Architecture

Roughly, the main idea of our approach to validation is to define, for each particular property, a distinguished view predicate which describes the accomplishment of that property. An attempt to validate a certain property p can then be made by attempting to satisfy the request of inserting the predicate corresponding to p. For instance, a successful attempt to insert the 0-ary predicate satisfiable shows that the database schema on which the insert request has been executed is satisfiable; a finitely failed attempt to insert satisfiable shows the unsatisfiability of the schema. Thus, the downward method is also used at definition time for validation purposes. See [DTU96] for the details of our approach to validation.

A validated schema is stored on disk by means of the *ECLiPSe Interface*. In this way, ECLiPSe gives us the support for storing disk-resident data efficiently. It is important to note that this is the only module that depends on the chosen back-end, i.e. ECLiPSe. The rest of FOLRE modules may not directly store nor retrieve information from ECLiPSe. All these accesses are performed by means of predefined calls to the interface module, which translates these calls into ECLiPSe primitives. Therefore, if we wanted to use a different back-end, we would only have to implement the corresponding interface module. Once the validated schema is stored, the *Augmented Database Generator* derives the corresponding Augmented Database.

Finally, the *Transaction Programs Generator* uses the Augmented Database to automatically derive transaction programs corresponding to the specified predefined update request. Such a request, together with the Augmented Database, implicitly configure an abstract search space that is explored at compile-time to produce an abstract syntax tree, from which the corresponding program is drawn. The derivation is done in such a way that the resulting program already takes into account, with special control instructions, the requested (view) updates, the constraints to be maintained and the constraints to be checked [PO95,Pas97]. These generated programs are also physically stored in the database. At execution time, users may instantiate the formal parameters with actual parameters and the updates given by the execution of the transaction programs are applied to the database (see section 5.3.2 for an example of a generated transaction program).

5.2 Query Manager

There is a large research effort on the field of query processing that has produced many systems that implement efficient techniques. We have simply selected one of these systems as our back-end platform. Therefore, in our system the Query Manager just needs to translate the query performed to the language of the back-end. This translation is also performed by the ECLiPSe Interface Module, as well as the interpretation of the obtained results. In this way, ECLiPSe gives us the support for querying disk-resident data efficiently. Hence, efficiency of query processing in FOLRE relies on the efficiency of the selected back-end.

In FOLRE we rely on classical Datalog syntax for queries. For example, to query for right residents but that are not employees we write: $\{Rr(x), \neg Emp(x)\}$ and to know whether John has an interview with IBM we write: $\{Int(John, IBM)\}$.

5.3. Update Manager

The Update Manager is the most important component of FOLRE. Its main purpose is to allow the user to successfully update base and view facts, which requires the management by this component of integrity constraints, views to materialize and conditions to monitor. Two kinds of updates are allowed by the system: on-line updates and predefined updates. Since they must be processed in a different way, we have an On-line Update Manager and a Predefined Update Manager.

5.3.1. On-line Update Manager

This component permits the user to request at run-time the application of a transaction to the deductive database. Therefore, this module must handle both downward problems (view updating and integrity maintenance) and upward ones (integrity checking, materialized view maintenance and condition monitoring). We deal first with downward problems and then with upward ones. This is appropriate since the result of applying the downward method, i.e. a transaction consisting of a set of base fact updates, is exactly the input to the upward one. Moreover, treatment of upward problems is structured in the following way: First, we deal with integrity checking; then, materialized view maintenance and condition monitoring are performed. In this way, the computation of the changes on the materialized views and conditions is only performed when constraints are not violated. Figure 3 summarizes the architecture of the On-line Update Manager, which is composed of the following three modules:

View Updating and Integrity Constraints Maintenance Module

Initially, the user requests the application of an on-line transaction which is composed of ground updates of base and derived facts. Updates of derived facts must be appropriately translated into updates of the underlying base facts. View updating is concerned with performing this translation successfully.

Much research has been devoted to this problem within the field of deductive and relational databases; see for example [KM90, TO95, Dec96]. In general, several translations that satisfy a view update may exist. In FOLRE, we follow the approach of obtaining all the translations that satisfy the request.

However, the application of some of the obtained transactions could induce the violation of some integrity constraint that the designer had specified to be maintained. Integrity maintenance [ML91, Wüt93, TO95, Dec96] consists of determining a set of additional base updates to be appended to these transactions such that the resulting sets satisfy all these integrity constraints.

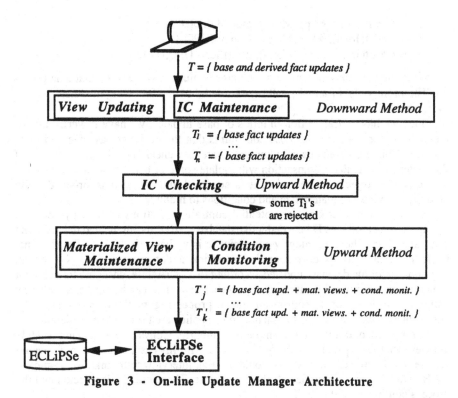

$T = \{$ base and derived fact updates $\}$

| View Updating | IC Maintenance | Downward Method |

$T_i = \{$ base fact updates $\}$

$\dots$

$T_n = \{$ base fact updates $\}$

| IC Checking | Upward Method |

some T_i's
are rejected

| Materialized View Maintenance | Condition Monitoring | Upward Method |

$T'_j = \{$ base fact upd. + mat. views. + cond. monit. $\}$

$\dots$

$T'_k = \{$ base fact upd. + mat. views. + cond. monit. $\}$

ECLiPSe ◄──► ECLiPSe Interface

Figure 3 - On-line Update Manager Architecture

In our system, the above two problems are handled together by our downward method. Given a user request to apply a transaction, the View Updating and Integrity Constraints Maintenance Module automatically translate this request into several transactions consisting only of base updates. Each obtained transaction guarantees the accomplishment of the view updates contained in the requested transaction and that the constraints that the designer had specified to be maintained remain satisfied.

More precisely, let D be a deductive database, A(D) its augmented database, T a requested transaction. Then, a *translation* of T is a set T' of ground base events such that: A(D) ∪ T' ⊨ T ; and A(D) ∪ T' ⊭ ιIc. The first condition states that the update request is a logical consequence of the database updated according to T', while the second condition states that the updated database will remain consistent since no insertion of the integrity constraints to be maintained will be induced.

T' is obtained by having some failed SLDNF derivation of A(D) ∪ {←T ∧ ¬ιIc} succeed. The possible ways in which a failed derivation may succeed correspond to the different translations T'_i that satisfy the request. Since several transactions can be obtained, the user may eventually discard some of them at the end of the execution of the View Updating and Integrity Constraints Maintenance module.

Example: Consider that the user wants to apply the on-line transaction T= {δRr(Joan), δApp(Maria)} to a database state that contains facts: Cand(Maria), App(Maria), Int(Maria, UPC), Comp(UPC), Cit(Joan).

The View Updating and Integrity Constraints Maintenance Module would obtain the translations:

$T_1 = \{ \delta Cit(Joan), \delta App(Maria), \delta Int(Maria, UPC) \}$
$T_2 = \{ \delta Cit(Joan), \delta App(Maria), \delta Comp(UPC) \}$
$T_3 = \{ \delta Cit(Joan), \delta App(Maria), \mu Int(Maria, UPC, UAB) \}$

Since the user may discard some obtained solution, we assume that s/he rejects T_2. Therefore, only T_1 and T_3 will be considered by the following modules.

Integrity Constraints Checking Module

Once we have a transaction in terms of base updates, we have to verify that its application does not violate those constraints that the designer has specified to be checked. This problem is usually known as integrity checking [SK88, GCM+94]. If the system detects that a transaction will violate some of these constraints, then this transaction is rejected. Otherwise, it is accepted and our system proceeds with determining views to materialize and conditions to monitor.

In our system, checking for potential contraint violations is done by applying our upward method. Let D be a deductive database, A(D) its augmented database and T a translation. Then, an integriy constraint Ic is violated if: $A(D) \cup T \models \iota Ic$. That is, Ic is violated if its corresponding insertion event predicate ιIc is a logical consequence of the database updated according to T. Therefore, checking for contraint violations is performed by simply querying ιIc. This query can be answered either by using a top-down or a bottom-up query processing method, when both the Augmented Database and the transaction to be applied are taken into consideration.

Example: Continuing our example, the Integrity Constraints Checking Module verifies whether T_1 and T_3 satisfy Ic1 and Ic4. In this case, transaction T_3 would violate Ic4 if applied, since Maria would have an interview with unknown company UAB. Translation T_1 satisfies all the constraints. Therefore, T_3 is rejected and the process continues only with T_1.

Materialized View Maintenance and Condition Monitoring Module

We then proceed by materializing views and monitoring conditions. Given a transaction, the materialized view maintenance problem consists in incrementally determining which changes must be performed to update accordingly the materialized views [CW91, GM95]. On the other hand, condition monitoring refers to the problem of incrementally monitoring the changes induced by a transaction on a condition that was specified by the designer [RCB+89, QW91].

Our system handles these two problems by applying our upward method. Let D be a deductive database, A(D) its augmented database and T a translation. Then, T induces an insertion on a materialized view V if: $A(D) \cup T \models \iota V$. Then induced insertions on a materialized view V are computed by simply querying ιV. Modifications and deletions on materialized views as well as changes on conditions to monitor are defined in a similar way.

Example: In our example transaction, changes induced to derived predicate Cand due to $T_1 = \{\delta Cit(Joan), \delta App(Maria), \delta Int(Maria, UPC)\}$ are determined. FOLRE detects that $\delta Cand(Maria)$ is the only induced change, which is due to the event fact $\delta Int(Maria, UPC)$. Then Cand(Maria) must be deleted from the materialized view and since deletions of Cand must be monitored, the associated text should be displayed.

Once our system has materialized the appropriate views and has monitored the relevant conditions, several overall final transactions may be obtained. At this point, the user selects one specific transaction to be physically applied to the database. The whole treatment of the on-line updates (and predefined updates) is completely performed without applying to any intermediate state of the database any of the transactions handled during the process.

Example: Since we have obtained only one final transaction T'$_1$ = {δCit(Joan), δApp(Maria), δInt(Maria,UPC), δCand(Maria)}, the following actions will be performed if the user accepts this solution:

- δCit(Joan): base fact Cit(Joan) will be deleted
- δApp(Maria): base fact App(Maria) will be deleted
- δInt(Maria,UPC): base fact Int(Maria,UPC) will be deleted
- δCand(Maria): materialized fact Cand(Maria) will be deleted
- Message "Maria has been deleted as a candidate" will be displayed

5.3.2. Predefined Update Manager

FOLRE includes also the possibility to handle predefined updates. This is concerned with the execution of the transaction programs corresponding to the specified predefined transaction requests.

Example: With request Enter-employee(Per) the designer wants a consistency-preserving transaction program such that after it is executed for a concrete person in parameter 'Per', we can guarantee that s/he is an employee, i.e. that inserts the person as employee. It must also guarantee that all constraints will remain satisfied after its application. From the above request and the database schema, our system generates the corresponding update transaction program, contained in figure 4.

	trek_text([temp(Per)], '
1	------------- if emp(Per) then
2	---------------|--- skip
3	---------------|- else
4	---------------|--- temp(Per) ,
5	---------------|----- if not rr(Per) then
6	---------------|-------|- { trr(Per) }
7	---------------|-------|--- either
8	---------------|-------|----|-- if ra(Per) then
9	---------------|-------|----|---|--- δcr(Per)
10	---------------|-------|----|---|- else
11	---------------|-------|----|---|--- if not cr(Per) then
12	---------------|-------|----|---|----|--- tra(Per)
13	---------------|-------|----|---|----|- else
14	---------------|-------|----|---|----|--- tra(Per) ,
15	---------------|-------|----|---|----|--- δcr(Per)
16	---------------|-------|----|---|--- end_if
17	---------------|-------|----|-- end_if
18	---------------|-------|----|- or
19	---------------|-------|----|-- tcit(Per)
20	---------------|-------|--- end_either
21	---------------|----- end_if ,
22	---------------|----- if app(Per) then
23	---------------|-------|- abort
24	---------------|----- end_if
25	------------- end_if
	'). % end of trek text

Figure 4 - Transaction Program Code Example

Line 1 above controls if the person provided is already an employee, in which case line 2 exits the transaction without any updating. Otherwise, line 4 proposes to insert him/her as such. Then two constraints may be affected: Ic1, which has to be maintained, and Ic2, that must be checked.

With regard to the maintenance of Ic1, if we want to insert someone as employee (line 4) without right of residence (line 5), then we must grant him/her this status (lines 6 to 20) in order to maintain consistency. For this, we initially draw the proposal that ιRr(Per) should be pursued (comment in line 6), which is followed by the translation of such view update into the needed base updates (lines 7 to 20).

For this view update transaction, there are two alternatives: we can give the right of residence to a person either by making him/her a non-criminal registered alien (lines 8 to 17) or by granting citizenship to such an individual (line 19).

The code generated for checking Ic2 states that, if we want to insert as employee (line 4) some applicant (line 22), then consistency is to be preserved in this case by aborting the transaction (line 23), since no integrity maintenance is allowed.

The previous example shows how our system addresses in an integrative way also at compile time view updating and integrity checking and maintenance. For details on formal procedures and examples, see [PO95, Pas97]. We plan to extend the current capabilities of our predefined updates to the rest of the stated problems (view materializacion and condition monitoring).

The *Predefined Update Manager* is the system component that allows the user to apply at execution time predefined transaction requests by executing their corresponding transaction programs. Figure 5 shows the architecture of this module.

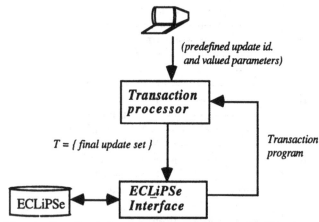

Figure 5 - Predefined Update Manager Architecture

To update a deductive database using a predefined parameterized transaction, the user must select the corresponding predefined transaction request and provide actual values to its parameters. The Transaction Processor uses these values to execute the corresponding transaction program, and generates a set of ground updates to be applied to the database.

Besides providing values for parameters, some further intervention will usually be expected from the user at run-time. For example, in the transaction of figure 4 s/he would hold all choice responsibility when confronted with 'either' instructions.

6. Conclusions and Further Work

We have described the architecture of the FOLRE system, whose main goal is to extend the functionality of current deductive database systems with more advanced updating capabilities like view updating, integrity checking, integrity maintenance, materialized view maintenance and condition monitoring; as well as the treatment of on-line and predefined updates. We have shown how all these capabilities are handled in an integrative way by considering a unique set of rules that define the difference between two consecutive database states. These rules can be interpreted in two different ways. Their *upward interpretation* defines changes on derived predicates induced by changes on base predicates; while the *downward interpretation* defines changes on base predicates needed to satisfy changes on derived predicates. Database updating problems can be dealt with by means of these two interpretations.

We are now investigating on how to increase the efficiency of some modules, which will probably imply the redesign of some of the system components. For instance, we are currently trying to merge the modules for view updating, integrity checking and integrity maintenance into a single module when dealing with on-line updates [MT97]. Further extensions are also needed for handling recursively-defined view predicates, since in this case our current system may enter in an infinite loop when dealing with view updating and integrity maintenance. Other needs for future research include extending the Transaction Programs Generator to deal also with materialized views and conditions to monitor; and incorporating some kind of database domain knowledge to guide the handling of on-line updates.

Our FOLRE prototype has been implemented on a Sun OS and currently includes all the modules described in this paper except for the schema Validator. Although it is not yet to be considered as a final system, we hope that it will help to fill what we believe to be an important gap within DDBMS prototypes and products in particular, and more generally within database technology.

Acknowledgements

We want to thank the other members of the FOLRE team, C.Farré, C.Martín and J.Sistac, for important contributions to this project, as well as to D.Costal, C.Quer, M.R. Sancho and A.Olivé for many useful comments and discussions. This paper has been partially supported by the PRONTIC program project TIC94-0512.

References

[CW91]   Ceri, S.; Widom, J. "Deriving Production Rules for Incremental View Maintenance", *17th. Int. Conf. on Very Large Databases (VLDB)*, Barcelona, 1991, pp 577-589.

[Dec96]   Decker, H. "An Extension of SLD by Abduction and Integrity Maintenance for View Updating in Deductive Databases", *Joint International Conference and Symposium on Logic Programming (JICSLP)*, Bonn (Germany), 1996.

[DTU96]   Decker, H.; Teniente, E.; Urpí, T. "How to Tackle Schema Validation by View Updating", *Int. Conf. on Extending Database Technology (EDBT)*, Avignon, France, 1996, pp. 535-549.

[ECL94]   *ECLiPSe User Manual*, Technical Report, ECRC, 1994.

[FLV96]   Friesen,O.; Lefebvre, A.; Vieille, L. "Validity: Applications of a DOOD System", *Int. Conf. on Extending Database Technology (EDBT)*, Avignon, France, 1996, pp. 131-134.

[GCM+94] García, C; Celma, M.; Mota, L.; Decker, H. "Comparing and Synthesizing Integrity Checking Methods for Deductive Databases", *10th Int. Conf. on Data Engineering (ICDE)*, Houston, USA, 1994, pp. 214-222.

[GM95] Gupta, A; Mumick, I.S. "Maintenance of Materialized Views: Problems, Techniques and Applications", *Data Engineering*, Vol. 16, No. 2, 1995.

[KM90] Kakas, A.; Mancarella, P. "Database Updates through Abduction", *Proc. of the 13th Int. Conf. on Very Large Data Bases (VLDB)*, Brighton 1987, pp. 61-70.

[LT84] Lloyd, J.W.; Topor, R.W. "Making Prolog More Expressive". Journal of Logic Programming, 1984, No. 3, pp. 225-240.

[Min96] Minker,J. "Logic and Databases: a 20 Year Retrospective", *Int. Workshop on Logic in Databases (LID)*, San Miniato (Italy), 1996, pp. 5-52.

[ML91] Moerkotte, G; Lockemann, P.C. "Reactive Consistency Control in Deductive Databases", *ACM Transactions on Database Systems*, Vol. 16, No. 4, December 1991, pp. 670-702.

[MT93] Mayol, E.; Teniente, E. "Incorporating Modification Requests in Updating Consistent Knowledge Bases", *4th Int. Workshop on the Deductive Approach to Information Systems and Databases (DAISD)*, 1993, pp. 335-360.

[MT97] Mayol, E.; Teniente, E. "Structuring the Process of Integrity Maintenance", *8th Database and Expert Systems Applications (DEXA'97)*, Toulouse, 1997.

[Oli91] Olivé, A. "Integrity Checking in Deductive Databases", *Proc. 17th Int. Conf. on Very Large Data Bases (VLDB)*, Barcelona, 1991, pp. 513-523.

[PO95] Pastor, J.A.; Olivé, A. "Supporting Transaction Design in Conceptual Modelling of Information Systems", *Conf. on Advanced Information Systems Engineering (CAiSE)*, Jyväskylä, 1995, 40-53.

[Pas97] Pastor, J.A. "Automatic Synthesis of Update Transaction Programs in Deductive Databases", Ph.D. Thesis , Barcelona, January 1997.

[QW91] Qian, X.; Wiederhold, G. "Incremental Recomputation of Active Relational Expressions", *IEEE Trans. on Knowledge and Data Engineering*, Vol. 3, No. 3, September 1991, pp. 337-341.

[RCB+89] Rosenthal, A.; Chakravarthy,S.; Blaustein, B.; Blakeley, J. "Situation Monitoring for Active Databases", *15th Int.Conf. on Very Large Databases (VLDB)*, Amsterdam, 1989, pp. 455-464.

[RU95] Ramakrishnan, K.; Ullman, J. "A Survey of Research on Deductive Database Systems", *Journal of Logic Programming*, 23(2), 1995, pp. 125-149.

[SSU96] Siilberschatz,A.;Stonebraker,M.;Ullman,J."Database Research:Achievements and Opportunities Into the 21st. Century". Int. Workshop on Logic in Databases, San Miniato, Pisa, 1996, pp. 245-248.

[SK88] Sadri, F.; Kowalski R. "A Theorem-Prover Approach to Database Integrity", in J. Minker ed., *Foundations of Deductive Databases and Logic Programming*, Morgan-Kaufman, 1988, pp. 313-362.

[TO95] Teniente, E.; Olivé. A. "Updating Knowledge Bases while Maintaining their Consistency", *The VLDB Journal*, Vol. 4, Num. 2, 1995, pp. 193-241.

[TU95] Teniente, E.; Urpí, T. "A Common Framework for Classifying and Specifying Deductive Database Updating Problems", *11th Int. Conf. on Data Eng.*, Taipei (Taiwan), 1995, pp. 173-183.

[UO92] Urpí, T.; Olivé, A. "A Method for Change Computation in Deductive Databases", *18th Int. Conf. on Very Large Data Bases*, Vancouver, 1992, pp. 225-237.

[VLD94] *Special issue on prototypes of deductive database systems*, Journal of Very Large Databases, Vol. 3, No. 2, 1994.

[VPK+90] Vieille, P.; Bayer, P.; Küchenhoff, V.; Lefebvre, A. "EKS-V1, a Short Overview", *AAAI'90 Workshop on KB Management Systems*, 1990.

[VRK+94] Vaghani, J.; Ramamohanarao, K.; Kemp, D.B. et al. "The Aditi Deductive Database System", *The VLDB Journal*, Vol. 3, Num. 2, 1994, pp. 245-288.

[Wüt93] Wüthrich, B. "On Updates and Inconsistency Repairing in Knowledge Bases", *Int. Conf. on Data Engineering, Vienna (ICDE)*, 1993, pp. 608 - 615.

An Introduction to the TriggerMan Asynchronous Trigger Processor[†]

Eric N. Hanson and Samir Khosla[‡]

301 CSE

CISE Department

University of Florida

Gainesville, FL 32611-6120

(352) 392-2691

hanson@cise.ufl.edu

http://www.cise.ufl.edu/~hanson

Abstract

A new type of system for testing trigger conditions and running trigger actions outside of a DBMS is proposed in this paper. Such a system is called an *asynchronous trigger processor* since it processes triggers asynchronously, after triggering updates have committed in the source database. The architecture of a prototype asynchronous trigger processor called TriggerMan is described. TriggerMan is designed to be able to gather updates from a wide variety of sources, including relational databases, object-relational databases, legacy databases, flat files, the web, and others. TriggerMan achieves the ability to gather updates from so many sources using an extensible data source mechanism. TriggerMan can make use of the asynchronous replication features of commercial database products to gather updates: When cooperating with a source DBMS with direct support for asynchronous replication, TriggerMan can gather updates in an efficient and robust manner. TriggerMan supports simple, single-table (single data-source) triggers, as well as sophisticated multiple-table (multiple-data-source) triggers. It also will support temporal triggers using an extensible temporal function mechanism.

1.   Introduction

There has been a great deal of interest in active database systems over the last ten years. Many database vendors now include active database capability (triggers) in their products. Nevertheless, a problem exists with many commercial trigger systems as well as research efforts into development of database triggers. Most work on database triggers follows the event-condition-action (ECA) rule model. In addition, trigger conditions are normally checked and actions are normally run in the same transaction as the triggering update event. In other words, the so-called immediate binding mode is used. The main difficulty with this approach is that if there are more than a few triggers, or even if there is one trigger whose condition is expensive to check, then update response time can become too slow. A general principle for designing high-throughput transaction processing (TP) systems put forward by Jim Gray can be paraphrased as follows: *avoid doing extra work that is synchronous with transaction commit* [Gray93]. Running rules just before commit violates this principle.

Moreover, many advances have been made in active database research which have yet to show up in database products because of their implementation complexity, or

---

[†] This work was supported by the United States Air Force Rome Labs and NCR/Teradata.

[‡] Currently with Informix Software Corporation, samir@informix.com.

because of the expense involved in testing sophisticated trigger conditions. For example, sophisticated discrimination networks have been developed for testing rule conditions [Hans96]. In addition, techniques have been developed for processing temporal triggers (triggers whose conditions are based on time, e.g. an increase of 20% in one hour). Neither of these approaches has been tried in a commercial DBMS.

In this paper, the author proposes a new kind of system called an *asynchronous trigger processor*, or ATP. An ATP is a system that can process triggers asynchronously, after updates have committed in a source database, or have been completed in some other data source. Processing triggers asynchronously avoids slowing down update transactions with trigger processing logic. Moreover, since an ATP could be used with many different source DBMSs, the effort to develop the trigger processing code could be amortized over use with more applications. Really, an arbitrary application program can be used to transmit descriptions of database updates (update descriptors) to the ATP, and triggers can be processed on top of these update descriptors. The ability to process triggers based on updates from many different sources can help make it economically viable to implement sophisticated trigger processing code.

We are currently developing an ATP called TriggerMan as a vehicle for investigating issues related to asynchronous trigger processing. A simple subset of the functionality discussed in this paper has been implemented. We are actively doing the detailed design and implementation of the more advanced features of TriggerMan.

Part of the motivation for TriggerMan has been the surge in popularity of asynchronous replication features in commercial database systems. In actual practice, to achieve replication of data in a distributed DBMS, most database customers greatly prefer asynchronous replication to a synchronous replication policy based on distributed transactions using two-phase commit. The reason for this is that update availability and response time are both better with asynchronous replication. This was a motivating factor behind the choice to move to an external, asynchronous trigger processor, which also would avoid slowing down updates. Furthermore, as shall be explained later, the update capture mechanism built in to asynchronous replication systems can be used to send update descriptors to an ATP.

With respect to related research, many active database systems have been developed, including POSTGRES, HiPAC, Ariel, the Starburst rule system, A-RDL, Chimera, and others [Wido96]. In addition, there has been a notion of "de-coupled" rule condition/action binding mode for some time, as introduced in HiPAC [McAr89]. However, the implicit assumption regarding de-coupled rule condition evaluation and action execution was that the DBMS itself would still do the needed work. This paper outlines an alternative architecture that would off-load rule condition testing and action execution to a separate system.

Ultimately, the proposed TriggerMan/ATP architecture will provide an "active information server" capability that can support a wide variety of applications. This architecture will be able to support different tasks that involve monitoring of information sources, filtering of data, and selective propagation of information. TriggerMan can be used to augment traditional data management applications, as well as support new, distributed, heterogeneous information systems applications.

TriggerMan will be extensible in a number of ways, including the ability to add new data sources, new data types, and new temporal functions. To handle extended data types, the approach used will be similar to that used in object-relational database systems such as Informix Universal server.

2. The TriggerMan Command Language

Commands in TriggerMan have a keyword-delimited, SQL-like syntax. TriggerMan supports the notion of a connection to a remote database or a generic data source program. A connection description for a remote database contains information about the host name where the database resides, the type of database system running (e.g. Informix, Oracle, Sybase, etc.), the name of the database server, a userid, and a password. A single connection is designated as the default connection. There can be multiple data sources defined for a single connection. Data sources can be defined using this command:

> define data source [connectionName.]sourceName [as localName]
> [(attributeList)]
> [propertyName=propertyString,
> ...
>   propertyName=propertyString]

Suppose a connection "salesDB" had been defined on a remote database called "sales." An example data source definition for the table "sale" in the sales database might look like this:

> define data source salesDB.sale as sale

This command would read the schema from the salesDB connection for the "sale" table to gather the necessary information to allow triggers to be defined on that table.

Triggers can be defined using the following command:

> create trigger <triggerName> [in *setName*] [-inactive]
> from *fromList*
> [on *eventSpec*]
> [start time *timePoint*]
> [end time *timePoint*]
> [calendar *calendarName*]
> [when *condition*]
> [group by *attr-list*]
> [having *group-condition*]
> do *action*

Triggers are normally eligible to run as soon as they are created if a triggering event occurs. However, if the -**inactive** flag is specified the trigger remains ineligible to run until it is enabled later using a separate **activate trigger** command. The **start time** and **end time** clauses define an interval within which the trigger can be eligible to run. In addition, the name of a calendar object can be specified as part of a trigger. A calendar indicates "on" and "off" time periods. For example, a simple business calendar might specify "on" periods to be Monday through Friday from 8:00AM to 5:00PM. A trigger with a calendar is only eligible to be triggered during an "on" period for the calendar. In addition, whether a trigger is eligible to be triggered is determined by the logical AND of the eligibility criteria determined by (1) whether the trigger is active or not, (2) whether the current time is between the start time and end time, and (3) whether the associated calendar is in an "on" time period.

Triggers can be added to a specific trigger set, otherwise they belong to a default trigger set. The **from**, **on**, and **when** clauses are normally present to specify the trigger condition. Optionally, **group by** and **having** clauses, similar to those available in SQL [Date93], can be used to specify trigger conditions involving aggregates or temporal functions. Multiple remote tables (or other data streams) can be referenced in the **from** clause. This allows multiple-table triggers to be defined.

An example of a rule, based on an **emp** table from a database for which a connection has been defined, is given below. This rule sets the salary of Fred to the salary of Bob:

```
create trigger updateFred
from emp
on update emp.salary
when emp.name = "Bob"
do execSQL "update emp set salary=:NEW.emp.salary where emp.name=
'Fred'"
```

This rule illustrates the use of an execSQL TriggerMan command that allows SQL statements to be run against data source databases. The :NEW notation in the rule action (the **do** clause) allows reference to new updated data values, the new emp.salary value in this case. Similarly, :OLD allows access to data values that were current just before an update. Values matching the trigger condition are substituted into the trigger action using macro substitution. After substitution, the trigger action is evaluated. This procedure binds the rule condition to the rule action.

An example of a more sophisticated rule (one whose condition involves joins) is as follows. Consider the following schema for part of a real-estate database, which would be imported by TriggerMan using **define data source** commands:

```
house(hno,address,price,nno,spno)
salesperson(spno,name,phone)
represents(spno,nno)
neighborhood(nno,name,location)
```

A rule on this schema might be "if a new house is added which is in a neighborhood that salesperson Iris represents then notify her," i.e.:

```
create trigger IrisHouseAlert
on insert to house
from salesperson s, house h, represents r
when s.name = 'Iris' and s.spno=r.spno and r.nno=h.nno
do raise event NewHouseInIrisNeighborhood(:NEW.h.hno, :NEW.h.address)
```

This command refers to three tables. The **raise event** command used in the rule action is a special command that allows rule actions to communicate with the outside world [Hans97]. Application programs written using a library provided with TriggerMan can register for events. When triggers raise events, the applications registered for the events will be notified. Applications can run on machines running anywhere on the network that is reachable from the machine where TriggerMan is running.

3.   System Architecture

The general architecture of the TriggerMan system is illustrated in Figure 1. Each box in this diagram represents a system component. These components can run on the same machine or different machines. Most components are single processes. The exception to this is the TriggerMan server component, which has a parallel internal structure, consisting of a number of virtual processors, or *vprocs*. The vprocs communicate with each other via message passing. Hence, the TriggerMan server code can be made to run with little modification on shared-memory multiprocessors, shared-nothing machines, and collections of SMP machines connected by an interconnect. The first parallel implementation is designed to run on an SMP. The vproc concept has been used before successfully in the implementation of parallel DBMS software, such as the Teradata system [Witk93].

In the current TriggerMan system that runs on an SMP, vprocs are software objects that live in the same address space. Each vproc owns multiple threads, including:

- a *matching thread* that processes update descriptors arriving from data sources to see if trigger conditions are satisfied,

- a command server thread that handles requests from client applications, and

- *rule action execution threads* to run rule actions.

The number of vprocs is normally made equal to the number of real processors in the system. In the current implementation, single-table triggers are allocated to different vprocs in a round-robin fashion to allow parallel condition testing. A special client application called the Console allows a user to start the system, shut down the system, create triggers, define data sources, and run other commands supported by TriggerMan. Multiple threads, spread across the vprocs, allow parallel testing of trigger conditions on an SMP machine.

Two libraries that come with TriggerMan allow writing of client applications and data source programs. These libraries define the TriggerMan *client application programming interface* (API) and the TriggerMan *data source API*. The console program and other application programs use client API functions to connect to TriggerMan, issue commands, register for events, and so forth. Data source programs, such as a generic data source that sends a stream of update descriptors to TriggerMan, or

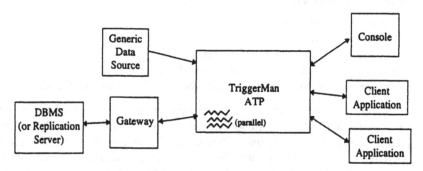

Figure 1 Architecture of the TriggerMan asynchronous trigger processor.

a DBMS gateway program that gathers updates from a DBMS and sends them to TriggerMan, can be written using the data source API.

4. Data Source Design

A flexible strategy is being designed to gather streams of update descriptors or other messages from data sources. A simple, generic data source could be an application that sends a stream of new data values to TriggerMan. Such a generic data source, as illustrated in Figure 1, would be a program written using the data source API. A more sophisticated data source could gather a stream of update descriptors from a database by cooperating with the replication services provided by the DBMS. E.g. with Sybase, a gateway program, as shown in Figure 1, could be written using the TriggerMan data source API and the Sybase replication API [Syba96]. This Gateway program would transmit update descriptors received from the Sybase replication server and propagate them to TriggerMan. A different gateway program could be written for each potential DBMS that might serve as a data source. For databases for which no replication service exists, a gateway program could be written that would query the database periodically and compare the answers to the queries to produce update descriptors to send to TriggerMan [Chaw96]. Alternatively, the gateway could trap inserts, updates and deletes using simple triggers in the source DBMS. Reading the database log is another alternative, but it is not usually realistic because DBMS vendors normally have a proprietary log format that other systems are not allowed to read, since the vendor reserves the right to change the log format.

TriggerMan will maintain catalogs and other persistent state information using a transactional DBMS. To preserve transaction semantics, the first approach to handling the stream of updates from a DBMS will be to apply the updates in TriggerMan, and run the resulting trigger actions, in commit order. The Sybase replication server, for example, presents updates in commit order, making this strategy feasible. The maximum transaction ID handled so far by TriggerMan will be recorded along with updates to TriggerMan's internal state information in a single transaction. If this transaction fails, the updates will be rolled back and will be re-applied later. Maintaining the maximum transaction ID applied so far will make sure TriggerMan does not forget to handle a transaction from the primary database.

An issue that will be addressed in the future is how to deal with high update rates in the data source databases. If updates are taking place at a high rate in the source DBMS, TriggerMan might not be able to keep up with the source if it must handle the updates in commit order. This is because it might not be possible to get enough concurrency or parallelism in the ATP if the updates are handled serially. Possible solutions to this problem will be considered, such as relaxing the requirement to handle updates in commit order (for database data/data sources) or in the order of arrival (for generic data sources). Piggybacking multiple update descriptors in a single message to the TriggerMan server and in a single broadcast to the vprocs may also make it possible to handle higher update rates.

5.   Temporal Trigger Support

Temporal triggers are triggers whose conditions are based on changes in a value or set of values over time. For example, a temporal trigger could be defined to fire if the sales from a particular store rise by more than 20% in one month. Prior work on temporal triggers has focused on logic-based trigger languages [Sist95]. The difficulty with these languages is that the user must specify the trigger in a logic-based notation, and logic-based languages with quantifiers may be difficult for typical application developers to master. Moreover, certain kinds of temporal conditions may be quite useful, yet be extremely difficult or impossible to specify using temporal logic. For example, one might envision a temporal trigger that would fire if the price of a stock had a "spike" in value, where the definition of "spike" is based on some application-specific mathematical criteria, such as "the average root mean square difference on a point-by-point basis between the actual sequence of values (curve) and an ideal spike is less than a threshold value." An example of an ideal spike and what an observed spike might look like is given below:

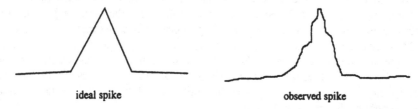

ideal spike   observed spike

The capability to detect a spike based on mathematical criteria would be much easier to express using an algorithmic language like C, C++, Java, or FORTRAN than using temporal logic. Moreover, temporal functions written in C, for example, may be able to evaluate temporal trigger conditions much more efficiently than the equivalent temporal logic-based condition evaluator.

Rather than use a temporal-logic-based language, we propose to use a set of basic temporal functions, including **increase, decrease** and several others, as well as temporal aggregates such as the **sum** and **count** of values over a certain time window. The benefit of using temporal operators to specify trigger conditions is that they are declarative, and relatively simple to understand – you say what you want, not now to achieve it. The implementation of the basic temporal functions will be provided as a standard part of the system. In addition, a *temporal function extensibility mechanism* is being developed to allow sophisticated application developers to write code to implement new temporal functions and register this code with the TriggerMan system. The extension code will be dynamically linked by the TriggerMan server when needed.

As mentioned earlier, the TriggerMan trigger language supports temporal condition specification through the use of the **group by** and **having** clauses familiar to users of SQL. For example, the following trigger will fire when there is an increase or decrease of more than 20% in the price of IBM stock in a six month period.

```
create trigger BigIBMchange
from stock
when stock.symbol = "IBM"
having increase(stock.price, "20%", "6 mo") or
   decrease(stock.price, "20%", "6 mo")
do raise event BigChange ("IBM")
```

The above trigger can be generalized to all "technology" stocks by introducing a **group by** clause and modifying the **when** clause, as follows:

```
create trigger BigTechStockChange
from stock
when stock.category = "technology"
group by stock.symbol
having increase(stock.price, "20%", "6 mo") or
   decrease(stock.price, "20%", "6 mo")
do raise event BigChange (:NEW.stock.symbol)
```

The **group by** capability is powerful since it allows triggers for multiple groups to be defined using a single statement.

Temporal functions can return boolean values (temporal predicates) and scalar values, such as integers and floating point numbers. These types of temporal functions can be composed in the **having** clause to form compound temporal conditions. For example, the following temporal function might compute a moving average of a value over a time window of width window_size:

```
moving_avg (expr,window_size)
```

The following example shows how this function could be used in conjunction with the **increase** function to detect when the 10-day moving average of the price of Oracle stock increases by more than 15%:

```
create trigger ORACLE_TREND
from stock
when stock.symbol = "ORCL"
having increase(moving_avg(stock.price, "10 days"), "15%")
do ...
```

Values of temporal aggregates computed in the **having** clause will sometimes need to be used in the trigger action. The trigger language needs a way to support this form of condition/action binding. When it is not ambiguous, the name of the temporal aggregate function can be used in the trigger action, as in the following example:

```
create trigger HighYearlySales
from sale
group by sale.spno
having sum(sale.amount, "1 yr") > 1000000
do execSQL "append to highSales(:NEW.sale.spno, :NEW.sum, Date())"
```

If the same function appears multiple times, the **as** operator can be used to bind names to the values produced by those functions, e.g.:

```
create trigger HighSalesAndCommssions
from sale
group by sale.spno
having sum(sale.amount, "1 yr") as s1 > 500000
and sum(sale.commission, "1 yr") as s2 > 50000
do execSQL "append to highSales(:NEW.sale.spno, :NEW.s1, :NEW.s2,
Date())"
```

5.1. Adding New Temporal Functions

The temporal function mechanism in TriggerMan is designed to be extensible. A new temporal operator can be defined using this notation:

define temporal function returnType funcName (argumentDefinition)
dynamicLinkLibraryName functionPrefix

The dynamicLinkLibraryName is the name of the dynamic link library (DLL) where relevant functions are kept. The DLL consists of compiled C code. The functionPrefix is the prefix of the name of all functions that are relevant to the temporal operator being defined. A temporal function's argument list can specify normal arguments, as well as initialization arguments used to initialize the state of the temporal function. Initialization arguments are preceded by the keyword **init**. A default value can also be provided for **init** arguments. For example, a new function to compute an exponential average could be registered with the system like this (the C:\tmanlib\expavg.dll file is a dynamic link library):

define temporal function double expavg (double newValue,
init double multiplier = 0.9) "C:\tmanlib\expavg.dll" "double_expavg"

Also, functions can be overloaded. For example, expavg can be re-implemented for different types, such as float, and the system will automatically use the right function depending on the data types with which it is called.

Functions with the proper formats and naming conventions need to be available in the dynamic link library to implement a temporal function. This kind of extensibility technique is similar to that used in extensible database systems such as POSTGRES [Ston90] and the Informix Universal Server [Info97]. To test the condition of a temporal trigger, state information related to the temporal trigger condition must be maintained. For example, state could simply be a number and a multiplier for a simple exponential average. For most temporal triggers involving temporal aggregates such as **increase**, **decrease** etc., the state of the trigger will be a time series. In addition, if there is a **group by** clause, one piece of state information (normally a time series) must be maintained for each group. The functions required in the DLL used to implement a temporal operator must be able to create a temporal trigger state object, delete the object, update the state of the object based on the arrival of new data or the passage of time, and get the current value of the temporal operator.

We use the C language to define the interface to a temporal operator's state object. C is used instead of C++ or Java [Arno96] because (1) we want very high performance, meaning that fully compiled code is required, ruling out Java, and (2) because dynamic linkers in Windows NT and Solaris (Sun Unix) support dynamic linking of C much better than dynamic linking of C++. In addition, we provide a reusable time-series abstract data type implemented in C for use by developers of new temporal functions, as well as for our own internal use.

Full details of the formats of the C functions required in a DLL to define the behavior of a temporal operator are not given here. A general description of the functions required (but not a complete list) is as follows:

constructor	A function to build the internal state object for a temporal trigger (or a single group of a temporal trigger in case a **group by** clause is used). Usually the state object will contain a time series.
destructor	A function to free the space used by a temporal trigger state object when it is no longer needed (e.g. when a trigger is dropped).
provide new history value	A function to take a new value and time stamp to update the history information (usually a time series) contained in the state object
provide new current time value	A function to provide a new value of the current time. This can be thought of as a "clock tick" function. The state object should be updated as needed based on this new time value (e.g. to trim off some of the oldest history values that have moved out of the time window of interest). This function will be called periodically for some operators, such as "holds(emp.salary, ">30000", "2 years")". With "holds" and some other temporal operators, it may be necessary to fire even if no new history value arrives.
get current value	Get the current value of the temporal operator (the result may be true/false or some other data type).

A protocol for firing temporal triggers needs to support both triggering when update events occur, and triggering when timers expire. The interface above allows TriggerMan to trigger both on update events and on timer expiration, as needed.

6. Support for Multiple-Table and Parallel Trigger Condition Testing

Allowing triggers to have conditions based on multiple tables greatly increases the power and expressiveness of the trigger language. However, efficiently testing multiple-table trigger conditions is a challenging problem. As part of prior work, we have developed an optimized multiple-table trigger condition testing mechanism known as the Gator network, a generalization of the TREAT and Rete networks used for rule condition testing in production rule systems such as OPS5 [Hans95]. We are investigating strategies that will allow development of a parallel version of the Gator network, as well as cost models and caching strategies specific to the environment of an asynchronous trigger processor. These new cost models and caching strategies are needed since TriggerMan runs in an separate address space and possibly on a separate machine from the DBMS or other data sources.

A parallel Gator network capability will be developed for TriggerMan to allow multiple table rule condition testing. A related approach has been successfully used to perform parallel rule condition matching in main-memory production systems using a Rete network [Forg82] organized as a global distributed hash table, or GDHT [Acha92]. The idea behind this strategy is as follows. A Gator network tree structure will be constructed for each trigger. Gator networks consist of nodes to test selection and join conditions, plus "memory" nodes that hold sets of tuples matching one or more selection and join conditions. For example, consider the following table schemas, trigger definition, and one possible Gator network for the trigger:

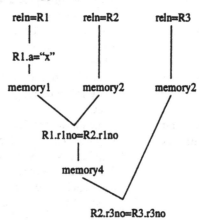

```
R1(r1no,a,b)
R2(r1no,r3no)
R3(r3no,c,d)

create trigger T1
from R1, R2, R3
when R1.r1no=R2.r1no
and R2.r3no=R3.r3no
and R1.a = "x"
then do ...
```

In this Gator network, memory1 logically contains the result of

select * from R1 where R1.a= "x"

Similarly, memory4 logically contains the result of

select * from R1, R2 where R1.a = "x" and R1.r1no=R2.r1no

In addition, memory nodes can be either stored or virtual. A stored node is like a materialized view. It actually contains the specified tuples. A virtual node is like a real view. It only contains a predicate defining which tuples should qualify. It does not contain the real tuples. Memory nodes at the leaf level, drawn at the top of a Gator network, are called alpha memory nodes. Inner memory nodes, holding join results, are called beta memory nodes. Only alpha memory nodes can be virtual.

A detailed discussion of how discrimination networks can be used for multiple-table trigger condition testing on a single processor can be found in [Hans96]. An outline of our approach to implementing a Gator network in parallel on a shared-nothing machine consisting of a set of vprocs is as follows:

1. The selection predicates will be allocated round-robin among the processors.
2. The tree shape of the network will be replicated on every vproc. The contents of alpha and beta nodes will not be replicated.
3. Stored memory nodes will be horizontally partitioned across the vprocs on a single attribute, normally a join attribute, using hash partitioning.

4. Stored memory nodes will be cached in their entirety in memory in TriggerMan on first use. Virtual memory nodes will never be cached. An LRU replacement strategy will be used with an entire memory node as the cache replacement granularity. (More sophisticated caching policies that allow caching a subset of a memory node are being considered).

5. For other attributes for which a fast access path is required to a memory node, such as additional join attributes or the primary key, parallel secondary hash partitions will be created. These are analogous to secondary indexes in a single-processor DBMS. For a memory node N(nno, X, ...) if the node has a primary partition on X, then a secondary partition on the nno (primary key) field can be formed by creating a table N_nno_index(nno,vproc_number) and doing a primary hash partition of N_nno_index on nno. A row in N_nno_index tells which vproc contains the tuple with a particular value of nno. This allows deletion of a tuple in N given its key (nno) value with two point-to-point messages, one to look up the processor where the tuple lives using N_nno_index, and one to actually delete the tuple.

6. Pattern matching will operate as follows:

   a. When a tuple update arrives, a description of the update will be packaged as a "token" and will be broadcast to all the vprocs. A token contains a tuple or an old/new tuple pair, along with a tag describing what kind of operation was performed (insert, delete or update). If the operation is an update, then the identification of which fields were updated will also be included in the token.

   b. Each vproc will test the token against its local collection of selection predicates. Event conditions from the **on** clause and regular selection conditions from the **when** clause will both be treated logically as selection conditions on tokens.

   c. For each matching selection predicate, the token will be forwarded onward down the network. For a single-table trigger, a match against the selection predicate for the trigger causes the trigger action to fire. The trigger action is executed once for each matching tuple, on the processor where the match is detected.

   d. For a multiple-table trigger, a match of a token against a selection predicate causes an update to the memory node below the selection predicate, and then the token is joined to a neighboring memory node (see below for a discussion of parallel joins of tokens to memory nodes). Resulting joining pairs of tuples (intermediate tokens) are then propagated down the network. When a token arrives at the bottom of the network (the P-node) the trigger action is run for that token.

In general, the following operations may need to be performed on a memory node: (1) insert a tuple, (2), delete a tuple and (3) join a tuple to the node. Each of these operations can be performed using one or two point-to-point messages from one vproc to another based on the hash partitioning scheme used. Consider memory2 from the Gator network shown earlier. Tuples may need to be inserted into or deleted from memory2. In addition, a tuple may sometimes be joined to memory2. This requires finding all the memory2 tuples such that memory2.r1no=CONSTANT for some constant value extracted from the r1no field of the tuple being joined to memory2. In this example, memory2 would be hash partitioned across the vprocs on the r1no column. Hence, to find all memory2 tuples satisfying memory2.r1no = CONSTANT, a vproc must do the following. First, use the hash function h used to define the partition of memory2 to find h(CONSTANT), yielding a value P, a vproc number. Any memory2 tuples that join to the current tuple must be stored on vproc P due to the way memory2 is partitioned. Send the tuple being joined to memory2 to vproc P. The join can them be completed locally on vproc P.

An additional issue is how to deal with non-equijoins. These are joins for which the join predicate is something other than the = operator. For example, the following trigger has a non-equijoin condition:

```
create trigger NonEquiJoinExample
from R1, R2
when R1.X >= R2.lowerBound and R1.X < R2.upperBound
do ...
```

For triggers like this, it is not possible to define a partitioning that can be used effectively to speed up join processing. Hence, in cases like this, broadcasts will be used to join a token to a memory node in parallel. Memory nodes will still be horizontally partitioned.

It is a good idea to avoid broadcasts and use a point-to-point messaging scheme instead when possible. This will avoid unnecessary CPU utilization. With point-to-point messaging, a parallel speedup can still be obtained because multiple tokens can be processed simultaneously on different processors.

We have outlined the basic pattern matching strategy for select/join trigger conditions. Fully detailed algorithms for all aspects of join condition testing and temporal condition testing are left for a future paper.

7.   Extensibility

TriggerMan is designed to be extensible. This will include support for new data types and operators, in addition to new temporal functions. Support for extended data types such as images, time series, web pages, text, etc. within a database management system has been supported in POSTGRES [Ston90] and Informix Universal Server [Info97] and is being included in other commercial database products. This feature is beginning to be used to add multimedia and object management capability to real-world database applications. The approach taken to support extensibility has been to define a dynamic link library of C functions with a certain format, including (1) constructor and destructor functions, (2) functions for translating an instance of a type from internal to external format, (3) functions for performing operations on instances of a type, (4) functions for estimating the cost of performing certain operations, etc. This library is then registered with the DBMS and dynamically linked when needed. As an example, an extended data type called Document could be created, and triggers could be defined on a stream of documents arriving from an intelligence-gathering source, implementing a form of selective dissemination of information using TriggerMan.

If possible, the approach to handling extended data types in TriggerMan will be to use the standard extensibility format used by Informix, and introduce commands to register new types with the system. If this is done, the same DataBlade modules used by Informix can be used by TriggerMan. Using the existing Informix type extension standard in TriggerMan is preferred to defining a new standard for extended types, since existing extended types that have already been implemented for Informix could be used with TriggerMan. However, we will define our own type extension module format if necessary. As part of the TriggerMan project, issues related to moving large objects between a DBMS and TriggerMan, caching the internal representation of large objects, and evaluating expensive predicates within the TriggerMan server will be investigated.

8. Performance of Initial Prototype

A version of the prototype TriggerMan server, consisting of roughly 20,000 lines of C++, is already operational. It implements single-table triggers, but has no persistent catalogs or ability to directly communicate with a DBMS via a replication server gateway. It supports parallelism using the concept of virtual processors (vprocs), making the code portable to both SMP

```
for {set i 2} {$i <= 2700} {incr i 2} {
    createTrigger t$i in ts1 {
    from EMPLOYEE
    on {insert EMPLOYEE}
    when {EMPLOYEE.salary = [expr 2700 % $i]}
    do {}} # no trigger action was run so only
}          # condition testing would be timed
```

and shared-nothing parallel computers. Performance tests were run on a dual-processor 75Mhz Sun SPARCstation 20. Originally, the TriggerMan command language was implemented as an extension of Tcl. We have since implemented a command-language parser so Tcl is not a required component of TriggerMan, and commands have a more natural, SQL-like syntax. At the time the tests were done, the createTrigger command was implemented as an extended Tcl command. The performance tests were done in the following manner. A single EMPLOYEE data source was defined. A total of 1350 triggers were then created using the Tcl program shown inset.

The triggers created fire when the inserted employee has a salary equal to some constant. The [expr 2700 % $i] expression is evaluated before the trigger is created. The % symbol is the modulo operator. There are 24 triggers that will fire when the inserted salary is zero. Triggers are allocated round-robin to the different vprocs. The tests were run first with one vproc, then with two. With one vproc, only one of the processors is used for rule condition testing. With two, both processors are used. The results are summarized in the following table:

Number of Processors Used (number of vprocs).	Average Condition Testing Time for All Triggers	Average Condition Testing Time Per Trigger
1	13.5 msec	10 µsec
2	7.5 msec	5.6 µsec

No selection predicate indexing strategy [Hans90,Hans96b] is currently used. A selection predicate index could dramatically increase performance for this example. This example shows that performance will be quite good for single data source triggers even when their conditions are not or cannot be indexed, as long as the number of triggers is not huge.

The TriggerMan code is now being ported to Windows NT, which will become our primary development platform. Code will be written in a way so that the system will be portable to NT and Solaris. Access to a database for storing TriggerMan's catalog information and other persistent state will be done using the ODBC interface so that TriggerMan will work with multiple different DBMS products.

9. Conclusion

The research outlined here seeks to develop principles that will allow the effective construction of asynchronous, or "outboard" trigger processing systems. A prototype ATP called TriggerMan is being implemented as a vehicle to explore asynchronous trigger processing issues and to validate the design approach introduced here. TriggerMan, or a system like it, could be useful in situations where current trigger systems are not. For example, TriggerMan could trigger on a stream of updates generated by a general application program that were never placed in any DBMS. Moreover, TriggerMan could place a trigger on two different data sources, one from a DBMS, and one from a program, performing an information fusion function. This type of function could be valuable in a number of heterogeneous information systems applications, e.g., in a chemical plant application, a trigger could correlate a stream of reactor vessel temperature and pressure values sent by an application with known dangerous combinations of temperature and pressure kept in a database, firing when it saw a dangerous combination. The main benefit of an ATP system is that it can allow sophisticated, "expensive" triggers (e.g. multiple-table and temporal triggers) to be defined against a database and processed using the best available algorithms, without adversely impacting on-line update processing. This could greatly expand the benefits of trigger technology in demanding, update-intensive environments.

The results of the TriggerMan project could lead to a new type of system to support applications that need to monitor changes to information – an asynchronous trigger processor. In addition, an architecture for asynchronous trigger processing similar to the one described here could be incorporated directly into a DBMS. This would allow the benefits of asynchronous trigger processing, particularly good update response time *plus* sophisticated trigger processing capability, without the need to incur the cost of moving update descriptors across the boundary from the DBMS into another system. In addition, it would not be necessary to cross back to the DBMS to run trigger actions against database data. In summary, the work outlined here can help develop a new, useful kind of information processing tool, the ATP, and point the way to improvements in the active database capability of existing database management systems. In either case, it will become possible to develop powerful information monitoring applications more easily, and these applications will run with faster performance.

Bibliography

[Acha92]   Acharya, A., M. Tambe, and A. Gupta, "Implementation of Production Systems on Message-Passing Computers," IEEE Transactions on Knowledge and Data Engineering, 3(4), July, 1992.

[Arno96]   Arnold, K., J. Gosling, *The Java Programming Language*, Addison Wesley Longman, 1996.

[Chaw96]   Chawathe, S., A. Rajaraman , H. Garcia-Molina , and J. Widom, "Change Detection in Hierarchically Structured Information," Proc. ACM SIGMOD Conf., 1996.

[Date93]   Date, C. J. And Hugh Darwen, *A Guide to the SQL Standard*, 3rd Edition, Addison Wesley, 1993.

[Forg82]   Forgy, C. L., Rete: "A Fast Algorithm for the Many Pattern/Many Object Pattern Match Problem," *Artificial Intelligence*, vol. 19, pp. 17-37, 1982.

[Gray93]   Gray, Jim, *Transaction Processing, Concepts and Techniques*, Morgan Kaufmann, 1993.

[Hans90]   Hanson, Eric N., M. Chaabouni*, C. Kim and Y. Wang*, "A Predicate Matching Algorithm for Database Rule Systems," *Proceedings of the ACM-SIGMOD Conference on Management of Data, pp. 271-280*, Atlantic City, NJ, June 1990.

[Hans96]   Hanson, Eric N., "The Design and Implementation of the Ariel Active Database Rule System," *IEEE Transactions on. Knowledge and Data Engineering*, vol. 8, no. 1, pp. 157-172, Feb., 1996.

[Hans96b]   Hanson, Eric N. and Theodore Johnson, "Selection Predicate Indexing for Active Databases Using Interval Skip Lists," *Information Systems*, vol. 21, no. 3, pp. 269-298, 1996.

[Hans95]   Hanson, Eric N., S. Bodagala, M. Hasan, G. Kulkarni, J. Rangarajan, *Optimized Rule Condition Testing in Ariel Using Gator Networks*, University of Florida CISE Department TR 95-027, http://www.cise.ufl.edu, October 1995.

[Hans97]   Hanson, Eric N. et al., "Flexible and Recoverable Interaction Between Applications and Active Databases," *VLDB Journal*, 1997 (accepted).

[Info97]   "Informix Universal Server," http://www.informix.com

[McCa89]   "McCarthy, Dennis R. and Umeshwar Dayal, "The Architecture of an Active Data Base Management System," *Proceedings of the. ACM SIGMOD Conference on Management of Data.*, Portland, OR, June, 1989, pp. 215-224.

[Oust94]   Ousterhout, John, *Tcl and the Tk Toolkit*, Addison Wesley, 1994.

[Sist95]   Sistla, Prasad A. and Ouri Wolfson, "Temporal Triggers in Active Databases," *IEEE Transactions on Knowledge and Data Engineering*, vol. 7, no. 3, June, 1995, pp. 471-486.

[Ston90]   Stonebraker, Michael., Larry Rowe and Michael Hirohama, "The Implementation of POSTGRES," *IEEE Transactions on Knowledge and Data Engineering*, vol. 2, no. 7, March, 1990, pp. 125-142.

[Syba96]   Sybase Replication Server Technical Overview, Sybase Inc., 1996.

[Wido96]   Widom, J. and S. Ceri, *Active Database Systems*, Morgan Kaufmann, 1996.

[Witk93]   Witkowski, A., F. Carino and P. Kostamaa, "NCR 3700 – The Next-Generation Industrial Database Computer," *Proceedings of the 19th VLDB Conference*, Dublin, Ireland, 1993.

Logging and Post-Mortem Analysis of Workflow Executions Based on Event Histories

Andreas Geppert and Dimitrios Tombros

Department of Computer Science, University of Zurich
{geppert,tombros}ifi.unizh.ch

Abstract. Logging and post-mortem analysis of workflow executions are important tasks of a workflow management system. In this paper, we show how both tasks are addressed in EvE, a prototypical distributed system implementing event-driven workflow execution. Essentially, both tasks benefit from the concept of an *event history* as it is present in active database systems. By using event-based workflow execution, the workflow log actually corresponds to the event history, and post-mortem analysis is accomplished through querying the event history. In our approach, an analysis of the required information has led to the design and development of a workflow analysis query service.

1 Introduction and Motivation

Workflow management [11, 15] is concerned with the specification and enactment of business processes. Workflow management systems (WfMSs) are software systems that implement these tasks. In addition to the primary tasks of specification and execution of workflows, a workflow management system also has to support additional functionality, such as the simulation, analysis, and evolution of workflow specifications, as well as analysis and maintenance of audit trails of workflow executions. Keeping an audit trail (or synonymously, workflow log) is an essential task for several reasons. First, many organizations, such as banks, are obliged to keep records of their business operations. Second, workflow specifications need to be maintained as any other kind of software, too. The need to modify workflow specifications can stem from changing requirements or inefficiencies and bottlenecks detected in old specifications. Such problems as well as possible optimizations can be determined based on the analysis of the workflow log. The other way round, without precise information about previous workflow executions, it can only be speculated which optimizations and improvements should be undertaken.

In this paper, we show how logging and analysis is performed in EvE [13], a distributed system providing event-driven workflow execution. In event-driven workflow management [4, 6, 8, 14, 16], the technology of active database management systems (ADBMSs) [1] is used to express certain aspects of workflow management, such as control flow enforcement [14] or agent synchronization [4]. Below, we show how ADBMS-technology can be adapted for logging and analysis of workflow executions. Concretely, we utilize the concept of an event history, as it is maintained by some ADBMSs (e.g., SAMOS [10] and REACH [3]).

While we adopt the concept of event history from ADBMSs, the implementation of events and the event history must be modified/extended in three ways:

- further attributes of event occurrences must be defined and stored (e.g., the workflow in which it occurred, distribution information, etc.),
- the event history must be maintained in append-only mode (whereas an ADBMS typically removes event occurrences upon event consumption),
- the event history must be made explicit to allow queries.

Based on these extensions, workflow logging and analysis can be provided in a quite elegant way, resulting in synergies of active systems technology and workflow management concepts.

The remainder of this paper is organized as follows: in the next section, we present an overview of our approach to workflow management. In section 3, we introduce the notion of event history in EvE, which is the fundamental concept for logging and analysis. Section 4 describes how workflow analysis is performed using the event history, as well as the design and implementation of an analysis query service. Finally, section 5 concludes the paper.

2 Overview

2.1 Workflows

A *workflow type* is the enactable specification of a (business or design) process. The workflow specification defines the process steps. Execution dependencies between the steps are also defined. There are ordering, temporal, and output-data dependencies. A step can either be an elementary activity or in turn a workflow. In the first case, the activity is performed by a person or a software system. Both are henceforth summarized under the term *processing entity* (PE). The workflow specification assigns responsible PEs to activities. In the second case, a step is a subworkflow and thus has in turn a complex structure and defines steps, constraints, and responsible PEs. A *workflow instance* is a concrete workflow executed according to the definition of its type. A WfMS is a software system that supports workflow specification and enactment.

In Figure 1[1] we present as an example the processing of a health insurance claim (HIC). The workflow is initiated once the HIC mail arrives at a local insurance agency. A clerk working at the local agency creates a file containing the diagnosis, treatments, costs, and the insurance number (activity accept_case). If the claimed amount is below 300 Swiss Francs the HIC is directly accepted and paid (activity print_check). Otherwise, the HIC has to be processed at the central company clearing center. There a sub-workflow is started, which consists of activities that may be performed in parallel. One is to check whether some of

---

[1] The meaning of the symbols is as follows. 1-in-N-split: exactly one of the successor activities is executed. AND-split: all the successor activities are executed. OR-join: at least one of the predecessors must have terminated with a certain result. AND-join: all the predecessors must have terminated with specific results.

Workflow structure and activity input/output parameters:

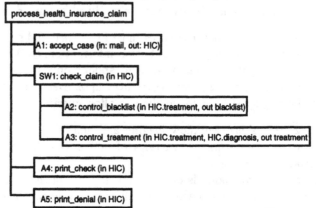

Activity execution dependencies:

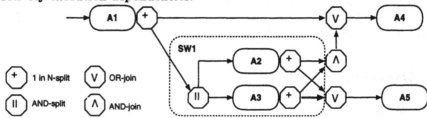

Fig. 1. The health insurance claim example workflow

the treatments are contained in a blacklist, in which case their coverage will be denied (activity `control_blacklist`). An activity of type `control_treatment` controls whether the treatment actually suits the diagnosis. If any of these controls fails, an entry is made in the customer record and a notification of the rejection is printed at the local agency (`print_denial`). Otherwise, a payment check can be printed at the local agency (`print_check`).

2.2 Brokers and Services

Besides workflow specification and enactment, further requirements such as the ability to integrate external systems and to reuse old artifacts (parts of specifications, mediation software) are important for WfMSs. All these requirements can only be met if various aspects of a WfMS-architecture are exactly defined:

- *components* representing PEs that take part in one of the workflows—the structural and informational aspect,
- *tasks* that can be performed by those components—the functional aspect,
- *parameterized* events through which components interoperate—the operational aspect, and

– *rules* determining how, when and under which constraints the components can/must perform the activities—the behavioral and temporal aspects.

We propose the Broker/Services Model (B/SM) [20] as a model for such architectures. Workflow specifications are mapped onto B/SM and are automatically augmented with the necessary elements to attain executability. B/SM is described in detail in [20] so that this section gives only a short description for the sake of comprehension.

Brokers represent components of a WfMS, i.e., they model PEs involved in the execution of one or more workflows in a way that allows them to interoperate. They are *reactive* and offer *services* to other brokers (their clients). Brokers can access the functionality of their peers through service requests. The set of activities that can be executed within a WfMS (i.e., its functionality) is described by services. A service is specified by a *signature* consisting of the service name, a set of typed input parameters bound at request time, a possible reply with its output parameters, as well as exceptions the request may cause (e.g. due to a service being temporarily unavailable). Broker behavior is defined in terms of event-condition-action (ECA) rules, which define their basic capabilities, i.e., reaction to request events, or to complex workflow-specific events such as the termination of multiple activities within a workflow. The supported composite event constructors are conjunction, sequence, disjunction, negation, repetition, and concurrency (i.e., two occurrences generated at different sites cannot be ordered temporally). In our example workflow we use the following brokers:

– a broker representing customers generating the requests to process health insurance claims
– insurance agents which provide the `accept_case` service (represented by the brokers `Worklist-Meier` and `Worklist-Hefti`). Their behavior is expressed by the rule:

```
ON    request(accept_case, mail)
IF    (HIC = create_claim(mail)) AND HIC.amount > 300
DO    request(control_blacklist, HIC.treatment)
      request(control_treatment, HIC.treatment, HIC.diagnosis)
```

– multiple PEs situated at the clearing center: a database application (broker `DBApp-RSA`) to check acceptance of the treatment (`control_blacklist`) and several experts (e.g., broker `Exp-Seehofer`) which can check the compatibility between treatment and diagnosis (`control_treatment`). If both controls are successful, the check can be printed as expressed by the rule:

```
ON    reply(control_treatment, treatment) AND
      reply(control_blacklist, blacklist)
IF    treatment="OK" AND blacklist="NO"
DO    request(print_check, HIC)
```

– a demon (broker `Printer`) providing printing services on printers at the insurance agency (`print_check`, `print_denial`).

A specific service is provided by one or more brokers and can be initiated by client brokers through request events. Service execution is terminated when the reply or one of the possible exception events defined for the service is generated. The brokers which provide a service requested during the execution of a workflow are determined by way of their basic capabilities as well as through *responsibility* predicates, which express organizational constraints (e.g., task delegation) or task-specific requirements (e.g., authorizing the payment of a large amount of money). Responsibilites only define the eligible PEs; in case there are multiple brokers eligible at runtime, it can be specified which of them should serve the request (e.g., randomly, or based on the current load of the candidates).

In typical cases, workflow activities consume input data, produce output data, and read and manipulate data items stored in some sort of data store. Thus, *production data* must flow through a workflow according to the workflow's definition. Most of the production data will be managed by external systems and in the general case, it is not justified to assume that the WfMS and the production data store are tightly integrated. However, the B/SM supports access of processing entities to these data through operations defined for their types.

In B/SM, workflows are defined by a name, a set of initiating requests and a set of terminating replies. The workflow structure and related execution constraints are defined by the reaction of certain brokers to specific situations (e.g., reaching a deadline). Workflows are executed by the execution of the services provided. A workflow starts executing when its *initiation event* occurs which is a request of the first service to be provided.

2.3 EvE

Brokers and consequently, workflows are executed through the use of the distributed event engine *EvE* [13]. A comprehensive description of EvE is beyond the scope of this paper; we thus introduce only its general concepts as far as needed for the understanding of this paper.

EvE's major purpose is to support brokers by providing event management, detection, storage, and broker notification in distributed environments. It needs several database functions (e.g., persistence, transactions, object management). Preferably an object-based system is used in order to prevent the impedance mismatch between the object-oriented broker model and the persistent platform. Furthermore, as previous experiments have shown, object-oriented ADBMSs are of little benefit, because they do not provide the sufficient functionality (e.g., with respect to event types), so that we decided to build EvE on top of the object manager Shore [5] and to implement the missing functionality ourselves.

EvE consists of various server nodes to which brokers are connected. The principle by which brokers use EvE is the following: broker ECA-rules are translated to rules stored and executed in EvE. When a broker generates a primitive event, it notifies its local EvE-server about the occurrence. EvE then performs composite event detection and determines brokers that have registered a notification interest for such primitive and potentially detected composite event occurrences which may result from this event. EvE then performes *task assignment* by determining those brokers that should react to the event (e.g., by executing a requested service). These brokers are then appropriately informed and react as defined by their ECA-rules (whereby these reactions can in turn generate new events, and so forth). An important task of EvE upon event detection is the maintenance of an event history in which all primitive and composite event occurrences are represented.

In the present paper, we will not consider in detail the technical aspects of event generation and (composite) event detection in EvE. It is sufficient to note that these actions take place in a distributed environment, a fact that has to be considered for the correct definition of the semantics of events [21].

3 The Event History in EvE

In this section, we introduce the event history in EvE and show how it can be used to accomplish workflow execution logging.

3.1 Structure of the Event History

Figure 2 how the relevant structures of event occurrences and the event history in OMT-notation (operations, attributes, and subclasses have been omitted).

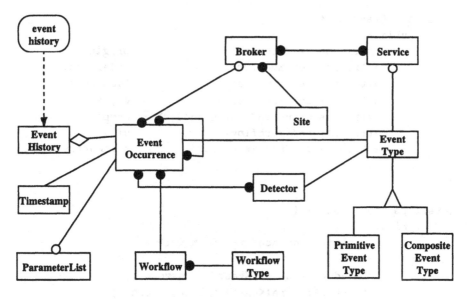

Fig. 2. Object Model of EvE Data Structures

An event occurrence has several attributes:

- a reference to the event type for which it occurred,
- a reference to the workflow in which it occurred,

- a reference to the broker which generated the event,
- a timestamp specifying at which point in time the event has been detected by an EvE-server,
- service-specific parameters in case of service request or reply events,
- a list of references to component events (in the case of composite events).

For each event type exists an event detector. In case of composite events, the detector maintains references to those component event occurrences that can still be used for event composition. Ultimately, the event history contains a sequence of event occurrence objects as components. Figure 3 shows the class definitions of event occurrences (**EventOcc**) and the event history in SDL-syntax [17].

The current naming and format of log entries in EvE is not compatible to the Workflow Management Coalition audit data specification standard [22] which also requires the logging of activity state information. It is however, straightforward to map the event information stored in EvE to the proposed abstract specifications. Although our model does not have to explicitly define activity states, activity instance state modification events can be mapped to service request, reply and exception events.

```
interface EventOcc {
    public:
        attribute ref<Broker>              origin;
        attribute ref<EventOcc>            refers_to;
        attribute ref<Timestamp>           timestamp;
        attribute ref<EventType>           etype;
        attribute sequence< ref<EventOcc> > comp;
        attribute ref<Workflow>            wfid;
        attribute ref<ParameterList>       parameters;
        ...
}

interface EventHistory {
    private:
        attribute sequence< ref<EventOcc> >   occs;
    public:
        int  addOcc(in ref<EventOcc> newocc);
        int  dump(in lref<char> filename) const;
        ...
}
```

Fig. 3. Interfaces EventOcc and EventHistory

3.2 Event Detection and Workflow Logging

Events are detected in EvE by dedicated event detectors. For composite event detection, we have adapted the technique of event graphs (which has originally been proposed for Sentinel [7] and has also been used in REACH [3]) to distributed systems. For event composition, the *chronicle* parameter context [7] is used, since this mode offers precisely the semantics required by workflow management (in the chronicle mode, the oldest appropriate component is chosen whenever there are multiple candidates for event composition).

During event detection, each detected (primitive or composite) event occurrence is also inserted into the event history. ADBMSs typically maintain only parts of the event history, e.g., by storing candidate component events in composite event detectors (e.g., SAMOS [10]). Event occurrences typically are removed as soon as the event occurrence has been consumed for event composition. In EvE, however, event occurrences are never removed (except upon explicit request from an administrator).

Summarizing, workflow logging actually means to maintain the event history. In fact, workflow logging is (operationally) for free, as it is done during event detection. We do not expect that EvE in general and the event history in particular will turn out as bottlenecks, because EvE is solely responsible for coordination of PEs (who perform the "real" work). In other words, EvE's tasks will consume only a fraction of the time needed by PEs to provide their services, and thus EvE will be able to serve large numbers of PEs in a timely manner. Moreover, EvE's approach to workflow enactment based on compiled ECA-rules is more efficient than those interpretating workflow specifications.

Note that over time the event history might grow very large and that it can contain information about workflows that have terminated long ago. If this information is no longer needed for analysis, it can be dumped to a file and removed from the history.

Table 1 shows a sample event history for the HIC-workflow. The example reflects three workflows (3245 through 3247).

4 Workflow Analysis

We now discuss the analysis of workflow executions based on the event history.

4.1 Evaluation Criteria

A number of criteria/queries can be used for the analysis and evaluation of an event history at a given time:

1. (a). How many workflows are currently active? (b). How many have terminated successfully? (c). For how many is termination still pending (i.e., no termination event has occurred)?

workflow id	event type	activity/service	origin	time
3245	Request	process_HIC	Customer	13.5./10:01
3245	Request	accept_case	Worklist-Meier	13.5./10:01
3246	Request	process_HIC	Customer	13.5./10:04
3246	Request	accept_case	Worklist-Hefti	13.5./10:14
3247	Request	process_HIC	Customer	13.5./10:16
3247	Request	accept_case	Worklist-Meier	13.5./10:26
3247	Reply	accept_case	Worklist-Meier	13.5./10:37
3247	Request	control_blacklist	Worklist-Meier	13.5./10:37
3247	Reply	control_blacklist	DB-App-RSA	13.5./10:49
3247	Request	print_denial	Worklist-Meier	13.5./10:51
3247	Reply	print_denial	Printer	13.5./10:52
3245	Reply	accept_case	Worklist-Meier	13.5./10:57
3245	Request	control_treatment	Worklist-Meier	13.5./10:57
3245	Request	control_blacklist	Worklist-Meier	13.5./10:57
3246	Reply	accept_case	Worklist-Hefti	13.5./10:59
3246	Request	print_check	Worklist-Hefti	13.5./11:00
3246	Except.(NOTAVAIL)	print_check	Printer	13.5/11:02
3245	Reply	control_blacklist	DB-App-RSA	13.5./11:04
3246	Request	print_check	Worklist-Hefti	13.5./11:55
3246	Reply	print_check	Printer	13.5./11:57
3245	Reply	control_treatment	Exp-Seehofer	14.5/08:43
3245	Request	print_check	Worklist-Meier	14.5./09:12
3245	Reply	print_check	Printer	14.5./09:13
3245	Reply	process_HIC	Worklist-Meier	14.5./09:13

Table 1. A sample event history

2. (a). How often did an instance of a specific workflow type execute. (b). How often did it terminate with a resulting termination event of a certain type?
3. What is the average/maximal/minimum execution duration of various workflow types?
4. What is the average/maximal/minimum execution duration of individual activities?
5. How often has a specific service (activity) been requested, or a subworkflow executed?
6. How often has a certain resource (PE) been involved in a workflow?
7. (a). What is the average/minimum/maximum delay time until a resource (processing entity) is available for the provision of a service? (b). Which resources become more often bottlenecks?
8. (a). How many and what types of exceptions have been raised during the execution of a specific workflow type? (b). Which requests cause more often exceptions?

Several of these criteria can be applied to all workflows, or to workflows of a specific type. The information obtained can typically be used in several ways:

- to find inadequate, incomplete, or incorrect specifications,
- to determine parts of workflow specifications that are worthwhile to be optimized, and
- to determine the existence and identify the location of bottlenecks.

4.2 Design of a Query Service for the Event History

The information that should be evaluated can be obtained by formulating and running queries on the event history created by the system. Some of the queries can be evaluated during the execution of a particular workflow to be analyzed, while others are only meaningful for postmortem evaluation. These queries can be categorized according to their purpose.

A first group of queries concerns the detection of semantic (specification) errors. The fact that workflows of a certain type often terminate with undesired results—representing a semantic failure (see query 2)—can indicate that the specification is incomplete, e.g., because conditions have been omitted. An overly high number of raised exceptions (query 8) occurring during the execution of a workflow type can indicate that exceptional situations are not addressed appropriately in the specification or that certain services are often not available in an adequate or timely manner.

The second group of queries helps to identify those workflows whose optimization is worth considering. For instance, if the answer to query 2 shows that a rather small number of instances of a certain workflows is executed (with respect to the total number of executed workflows), then optimizing this workflow type will probably not increase the overall throughput very much. The same conclusion can be drawn from query 3: if the average execution time is rather small, then optimizing the corresponding workflow specification might not improve overall system performance.

Bottleneck situations and inefficiencies may be identified by several queries (e.g., 5, 6, 7, and 8). Potential bottlenecks are processing entities, the resources they use for activity execution, as well as system infrastructure. Bottlenecks can be caused due to the following factors:

- high workloads such as many requests for time-consuming tasks as specified in the workflow,
- scarcity of resources leading to a limited choice of responsible and capable processing entities for given tasks,
- unavailability of system infrastructure (e.g., a network node on which the only capable broker for a specific service resides) leading to frequent exceptions and consequently new requests, and
- suboptimal task assignment strategies.

The presented queries can be combined to help the identification of service requests which cause more often an exception, which services are the most time consuming or have the largest variation in their execution time, and which processing entities are involved in the execution of such "problematic" services.

In order to support analysis, the WfMS has to support the extraction of the relevant information from the event history. For that matter, a set of base queries has been identified for EvE that is sufficient for this purpose. In a first step, these queries are specified in OQL. The next section shows how these queries are implemented.

Figure 4 shows a query that computes the times consumed by executions of an activity or workflow of a specific type (see query 4 above). The begin of the activity/workflow is given by the event named **W-request**, and its end is given by the event of type **W-reply**. This query computes execution times of the activity/workflow within executions of the workflow type WF. If execution times should be considered independent of the workflow within which they were executed, then the predicate in line 4 would be omitted.

If the average (minimum/maximum) execution time should be computed, then the average (mimimum/maximum) operators would be applied to the result of this query (i.e., avg, min, or max).

```
select   occ2->timestamp - occ1->timestamp
from     occ1 in eventhistory, occ2 in eventhistory
where    occ1->etype->name = W-request
         and occ1->workflow->wf_type->name = WF
         and occ2->replies_to = occ1
         and occ2->etype->name = W-reply
```

Fig. 4. A sample OQL-query against the event history

Further analysis of the queries shows that a set of "base" queries can be determined that occur in many complex queries used for analysis. For instance, the base query **searchWorkflow(W, E)** finds all event occurrences of E that have occurred in workflow executions of type **W**. These base queries can be combined and reused in a meaningful way in many different analysis scenaria. We used this fact to simplify the implementation of an interface which can be used for the analysis of workflows.

4.3   Implementation of the Query Service

Ideally, the storage system would provide for a query language such as OQL or SQL. However, object managers typically do not support queries, and among the object-oriented DBMSs only O$_2$ [2] fully implements OQL. We reclined to move to that platform due to, e.g., better extensibility in Shore [5]. Likewise, using a relational DBMS was not considered either, for similar reasons and in order to avoid the impedance mismatch between the B/SM and the storage platform.

Thus, the queries either had to be hard-wired in the analysis interface, or otherwise a full-blown query language would have to be implemented. Due to the fact that queries are always directed against the same extension (namely, the event history), we decided against the second alternative and pursued a mixed approach. The base queries mentioned above have been implemented as methods of the class **EventHistory**. All these queries produce as their result sets of event occurrences which can thus be easily combined using normal set operations (also implemented in the analysis interface). In order to improve response time for analysis queries, we use the indexing and clustering facilities of Shore.

Figure 4.3 shows the signatures of the base queries. Each query returns a set of event occurrences. As noted above, complex queries can be formulated, by applying on the results of the base queries the conjunction (**AndJoin**) or disjunction (**OrMerge**) operators.

```
interface EventHistory {
    ...
    set<EventOcc> SearchWorkflow(in lref<char> wfName,
                                in lref<char> eType) const;
    set<EventOcc> SearchBetween(in long fromTime, in long toTime,
                                in lref<char> eName) const;
    set<EventOcc> SearchBefore(in long fromTime,
                                in lref<char> eName) const;
    set<EventOcc> SearchAfter(in long untilTime,
                                in lref<char> eName) const;
    set<EventOcc> SearchReferring(in lref<char> eName,
                                in ref<EventOcc> refTo) const;
    set<EventOcc> SearchBroker(in lref<char> bName,
                                in lref<char> eName) const;
    set<EventOcc> SearchSite(in lref<char> siteName,
                                in lref<char> eName) const;
    set<EventOcc> AndJoin(in set<EventOcc> set1,
                                in set<EventOcc> set2) const;
    set<EventOcc> OrMerge(in set<EventOcc> set1,
                                in set<EventOcc> set2) const;
}
```

Fig. 5. Signatures of Query Implementations

The provided base queries are used to implement any of the queries described in section 4.1. For example, query 1 (a) can be implemented by combining **SearchWorkflow()** and **SearchReferring()** to find out which of the initiated workflows (i.e., those for which the initiation event set is not empty) have successfully ended (i.e., also a termination event is logged in the event history). Similarly, **SearchBroker()** can be used in combination with **SearchWorkflow()** and **SearchReferring()** to determine which brokers are most often involved in an unsuccessful request (causing an exception).

The complex queries as well as computations and aggregation operations are implemented in the analysis application programs.

In order to prelimiarily test the performance of the analysis query interface, we have run several test queries on a synthetic event history (see Fig. 6). The tests were executed on a SUN Ultra 1 (128 MB main memory, 167 MHertz processor) under Solaris; results are given as wallclock time in seconds.

Query Q1 retrieves all occurrences of a certain type having occurred within a given time interval. For this query, a full scan of the event history is neccessary. Q2 retrieves all occurrences of a certain type that have been generated within an instance of the HIC-workflow (query searchWorkflow). Finally, Q3 retrieves all occurrences of a certain type that have been generated by a specific broker within an instance of the HIC-workflow (queries searchWorkflow and searchBroker, then combined by AndJoin). 100 different workflow types have been defined. The workflow instances (500, 1000, 2000, and 5000, respectively) have been distributed evenly among these five types. Each workflow instance generated an average of 8 event occurrences.

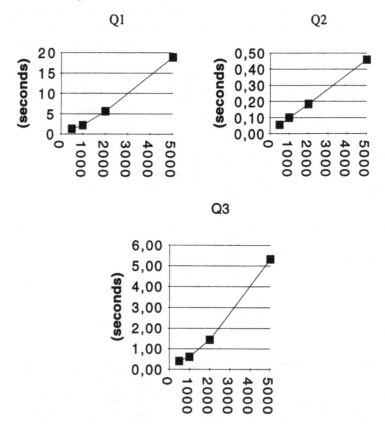

Fig. 6. Results of Analysis Query Performance Tests

Results are not satisfying when the whole event history has to be searched (as in Q1). If restrictions on workflow types, event types, and/or brokers are specified, then the query execution time can benefit from indexing. In addition, the rather high number of workflow types leads to more selective queries and therefore to smaller execution times (alternatively, if only 5 workflow types are defined but the same number of instances, then results are much worse especially when indexing is used). In our future work, we will investigate how to improve the performance of analysis queries.

In future experiments, we will compare these results with those obtained when using an OODBMS with a full-fledged query language. We will also test the performance of the event detectors using the Beast-benchmark [12].

4.4 Example

We conclude this section by showing through a sample scenario how workflow execution analysis helps to improve specifications and throughput.

Assume a workflow administrator has the impression that system throughput is rather low. He can check this by computing the average/minimal execution times of instances of the HIC-workflow (query 3.). He suspects that the activity control_treatment is responsible for delays. He can validate this hypothesis using queries 5. (for determining whether this activity has actually been executed frequently) and 4. (to determine how large the average execution time of the activity is). He might then discover that a large fraction of the execution of HIC-workflows is due to this activity. Finally, he uses query 6. for the people (insurance experts) that are responsible to execute the activity. The administrator then comes to the conclusion that the expert represented by the broker Exp-Seehofer is the bottleneck, because the activity is assigned very often to this resource (e.g., as this expert is the only one with certain capabilities such as expertise in specific treatments and diseases).

After this bottleneck has been discovered, the appropriate reaction would be to add one or more additional experts with the same capabilities, and to modify the task assignment such that the load is better balanced among these experts.

5 Conclusion

In this paper, we have shown how logging and analysis of workflow executions can be elegantly performed in a system that supports the notion of event history. Although logging and analysis are considered as important tasks of a workflow management system (e.g., [15]), and the Workflow Management Coalition has already drafted a standard for workflow logs [22], little work has been done in other event-driven approaches to workflow management. Non-event-driven commercial systems (e.g., Staffware [19]) usually provide rudimentary logging information in the form of an audit trail which is dumped to a file, whereas others such as COSA Workflow [18] store log records in a relational DBMS. To the best of our knowledge none provide sophisticated analysis tools.

In order to perform logging and analysis adequately in our context, several extensions and modifications have been necessary with respect to event histories maintained by ADBMSs:

- the event history must be made explicit, such that it can be queried,
- further event attributes have to be added for event occurrences (e.g., a reference to the component who generated the event, etc.),
- event occurrences should not be deleted from the history upon event consumption (this is similar to the model proposed in [9]).

From the point of view of active systems, our approach to workflow logging exploits synergies, since EvE as an active system has to maintain the event history anyway. Analysis is then possible by allowing queries against the event history. Further ways to use the knowledge in the history are possible; e.g., "replays" of single workflow executions based on the event sequence pertaining to the particular workflow. These tasks and further usages of the event history and the implementation of a graphical analysis tool are part of our future work.

Acknowledgements

We are indebted to our colleagues Klaus Dittrich and Markus Kradolfer for fruitful discussions and our students Patrick Brunschwig, Natalie Glaus, and Tom Haas for their great contributions to EvE. We also acknowledge the comments of the anonymous reviewers which helped us to improve the paper, as well as the funding of D. Tombros by the Swiss National Science Foundation in the context of the SPP-IuK project Swordies (no. 5003-045356).

References

1. ACT-NET Consortium. The Active Database Management System Manifesto: A Rulebase of ADBMS Features. *ACM SIGMOD Record*, 25(3), September 1996.
2. F. Bancilhon, C. Delobel, and P. Kanellakis, editors. *Building an Object-Oriented Database System. The Story of O2*. Morgan Kaufmann Publishers, 1992.
3. A. Buchmann, J. Zimmermann, J. Blakely, and D. Wells. Building an Integrated Active OODBMS: Requirements, Architecture, and Design Decisions. *Proc. 11th ICDE*, Taipeh, Taiwan, March 1995.
4. C. Bussler and S. Jablonski. Implementing Agent Coordination for Workflow Management Systems Using Active Database Systems. *Proc. 4th RIDE -ADS*, Houston, TX, February 1994.
5. M.J. Carey, D.J. DeWitt, M.J. Franklin, N.E. Hall, M.L. McAuliffe, J.F. Naughton, D.T. Schuh, M.H. Solomon, C.K. Tan, O.G. Tsatalos, S.J. White, and M.J. Zwilling. Shoring up Persistent Applications. *Proc. ACM-SIGMOD*, Minneapolis, May 1994.
6. F. Casati, S. Ceri, B. Pernici, and G. Pozzi. Deriving Active Rules for Workflow Management. *Proc. 7th DEXA*, Zurich, Switzerland, September 1996.
7. S. Chakravarthy, V. Krishnaprasad, E. Anwar, and S.-K. Kim. Composite Events for Active Databases: Semantics, Contexts and Detection. *Proc. 20th VLDB*, Santiago, Chile, September 1994.
8. U. Dayal. Organizing Long-running Activities with Triggers and Transactions. *Proc. ACM-SIGMOD*, Atlantic City, NJ, May 1990.

9. A.A.A. Fernandes, M.H. Williams, and N.W. Paton. A Logic-Based Integration of Active and Deductive Databases. *New Generation Computing*, 1996.

10. S. Gatziu and K.R. Dittrich. Detecting Composite Events in an Active Database System Using Petri Nets. *Proc. 4th RIDE-ADS*, Houston, TX, February 1994.

11. D. Georgakopoulos, M. Hornick, and A. Sheth. An Overview of Workflow Management: From Process Modeling to Workflow Automation Infrastructure. *Distributed and Parallel Databases*, September 1994.

12. A. Geppert, S. Gatziu, and K. Dittrich. A Designer's Benchmark for Active Database Management Systems: OO7 Meets the Beast. In *Proc. 2nd RIDS*, Athens, Greece, September 1995.

13. A. Geppert, M. Kradolfer, and D. Tombros. EvE, an Event Engine for Workflow Enactment in Distributed Environments. Technical Report 96.05, Department of Computer Science, University of Zurich, May 1996.

14. A. Geppert, M. Kradolfer, and D. Tombros. Realization of Cooperative Agents Using an Active Object-Oriented Database Management System. *Proc. 2nd RIDS*, Athens, Greece, September 1995.

15. S. Jablonski and C. Bussler. *Workflow Management. Modeling Concepts, Architecture, and Implementation*. Intl. Thomson Computer Press, London, 1996.

16. G. Kappel, P. Lang, S. Rausch-Schott, and W. Retschitzegger. Workflow Management Based on Objects, Rules, and Roles. *Bulletin of the IEEE Technical Committee on Data Engineering*, 18(1), March 1995.

17. The Shore Project Group. *Shore Data Language Reference Manual. Version 1.0.* Computer Science Department, University of Wisconsin, Madison, August 1996.

18. Software-Ley. *COSA Workflow, Product Description, Version 2.0 (in German)*, 1996.

19. Staffware House. *Staffware Workflow, System Overview*, 1996.

20. D. Tombros, A. Geppert, and K.R. Dittrich. Design and Implementation of Process-Oriented Environments with Brokers and Services. In B. Freitag, C.B. Jones, C. Lengauer, and H.-J. Schek, editors, *Object-Orientation with Parallelism and Persistence*. Kluwer Academic Publishers, 1996.

21. D. Tombros, A. Geppert, and K.R. Dittrich. Semantics of Reactive Components in Event-Driven Workflow Execution. *Proc. 9th CAiSE*, Barcelona, Spain, June 1997.

22. *Workflow Management Coalition Draft Audit Specification*, Document Number WFMC-TC-1015 (http://www.aiai.ed.ac.uk/WfMC/DOCS/if5/if59611.html), August 1996.

Rule Modelling and Simulation in ALFRED

Markus Schlesinger[1] and Georg Lörincze[2]

[1] University of Bern, Institute of Information Systems,
Engehaldenstr. 8, CH - 3012 Bern, Switzerland
schlesi@ie.iwi.unibe.ch
[2] University of Bern, Institute of Computer Science,
Neubrückstr. 10, CH - 3012 Bern, Switzerland
lorincze@iam.unibe.ch

Abstract. This paper presents rule modelling and simulation in the active database system ALFRED (**A**ctive **L**ayer **F**or **R**ule **E**xecution in **D**atabase Systems). In contrast to other systems, rules and user commands are represented *entirely* as enhanced Colored Petri Nets which we call Action Rule Flow Petri Nets (ARFPN). To achieve this, certain requirements had to be met such as a uniform model which is appropriate for the modelling of rule components, rule semantics, and rule triggering as well as for rule simulation. In this paper we describe how each rule component is represented as an ARFPN with respect to rule semantics. In addition, we discuss in detail the simulation of rule processing by means of an order workflow example.

1 Introduction

In recent years much research effort has been devoted to the area of active database management systems (ADBMS) ([15], [2], [7], [5], [8]). These systems extend traditional (passive) database management systems (DBMS) with the ability to react on certain situations by the execution of actions. Such behavior is called *active*. In ADBMS, active behavior is defined by *event-condition-action* (ECA)-rules [3]. An ECA-rule consists of an event, a condition, and an action. Events and conditions are used to represent situations. The event specifies when a rule is triggered, the condition describes a certain database state, and the action defines the response. The rule action is executed if the rule is triggered and the condition is satisfied.

In almost all ADBMS several different models are needed for rule representation and processing. These approaches have disadvantages like the existence of redundant rule data and the need for combining all models. In this paper we describe a model in which rules can be represented, analyzed, and processed entirely. This model is called ARFPN (**A**ction **R**ule **F**low **P**etri **N**ets) that extends Colored Petri Nets (CPN) and is employed in the ADBMS ALFRED (**A**ctive **L**ayer **F**or **R**ule **E**xecution in **D**atabase Systems). This system has a layered architecture and can in principle be put on top of every (passive) DBMS. ALFRED consists of a *User System* which the user works with and a *Processing System* in which user commands and rules are modelled, analyzed, and processed on the basis of ARFPN. This model can be used to represent rule semantics as well as to simulate rule processing.

The paper is structured as follows: Section 2 gives a brief overview of some important requirements which have influenced the development of ALFRED. It also contains a description of the architecture and the supported rule language. Section 3 introduces an order workflow example consisting of several rules. Section 4 explains how these rules are modelled on an ARFPN basis and Sect. 5 describes the simulation (processing) of rules by means of the defined workflow example. The paper is summarized in Sect. 6.

2 ALFRED

ALFRED is a project at the Institute of Information Systems of the University of Bern which started in 1995 ([12], [14]). This work is motivated by a Swiss National Science Foundation project. The aim was to examine the application of trigger concepts for enforcing business rules [11]. Several case studies were analyzed to determine the types of rules being employed in different organizations. Furthermore, some approaches for rule classification were developed and trigger mechanisms of commercially available DBMS have been compared ([10], [13]).

2.1 Requirements

ADBMS must meet some essential requirements [6]. First of all, an ADBMS is a DBMS itself which means that all the concepts provided by a passive DBMS are required for an ADBMS as well. Secondly, an ADBMS must support the definition and management of rules. Another requirement is that ADBMS must have execution models which allow the processing of rules considering the defined rule semantics. In the context of rule modelling and simulation, three important classes of requirements have influenced the design of ALFRED.

1. **Rule specification**
   ADBMS can be employed in organizations of different industries. In each organization, a set of business rules exists that prescribes how the business is done, i.e., statements about guidelines and restrictions with respect to states and processes in the organization [9]. Some of these business rules can be modelled as executable ECA-rules, others not because they contain components that cannot be processed in ADBMS. A main requirement for ALFRED was the support of a rule definition language which allows each business rule to be represented as an ECA-rule whether the rule can be (automatically) processed or not. This means that the rule language must support the definition of primitive and composite components for processing and linguistic components for the registering of non-processable rule parts. In addition to this, the rule language must support the specification of different rule execution semantics (e.g. *priorities* and *coupling modes*).

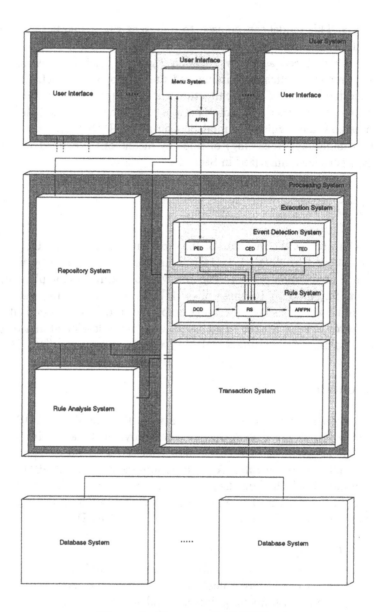

Fig. 1. Architecture of ALFRED

1 named *ARFPN*) which integrates triggered rules. The third subsystem is the *Dynamic Cycle Detection (DCD)* which monitors existing cycles at runtime. The *Transaction System* processes user commands and rules by evaluating conditions and executing actions in this system or in the underlying DBMS. Furthermore, transactions and locks for objects and data are created, monitored, and managed.

2. **Uniform model**

   In addition to rule execution, an ADBMS must allow the analysis of the rule base, e.g., to detect cycles and check their termination, to check whether the rule set is confluent, and whether rules are in conflict or rule components are redundant. To meet these requirements, rules and the corresponding data need to be represented in one uniform model.

3. **Rule simulation**

   The realized active behavior can differ from the desired one. For this reason, ADBMS should support a simulation tool to check the specified behavior. Such a tool enables the user to control rules, detect and eliminate errors and/or side effects. Furthermore, the simulation reveals the rules being triggered and their execution time points.

2.2 Architecture

To satisfy the requirements mentioned above, we have chosen to design ALFRED with an *enhanced layered* architecture. In this approach, each underlying DBMS need only support data definition and data manipulation commands which build the communication interface to ALFRED. The possibility of processing commands and rules necessitates additional consideration of rule characteristics like triggering dependencies and cycle detection. For this reason, parts of the underlying DBMS are not adequate and must be realized in the active layer. Examples are the management of transactions and locks. Therefore, the chosen architecture enables ALFRED to be put on top of every (passive) DBMS in principle.

As mentioned above, ALFRED consists of a *User System* and a *Processing System* (cf. Fig. 1) which are described briefly in the following ([12], [14]).

1. **User System**

   The *User System* is a graphical user interface [1] and consists of a *Menu System* and a translator called *AFPN (Action Flow Petri Net) Generation*. The *Menu System* allows the definition of rules and the interaction with the underlying DBMS. The translator (in Fig. 1 named *AFPN*) models each user command as a simple Petri Net (PN) that is passed to the *Processing System*.

2. **Processing System**

   This system consists of an *Execution System*, a *Rule Analysis System*, and a *Repository System*.

   (a) **Execution System**

   In this system, user commands and rules are modelled as ARFPN and processed step by step. To achieve this, the *Execution System* consists of three subsystems. The occurrence of each event is detected by the *Event Detection System* which consists of the *Primitive Event Detection (PED)*, the *Composite Event Detection (CED)*, and the *Time Event Detection (TED)*. The main processing is done by the *Rule System*. This includes the *Rule Simulation (RS)* which moves tokens through the generated ARFPN. Another component is the *ARFPN Generation* (in Fig.

(b) **Rule Analysis System**

After the definition or modification of rules, the rule set may be inconsistent – which must be avoided. For this reason, ALFRED supports the analysis of the rule base for the detection and termination of cycles, confluence, conflicts and redundancy.

(c) **Repository System**

The *Repository System* contains object and rule data for analysis and information retrieval.

2.3 Rule Language

The spectrum of active behavior is fixed by the rule language. This prescribes which types of events, conditions, and actions can be employed. Additionally, rule semantics can be specified.

The **ALFRED Rule Definition Language** (ARDL) consists of a *structural part* which defines the structure and the contents of a rule, and a *semantics part* for determining the processing of rules.

1. **Rule structure**

ARDL supports the definition of *event-based* (e.g. ECAA) and *pattern-based* (e.g. CAA) rule structures. Each component can be *linguistic, primitive,* or *composite*. Linguistic components are used to specify rule parts that cannot be processed automatically.

An event-based rule is triggered when the corresponding primitive or composite event is detected. Examples of primitive events are *data manipulation events, absolute time point events,* and *abstract events*. Composite events consist of primitive and/or (other) composite events that are combined by event operators. ARDL supports *boolean, choice, sequence, repetition, interval* and *time operators*.

Conditions determine what has to be checked. Primitive conditions are, e.g., **true, false**, *predicates*, and *queries*. Composite conditions consist of primitive and/or (other) composite conditions combined by the boolean operators **AND, OR** and **NOT**. Furthermore, composite conditions can be *functions* that return boolean values.

The action component of a rule specifies the response to a certain situation. Examples of primitive actions are *data manipulation actions, message actions* and *abstract actions* that are used to raise abstract events. Composite actions are sequences of primitive actions and others like *transactions, procedures* and *applications*.

2. **Rule semantics**

The semantics part of the ARDL consists of a set of statements that are applied to prescribe the rule processing. Examples of supported semantics are *execution time points* (**pre, post**), *execution granularities* (**instance, set**), *global priorities, coupling modes* (e.g. **immediate, deferred, detached independent**), *parameter contexts* (e.g. **recent, chronicle, cumulative**), *milestones* [2], and *contingency plans* [4].

3   Example of Workflow Modelling

We explain a simplified workflow example which is used throughout the next two sections to illustrate in detail how rules are mapped to ARFPN structures and to show the semantics of these structures.

We consider an order workflow in a mail-order house for clothing. During this workflow, several processes can be done automatically whereas others have to be initiated by employees. The workflow steps are:

1. **Arrival of order**
   An order of a customer initiates the business process. For the reason of simplicity, we assume an order to be in electronical form (e.g. e-mail) which can be (automatically) stored and processed.
2. **Checking of stock-in-trade**
   After an order has arrived, the system has to make sure that the stock-in-trade is large enough for the order to be carried out.
3. **Actualizing stock-in-trade**
   If there are sufficient articles for fulfilling the order, a competent employee must be charged with the task of gathering the articles. After this has been done, the system can update the stock-in-trade for these articles in the database.
4. **Generation of delivery note**
   After all the ordered articles are compiled, a delivery note must be generated.
5. **Generation of invoice**
   After the generation of a delivery note, an invoice can be generated and added to the delivery. At this point, the *accounting* and *delivery workflow* must be started.
6. **Finalization of order**
   At the end of an order processing, the system must finalize it (e.g. mark it as finished).

In ALFRED we define an ARFPN which describes this workflow and additional rules that guarantee the correct processing of an order (cf. Fig. 2). For the reason of simplicity, the rules are only drawn as black-boxes. In order to understand the process and the connection between the rules, we explain shortly the task of each rule:

- R_1: *arrival of order*
  This rule waits for the arrival of an order and updates the order data.
- R_2: *check stock-in-trade*
  This rule checks whether there are enough articles in the stock for the order to be carried out. If this is not the case, rule R_3 and R_4 are triggered and the *TED* is activated. Additionally, a competent employee is charged with the current order.
- R_3: *wait for new article*
  This rule waits for a new article to arrive and checks whether this article

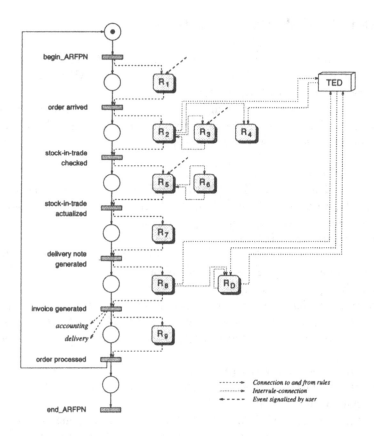

begin_ARFPN

order arrived

stock-in-trade
checked

stock-in-trade
actualized

delivery note
generated

invoice generated

accounting

delivery

order processed

end_ARFPN

Connection to and from rules
Interrule-connection
Event signalized by user

Fig. 2. Order workflow depicted as ARFPN (simplified)

corresponds to an ordered one. The arrival of a new article is signalized by
an employee.

- R_4: *delivery problems*
  This rule guarantees that the responsible employee is warned when an order
  has to wait too long for the arrival of new articles presently not available
  in-house. As this is a rule that depends upon a time value, it is connected to
  the *TED* which generates an abstract event on completion of the time delay
  originating from rule R_2.

- R_5: *wait and actualize*
  If we assume that the compilation of articles is not done automatically, the
  system has to wait until all the ordered articles are gathered. This must be
  signalized by an employee. After the gathering, the stock-in-trade has to be
  updated which triggers rule R_6.

- R_6: *ordering of new articles*
  If after an update the current stock is below a certain threshold, an order for
  new articles is generated.

- R_7: *generate delivery note*
  This rule generates and prints out a delivery note for the ordered articles.
- R_8: *generate invoice*
  This rule generates and prints out an invoice for the ordered articles, triggers rule R_D and activates *TED*.
- R_D: *dunning*
  This is a meta rule for the handling of dunnings. The rule is triggered by two abstract events. One event is used to pass the order identification and is raised by rule R_8 or R_D. The other event is signalized by the *TED* on completion of a predefined time delay. If this timespan elapsed (e.g. 30 days after delivery of invoice), the system automatically generates a dunning, retriggers the rule (for the second dunning) with the same order identification and resets the *TED* to the new time delay.
- R_9: *finalize order*
  At the end of the order workflow, the system has to finalize the order (e.g. mark it as finished, gather time information of run through time).

4 Rule Modelling

In this section we describe how rule structures, components, and semantics are represented as ARFPN in general and look in detail at the representation of rule R_5 (*wait and actualize*).

4.1 Structure

Rules can have different structures. Figure 3 shows how an ECAA-rule is modelled as ARFPN. The rule components are represented as dotted ellipses.

The modelling of an event component ends with a transition and a place that is called **End Of Event (EOE)**. To connect the event part to the condition component, a further transition (**Begin Of Condition (BOC)**) is employed that indicates the beginning of the rule condition. Because the evaluation of a condition may result in **true** or **false**, two places are needed to point out the result (**true-out**, **false-out**). The evaluation is done in a special transition (**End of Condition (EOC)**) which indicates the end of this component as well. To connect the action components to the condition part, two transitions are needed that are labelled **Begin Of Action (BOA)**. These are connected to the places representing the results of the condition evaluation. The end of an action component is represented as a transition (**End Of Action (EOA)**) as well. The rule ends with a place (**End Of Rule (EOR)**) which is connected to both **EOA** transitions.

4.2 Events

Linguistic and *primitive* events are modelled as (simple) places. To model *composite* events, we designed an appropriate ARFPN for every event operator. These nets are also used to represent composite events that are composed of more than

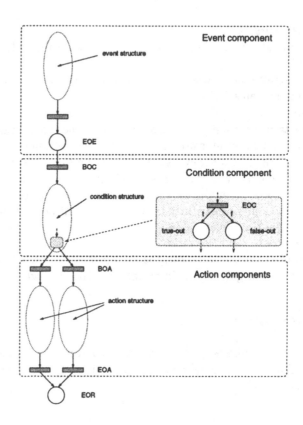

Fig. 3. ECAA-rule depicted as ARFPN

one operator. To guarantee their semantically correct modelling, additional constructs and algorithms were developed ([12], [14]).

The event component of rule R_5 is composite. It consists of two primitive events (**stock-in-trade checked** and **articles gathered**) and the boolean operator **AND** (cf. Fig. 4). This event is signalized if both primitive events are detected regardless of their order of occurrence. The event operator is modelled as a transition which is connected to the places representing the primitive events. This transition is firable if each place contains at least one token. The other transition and place (**EOE**) indicate the end of the rule event.

4.3 Conditions

ARFPN contain a (special) construct that permits the modelling of choices. This construct (cf. Fig. 4) consists of a transition and two places that are connected by labelled arcs (**t** and **f**). These places are called **true-out** to indicate satisfaction and **false-out** to point out violation. If such a *condition transition* is firable, the evaluation is done in the *Transaction System* that returns the result. After evaluation, the transition fires and gives a token to one of these places depending on the result.

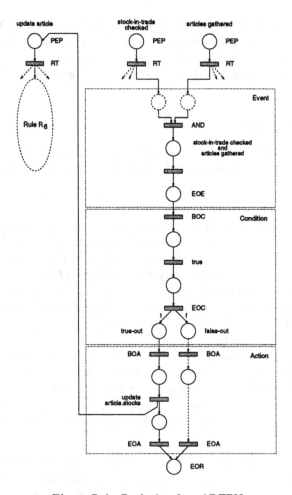

Fig. 4. Rule R_5 depicted as ARFPN

Linguistic and *primitive* condition types are modelled as (simple) transitions. *Composite* conditions are modelled using additional structures for the boolean operators as well as for programming constructs like *sequences*, *choices* and *loops*.

The condition component of rule R_5 is primitive and always satisfied (**true**). It is represented by a transition that is labelled with **true** (cf. Fig. 4). Note that the **false-out** place will never contain a token.

4.4 Actions

Linguistic and *primitive* actions are modelled as transitions. *Composite* actions are, e.g., sequences of primitive actions or procedures. The same additional constructs as mentioned in Sect. 4.3 are used to model these actions.

The action component of rule R_5 is primitive and consists of a data manipulation operation which updates the stocks of articles. It is modelled as a transition (cf. Fig. 4). Note that R_5 has only an action component for the **true** branch. The (degenerated) **false** branch is represented as a single place that will never be processed.

4.5 Rule Integration

Having defined the various components of a rule we now have to integrate the modelled rule into the rule set. For this reason, we need the following additional constructs:

1. **Replication structure**
   In case of a large rule set, a primitive event can participate in many composite events. It would not be efficient to remember all those places. Instead, a simple construct is added. Each type of primitive event is represented only by one place called **Primary Event Place (PEP)**. With the aid of a **Replication Transition (RT)**, the event will be copied as often as required. This approach has the advantage that only the locations of all **PEP** have to be known.

2. **Interrule connections**
   Rules can trigger other rules that have to be considered while processing. In ALFRED, we allow different *execution time points* (**pre** and **post**) and *granularities*. These rule semantics are realized by simple transitions that connect the rule to the corresponding **PEP**. For the sake of simplicity, these transitions are symbolically realized by action transitions in all figures shown in this paper.

In Fig. 4, the modelling of rule R_5 and the above mentioned structures are shown. In addition to the rule components, we can see the replication structure for the two primitive events and the connection to rule R_6. The replication structure of each primitive event consists of one **PEP** and one **RT**. The interrule connection is realized by a transition (**update article.stocks**) whose outgoing arc points to the **PEP** which represents the corresponding primitive event.

5 Rule Simulation

The behavior of a large rule set is difficult to understand. For this reason, ALFRED supports the simulation of rule processing to monitor the systems reaction given a user-defined start situation. This is entirely done in the *Processing System* wherein only rules are considered which are really needed. To determine this set of eligible rules, the ARFPN is processed step by step using runtime information supplied by the *Transaction System*.

On the basis of the workflow example introduced in Sect. 3, we discuss how the simulation is done. Therefore, we roughly show the beginning and the end of the workflow simulation and explain in detail the processing of rule R_5 by means of three snapshots.

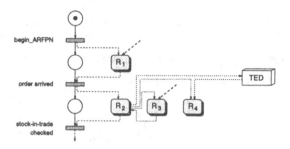

Fig. 5. First part of order workflow

5.1 Start of the Order Workflow Simulation

In Fig. 5, the first part of the order workflow is shown. The ARFPN on the left hand side starts with begin_ARFPN following the user commands order arrived and stock-in-trade checked. The rules depicted in the figure do not really exist in this ARFPN at this moment. They are only integrated into the structure dynamically at the time they are triggered.

The *AFPN Generation* sends the AFPN (without rules) to the *Primitive Event Detection (PED)* which looks for primitive events being activated by user commands. It detects such a correspondence between the first transition begin_ARFPN and rule R_1, for example. For each activation, the *PED* inserts an arc into the AFPN from the transition to the corresponding PEP. The enhanced AFPN (ARFPN) is then passed to the *Rule Simulation (RS)* where the token game starts. The begin_ARFPN transition can be fired and two new tokens will be created. One of them is put into the place before order arrived, the other one is moved to the corresponding PEP. Because rule R_1 is composed of two abstract events (begin_ARFPN, new order arrived) connected by AND, the *Composite Event Detection (CED)* has to wait for the occurrence of the second event. If this occurs, the rule is copied out of the rule set (*instantiation*) and integrated into the existing ARFPN by connecting the EOR place to the order arrived transition. If the processing of this rule is finished, the EOR place contains a token and hence the *RS* can fire the order arrived transition.

The same procedure will take place for the rule R_2 which even defines a cascading rule triggering. During the processing of R_2, rules R_3 and R_4 are integrated dynamically if necessary and a time value is passed to the *Time Event Detection (TED)*. After the delay elapses, *TED* will generate an abstract event which is signalized to the *CED*. With this approach, rule R_4 will be executed at a certain time in the future. After having processed rules R_2 and (possibly) R_3, the transition stock-in-trade checked can be fired.

5.2 Snapshot 1: Rule Triggering

Figure 6 shows the snapshot of the processing after firing the transition stock-in-trade checked. The connection between this transition and the PEP of the

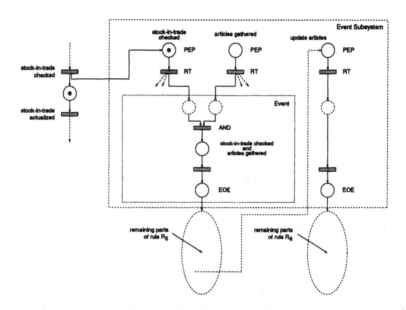

Fig. 6. Processing the event component of rule R_5

corresponding event has been made by the *PED* before the actual processing. When the *RS* fires the **stock-in-trade checked** transition, two new tokens are created. One is put into the place before the transition **stock-in-trade actualized**, the other one is moved to the **PEP**. The latter moving causes the calling of *CED* which plays the token game in the *Event Subsystem* (the parts from *all* rules between the places **PEP** and **EOE**) and reports rules being triggered.

In our example, the *CED* can fire the **RT** of the **stock-in-trade checked** event, then it has to wait for the abstract event **articles gathered**, which must be signalized by an employee. As long as this event is not activated, the processing of this workflow is suspended. Once it is raised, *CED* can fire the corresponding **RT** and moves the token into the following place. As there are enough tokens now for the firing of the **AND** transition, this will be done and the composite event is detected. The *CED* transports the token until it reaches the **EOE** of the rule, then it reports the identification of the triggered rule back to the *RS*.

The *Rule Simulation* passes the identifications with additional information (the location of the transition **stock-in-trade actualized**) to the *ARFPN Generation*.

5.3   Snapshot 2: Rule Instantiation

The *ARFPN Generation* instantiates the triggered rules and integrates them into the existing ARFPN with respect to the defined rule semantics. This instantiation is done because different *execution time points, execution granularities,* and *coupling modes* need to be realized.

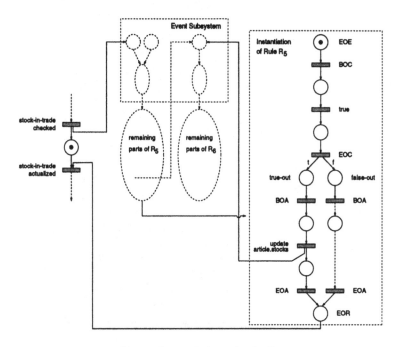

Fig. 7. Instantiation of rule R_5

Figure 7 shows the process of the instantiation and integration for rule R_5. The rule is copied only from its EOE place to its EOR place. The token residing in the original EOE is *moved* to the new EOE. Then the *ARFPN Generation* has to construct the back connection to the existing ARFPN, e.g., according to coupling modes. In R_5, we assume an **immediate** mode for the *event-condition* and *condition-action* coupling. Because of this, a connection is established from the EOR place to the **stock-in-trade actualized** transition. After this, the location of the new EOE is passed to *RS* which continues the simulation. Note that only after the integration of the rule instance the semantics of the ARFPN is correct again. For this reason, *RS* has to make sure that after the marking of a PEP, it first calls *CED* and then *ARFPN Generation* before it continues the processing.

RS can now continue with the token game. The condition of rule R_5 is always **true** and a token is put into the **true-out** place. Then the BOA transition can be fired. After this, the transition **update article.stocks** is fired. This is done by calling the *Transaction System (TS)* with the necessary action data (stored in the transition) and the parameters (stored in the token). After having processed the action on the database, *TS* informs *RS* which then continues the simulation.

5.4 Snapshot 3: Rule Integration

Because the **update article.stocks** transition is connected to a PEP (this connection was done at the rule definition time point and copied during the instantiation process), *CED* is called again to detect events. *RS* then gets the identific-

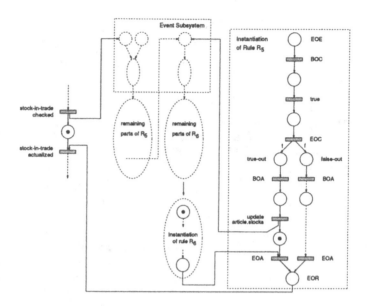

Fig. 8. Integration of rule R_6

ation of the triggered rule R_6 and passes it to the *ARFPN Generation*. The rule is then instantiated and integrated at the correct position (cf. Fig. 8).

RS continues to move tokens. First, rule R_6 is processed (all other transitions cannot be fired), then the **EOA** transition of rule R_5 is fired and eventually the **stock-in-trade actualized** transition can be processed. At this point both rules R_5 and R_6 have been executed.

5.5 End of Order Workflow Simulation

Figure 9 shows the last part of the order workflow. Rule R_7 is integrated after the firing of **stock-in-trade actualized** transition, same with rule R_8 and the firing of **delivery note generated** transition. Rule R_8 calls the *TED* with a time value and the location of the **PEP** to mark before it is connected to rule R_D.

The dunning meta rule R_D is based on a composite event connected by the boolean operator **AND**. After the defined time delay, the *TED* moves a token into the appropriate place and the *CED* starts to play the token game. The rule contains actions that trigger the rule again. This cascaded triggering is realized by new rule instances. We assume that this rule has a **detached independent** coupling mode between the event and condition component and an **immediate** mode between the condition and action part. This means that the condition and action are processed in a new transaction independent of the triggering one. For this reason there is no connection from rule R_D to R_8.

When RS fires the **invoice generated** transition, tokens are passed to two other workflows (*accounting* and *delivery*) and rule R_9 is integrated. The firing of the **order processed** transition creates two tokens. One token is put into

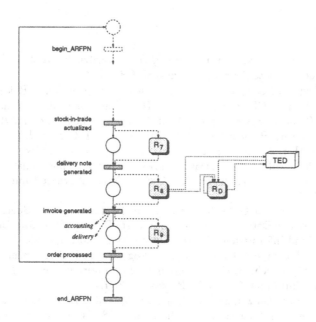

Fig. 9. Last part of order workflow

the place in front of **end_ARFPN**; by the firing of this transition, the employee is informed of the order being finished. The second token will be moved into the place in front of **begin_ARFPN** and the order process can restart.

6 Conclusion

In this paper we introduced the ALFRED system and the application of Action Rule Flow Petri Nets (ARFPN) that extend Colored Petri Nets for rule modelling and simulation. ALFRED is based on an enhanced layered architecture which enables it to be put on top of every (passive) DBMS in principle. We also described some important requirements for rule modelling and simulation and we briefly explained the architecture and subsystems of ALFRED as well as the rule definition language. This language supports the definition of business rules in terms of ECA-rules whether they can be (automatically) processed or not.

In contrast to other ADBMS, user commands and rules are modelled in AL-FRED in their entirety as ARFPN. Such a modelling guarantees that the rule processing is exactly prescribed and can be controlled. Additionally, we explained how the rule structures, components, and semantics like the cascading of rules are realized. For rule simulation, we introduced a simplified order workflow example which contains several rules. This example illustrates that rules which can be automatically executed as well as rules which have to be triggered by employees may be represented and processed by the ALFRED approach.

References

1. R. Blum. Entwurf und Implementierung einer Benutzerschnittstelle für ALFRED. Institute of Computer Science, University of Bern, 1997.
2. H. Branding, A. Buchmann, T. Kudrass, and J. Zimmermann. Rules in an Open System: The REACH Rule System. In N.W. Paton and M.H. Williams, editors, *Rules in Database Systems*, pp. 111 – 126. Springer, London et al., 1993.
3. S. Chakravarthy, B. Blaustein, A.P. Buchmann, M. Carey, U. Dayal, D. Goldhirsch, M. Hsu, R. Jauhari, R. Ladin, M. Livny, D. McCarthy, R. McKee, and A. Rosenthal. HiPAC: A Research Project in Active, Time-Constraint Database Management. Technical Report XAIT-89-02, Xerox Advanced Information Technology, 1989.
4. S. Chakravarthy and D. Mishra. Snoop: An Expressive Event Specification Language For Active Databases. Technical Report UF-CIS-TR-93-023, Department of Computer and Information Sciences, University of Florida, 1993.
5. O. Diaz, N. Patom, and P. Gray. Rule Management in Object-Oriented Databases: A Uniform Approach. In *Proceedings of the 17th International Conference on Very Large Data Bases*, pp. 317 – 326, Barcelona, 1991.
6. K.R. Dittrich, S. Gatziu, and A. Geppert. The Active Database Management System Manifesto: A Rulebase of ADBMS. In T. Sellis, editor, *Rules on Database Systems, Lecture Notes in Computer Science 985*, pp. 3 – 17. Springer, Berlin et al., 1995.
7. S. Gatziu and K.R. Dittrich. SAMOS: an Active Object-Oriented Database System. *IEEE Bulletin of the Technical Committee in Data Engineering: Special Issue On Active Databases*, 15 (1 - 4), pp. 23 – 26, 1992.
8. N.H. Gehani, H.V. Jagadish, and O. Shmueli. Event Specification in an Active Object-Oriented Database. In *Proceedings of the ACM SIGMOD International Conference on Management and Data*, pp. 81 – 90, San Diego, 1992.
9. H. Herbst. *Business Rule Oriented Conceptual Modeling*. PhD thesis, Institute of Information Systems, University of Bern, 1996.
10. H. Herbst and G. Knolmayer. Ansätze zur Klassifikation von Geschäftsregeln. *Wirtschaftsinformatik*, 37 (2), pp. 149 – 159, 1995.
11. G. Knolmayer, H. Herbst, and M. Schlesinger. Enforcing Business Rules by the Application of Trigger Concepts. In *Priority Programme Informatics Research, Information Conference Module 1, Secure distributed systems*, pp. 28 – 31. SNF, Bern, 1994.
12. G. Lörincze. Modellierung, Analyse und Simulation von Regeln in der aktiven Schicht ALFRED. Master's thesis, Institute of Computer Science, University of Bern, 1996.
13. M. Schlesinger. Vergleich aktiver Mechanismen in Ingres V6.4, Oracle V7.0 und Sybase V10.0. In H.-J. Scheibl, editor, *Softwareentwicklung - Methoden, Werkzeuge, Erfahrungen '95*, pp. 41 – 53. Technische Akademie Esslingen, Esslingen, 1995.
14. M. Schlesinger. *ALFRED: Konzept und Implementation einer aktiven Regelschicht für Datenbanksysteme*. Institute of Information Systems, University of Bern, 1997 (to appear).
15. J. Widom and S. Ceri. *Active Database Systems*. Morgan Kaufmann, San Francisco, 1996.

Using the Properties of Datalog to prove Termination and Confluence in Active Databases

Sara Comai[1]   Letizia Tanca[2]

[1] Politecnico di Milano, Dipartimento di Elettronica e Informazione
P.za L. da Vinci 32 - I-20133 Milano, Italy
comai@elet.polimi.it
[2] Università di Verona, Facoltà di Scienze MM.FF.NN
Cà Vignal, Strada le Grazie, 1 - I-37134 Verona, Italy
tanca@biotech.univr.it, tanca@elet.polimi.it

Abstract. An *active database system* is a DBMS endowed with *active rules*, i.e. stored procedures activated by the system when specific events occur. The processing of active rules is characterized by two important properties: *termination* and *confluence*. We say that the processing of a set of active rules *terminates* if, given any initial active database state, the execution of the rules does not continue indefinitely; it is *confluent* if, for any active database state, the final state does not depend on the order of execution of the rules. Finding sufficient conditions is a non-trivial problem and the lack of a structured theory for the design of a system of active rules makes the analysis of the two properties more difficult. In this work, we see ECA rules as an evolution of deductive rules: we translate the active rules into logical clauses, taking into account the system's execution semantics, then we try to transfer to the active process the known results about termination and determinism available in the literature for deductive rules: sufficient conditions for the two properties of the ECA rules to hold can be found.

1 Introduction

An *active database system* is a DBMS endowed with *active rules*, i.e. stored procedures activated by the system when specific events occur. Typically an active rule consists of three parts: the *event* part, which specifies a list of events, the *condition* part, which is a query on the database, and the *action* part, which generally consists of one or more updates or queries on the database. A rule having this form is called Event-Condition-Action rule (ECA rule). When its events occur, the rule is said to be *triggered*; when the condition has been evaluated the rule is said to be *considered*; if the consideration succeedes the rule action is *executed*.

Several active DBMS and research prototypes have been designed and implemented; many commercial systems provide a support for active rules, as for example Oracle 7 [21] and Illustra [16], and the new standard SQL3 [22] includes the definition of such rules. Since each system is characterized by different syntactic and semantic features, different active databases with similar active rules can show different behaviours.

A problem in the use of active rules is the fact that even for a specific active database system it is quite difficult to predict the behaviour of a set of rules: given an initial database state, the same set of rules can lead the database to different final states or can even be executed endlessly.

The processing of active rules is thus characterized by two important properties: *termination* and *confluence* [3, 4, 6]. We say that the processing of a set of active rules *terminates* if, given any initial active database state, the execution of the rules does not continue indefinitely; it is *confluent* if, for any active database state, the final state does not depend on the order of execution of the rules. In real applications, it is desiderable that the execution of a set of rules always terminate and, for a given initial database state, the resulting final database state be unique.

In general, the properties of termination and confluence are undecidable; finding sufficient conditions is a non-trivial problem and the lack of a structured theory for the design of a system of active rules makes the analysis of the two properties more difficult. Aim of this paper is to give sufficient conditions to guarantee that the two properties hold.

Since the computation of an active set of rules depends on the features of the specific system, the analysis of the properties of termination and confluence must take into account the semantics of the active rules; for this reason we consider an execution model describing the behaviour of active DBMS with different semantics and analyze the two properties on this model. This execution model, presented in [12], is based on a data model which extends the database with the notion of *eventbase*, recording all the events that occur during a transaction, and on an extended, logic-based syntax of the rules, which can describe the active rules of all the known real systems. We encode the rules of the system of interest in this core format, and then give sufficient conditions for termination and confluence of the set of rules in this format. These conditions can straightforwardly be imposed on the original rules.

As the deductive database language Datalog, together with its extensions, has strong theoretical foundations, we translate the active rules into Datalog clauses, and try to transfer the known results about termination and determinism available in the literature for the deductive process to the active process: if a correspondence between the two kind of processes can be established, sufficient conditions for the two properties of the active rules to hold can be found. In our analysis we consider different kinds of active rules, having different semantic features, thus providing a general analysis.

Different priority assignments for rules are provided, which guarantee both properties. The most relevant contribution of this paper is the explicit introduction of the system's execution semantics in the analysis of termination and confluence; thus, we can see how the specific semantics influences the two properties. This way, the results can be applied to many system, and are quite general.

We believe that our method can be included in a design tool as a mechanism for rule analysis. The different prioritizations derived by the method may be suggested to the rule programmer, who can apply the prioritization that is most coherent with his/her intended semantics. Though many systems do not offer an explicit priority mechanism, often priorities can be forced by careful rule programming, thus we do not believe that this is a limit to the generality of our approach.

The paper is structured as follows: in Section 2 we present related work on termination and confluence; in Section 3 we introduce the semantics of the active database systems: the most important semantic dimensions considered in this paper are shown, and a model to describe the semantics of any active database system is presented. On the basis of this model, the properties of termination and confluence are defined in Section 4 and sufficient conditions to guarantee the two properties are provided. In Section 5 we draw the conclusions.

2 Related Work

Several studies on the properties of termination and confluence have been proposed in the literature for Condition-Action and ECA rules. Some approaches derive from Logic Programming ([20, 27, 18, 13, 26]), others are founded upon the analysis of the triggering, the activation or the execution graphs ([3, 4, 25, 18]); other approaches are based on Relational Algebra [7, 5], on Abstract Interpretation [8], or study the interaction among groups of rules [6].

The Logic Programming approach is based on the fixpoint semantics of the Logic Programs obtained by viewing production rules as deductive ones [10]: this semantics is defined for rules having only the condition and the action part and allows the use of recursive rules. As the active rule semantics is richer than the semantics of production rules, new, extended semantics for active rules have been proposed: some of these semantics (e.g. the PARK semantics [13] and the durable change semantics [26]) always guarantee the termination of the execution process, but it is not straightforward to apply some results to real active database systems.

The PARK semantics [13] is the result of the integration of the inflationary fixpoint semantics with the conflict resolution strategy, which is seen as a parameter of the semantics. The PARK semantics inhibits the generation of inconsistencies: these arise when two firable rules try to insert and to delete the same information: one of the two conflicting rules is blocked and rule processing is started again from the initial database state without the blocked rule. The rules to be blocked are chosen with a conflict resolution strategy. In this way, termination is always guaranteed; instead the property of confluence depends on the conflict resolution strategy used by the system. Our approach, studying the sequential execution of active rules, does not consider this kind of inconsistencies: indeeed, inhibiting the execution of a rule is not possible in real systems.

The durable change semantics [26] is based on Datalog$_{1s}$: events of ECA rules are represented by tuples in the so-called *delta* relations and can trigger the rules only if their effects are durable and persist until the end of the transaction. This method solves the termination problem, since conflicts among events do not produce persistent changes but not the confluence problem. The author provides an analysis for termination based on a rule precedence assignment and concentrates on a propagation policy of the changes occuring in a transaction (e.g. after the deletion of a tuple, other tuples are deleted) and not on the programs which can undo the changes occurred during a transaction.

In the other works based on the fixpoint semantics, termination can be guaranteed only for particular classes of systems. For example, in Statelog [20], an extension of stratified Datalog, the class of Δ-monotone Statelog, where each relation is either nondecreasing or nonincreasing, is studied. This class satisfies some properties that ensure termination.

In [27], a semantics for the class of relational databases which reach a unique fixoint is given: to belong to this class the system has to satisfy the condition of non-interference among Condition-Action rules. This condition can be easily checked, but is very restrictive.

The approach based on triggering, activation or execution graphs is generally used to isolate rules which may not ensure termination.

The first work is that of [3]: a static analysis model for the ECA rules of the Starburst system is proposed. Termination is analyzed by using the triggering graph, a directed graph whose nodes represent the rules and whose edges indicate that a rule produces an event that may trigger another rule. Rule execution terminates if the graph is acyclic, and may not terminate if there is at least one cycle. The confluence analysis is done on the execution graph, whose nodes represent the states and whose oriented edges are labeled with the name of the rule whose executions make the system pass from one state to another state. All the possible execution sequences are represented. A set of active rules is confluent if all possible sequences lead the database to the same final state, i.e. if the execution graph has a unique final state. If the rules commute in pairs and the execution graph is acyclic the rule execution process is confluent.

Less restrictive conditions for termination of ECA rules are proposed in [4]: the analysis of the triggering graph is integrated with the analysis of the activation graph. Its nodes represent the rules and the edges indicate that the action part of a rule can verify the condition part of another rule. The rule execution may not terminate if the two graphs have a common cycle.

Another algorithm to simplify the analysis of the triggering graph in an object-oriented database is presented in [25]. If the triggering graph presents some cycles, all the action operations which update the same object are grouped in one complex operation: if this operation is monotonic some edges can be deleted from the graph.

Still another approach to termination analysis, which tries to eliminate some edges from the triggering graph, is presented in [18] for an active object-oriented database: it is based on the notion of logic "triggering formulae". Depending on the satisfiability of these formulae, the edges of the graph have to be maintained or can be deleted: a "refined triggering graph" is obtained.

A less conservative algorithm to determine if a rule set terminates and is confluent, and which can be integrated with the graph analysis, is proposed in [7, 5]: it propagates the effect of the action part of an active Condition-Action rule to the condition part of another rule. Both the condition and the action part are expressed in an extended relational algebra.

A different approach is proposed in [6]: an abstract model is presented to describe the behaviour of a complex set of active ECA rules divided in disjunct strata. Each stratum can be studied locally and the whole set of rules can be studied as a function of the interactions among strata: several stratification criteria, which guarantee the termination of the whole rule set, are explained.

An analysis which takes into account different semantic choices is that of [24]: it considers both the instance-oriented and the set-oriented activation modality in an OODBMS endowed with rules with implicit events. Decidability properties for termination and confluence of rule processing are studied.

Our analysis considers other semantic dimensions too in order to provide some results valid for most of the active database. In this work we do not consider the semantic choices used only by very few systems, for which the analysis should be extended. Another feature of our approach is to try to exploit the results about termination and confluence of other systems, as it is done for example in [17], where ECA rules are modelled as term rewriting rules, or in [8], where the analysis is reconducted to abstract interpretations.

3 Semantics of Active Databases

As ECA rules behave differently depending on the specific system [12], the execution process of ECA rules cannot be easily defined by means of a unique algorithm. In [12] a very simple algorithm describing the semantics of a transaction and rule execution is introduced, and applied to the active rules, rewritten in a form which expresses explicitly all their semantic features.

3.1 Semantic Dimensions in Active Databases

From an analysis of existing active database systems, we can determine several features of the behaviour of ECA active rules. In [12] all the possible semantics dimensions are treated exhaustively. In this paper we consider, among the possible dimensions, the most relevant to the problems of termination and confluence:

Rule activation granularity: it is *instance-oriented* if one rule is triggered for each tuple/object affected by the event, *set-oriented* if a single rule is triggered for a set of tuples/objects (for example a relation) affected by the same event.

Composite events: we consider only disjunctions of elementary events.

E-C coupling mode: it is *immediate*, if the condition is evaluated as soon as the update that has triggered the rule terminates, or *deferred*, if the condition is evaluated at the end of the transaction which has triggered the rule.

Atomicity of rule execution: rule execution is *interruptable* if, when a triggering event is generated from within the action part of an executing rule, the rule that produced the triggering event is suspended; it is *atomic* if the triggering event is "frozen" until the termination of action execution.

Event consumption: triggering events produced in a transaction can retain the capability of triggering rules or lose this capability after rule execution. In the former case no event consumption is performed, in the latter case the triggering events are *consumed* and cannot trigger the rule any more; they can be consumed at *consideration*, i.e. after condition evaluation, or after *action execution*, i.e. when the rule is fired. However, since all the current systems consume events at consideration, we consider only this option. Moreover, events can be consumed *locally*, i.e. for the rule triggered by it, or *globally*, if one rule can consume its events and those of other rules not yet processed.

3.2 Data Model

According to [12], all the semantic dimensions that characterize the behaviour of the ECA rules can be uniformly encoded into a low-level, logic-based syntax, called *core syntax* (see Section 3.3). Rules written using this syntax are called *core rules* and can be processed by a unique execution algorithm based on the following data model.

An *active database* contains a set of rules and two more components: the *database* (DB), which represents the passive, traditional database, and the *event-base* (EB), which stores the events and the information relevant to the database history. These two components are tightly connected by the definition of update of an active database: an update operation modifies the *database* (by introducing, deleting or replacing an element), and the *eventbase* (by recording the corresponding events). We extend the notion of *state s* of an active database: it consists of the database state and the eventbase state: $s = (DB, EB)$.

In the *eventbase* relations EVENT and ACTIVE are stored.

Relation *EVENT(EID, type, elem, ts)* records all the events occurred in the transaction. EID is the event identifier, *type* is the name of the event type, *elem* is the data element affected by the event (the object identifier in the object oriented model, the whole tuple in the relational model), and *ts* is a timestamp, which indicates the temporal instant of event occurrence. No event is ever deleted, since some systems require the possibility to query the past history.

Relation *ACTIVE(EID, rule)* indicates which rules (*rule*) are triggered by an event (*EID*). In general, one EID may correspond to more than one rule. Tuples are inserted when an event occurs which triggers a rule, and are deleted if in the system's semantics events are consumed.

This model can be used both for the relational model and for the object-oriented model. In the sequel of the paper we focus on the *relational model*.

3.3 Core Active Rules

A core active rule consists of the event, condition and action parts, possibly followed by a priority declaration needed to reflect ECA rule priorities.

The core rule has the general form:

$$ebq(\vec{y}_1); \; db/ebq(\vec{x}_2, \vec{y}_2) \longrightarrow TU(\vec{x}_3, \vec{y}_3*)$$

where $\vec{x}_j$ is a vector of input variables and $\vec{y}_i$ is a vector of output variables .

The **event part** $ebq(\vec{y}_1)$ (eventbase query), with $\mid \vec{y}_1 \mid \geq 0$, is a logical formula interpreted over the eventbase. If the formula is satisfied, the rule is triggered and the free variables $\vec{y}_1$ (if present) are bound to the identifiers of triggering events to be used in other parts of the rule.

The **condition part** $db/ebq(\vec{x}_2, \vec{y}_2)$ (database/eventbase query) is the translation of the condition part of the original active rule, where $\vec{x}_2 (\subseteq \vec{y}_1$ for safety) are input variables bound in the event part and used in the condition, and $\vec{y}_2$ are output variables (if present) whose bindings are computed in the condition and transferred to the action.

The **action part** $TU(\vec{x}_3, \vec{y}_3*) \equiv TU_1(\vec{x}_{3_1}, \vec{y}_{3_1}*); \ldots; TU_n(\vec{x}_{3_n}, \vec{y}_{3_n}*)$ is a sequence of non-interruptable updates on the database and eventbase (Transaction Units, See 3.4) where $\vec{x}_{3_i}(\subseteq \vec{y}_1 \cup \vec{y}_2$ for safety) are input variables bound to the identifiers of the events to be consumed and to items retrieved by the condition (which must be acted upon in the action), and $\vec{y}_3*$ are variables whose values are *invented* by the system [9, 15, 1], i.e. created at execution time. Each elementary update of the original action sequence is followed by an update to the eventbase that introduces the event it generates.

A set of rules from any existing system can be semi-automatically translated [12] into the corresponding set of core rules provided that one has analyzed all the semantic choices taken by that system. Here we show how to translate the semantic dimensions considered in this paper.[3]

Rule activation granularity: the event part of the rule must query relation EVENT to check for the event occurrence, and relation ACTIVE to see if that event is active for that rule. If the rule is *set-oriented* it is triggered if one or more events of the same type have arisen ($\exists$ EID active*(EID, "rule")* $\wedge$ $\exists$ TS event*(EID, "type", elem, TS)*, so the variable EID used in the event part is existentially quantified; if it is *instance-oriented* one rule instance for each single event has to be triggered, so variable EID is free, to be bound to each single instance of the same event type.

E-C coupling mode: if the E-C coupling mode is *deferred*, the rule must check the occurrence of the "commit" event, which arises and therefore is recorded at the end of a transaction ($\exists EID1, TS1$ event$(EID1, "commit", "NULL", TS1)$), otherwise no such check is needed.

Atomicity of rule execution: if rule action execution is *atomic*, at the beginning of the action part of each atomic rule the event "BeginAction" is inserted, and removed at the end of the action . In the event part of each rule the presence of the event "BeginAction" must be tested, which indicates that some atomic rule is still running ($\forall EID1, X1, TS1 \neg$event$(EID1, "BeginAction", X1, TS1)$). If the rule is interruptable its core version does not contain the insertion and deletion of the event "BeginAction" in the action part.

Event consumption: to model *event consumption*, tuples from relation ACTIVE

---

[3] Notice that, in analogy with the deductive database style, the relations of the database/eventbase are written as literals whose ordered list of arguments represent the attributes of the relation.

are deleted in the action part of the rule (*delete(active(EID, "rule")))*. To model event *consumption at consideration* two rules are needed: a first rule, containing the event, the condition and the action part of the original rule, which consumes the triggering event(s) for itself and for the second rule, and a second rule, containing the same event part as the original rule and the negated condition part of the original rule (so that the conditions of the two core rules are mutually exclusive), whose action part also consumes the triggering event(s) for both R1 and R2.

Example I: Suppose that a person who wants to participate to a conference pays his/her participation fee: the payment is recorded in the relation *Payment* of the database and the event corresponding to the insertion of the record is registered in the eventbase. Consider a rule *Participants_list*, which, after the insertion of a tuple in relation *payments*, inserts the data of the person who has made a request (recorded in relation *request*) for participating in a conference in relation *participants*.

We show the rule written in Postgres [23], having E-C coupling mode immediate, granularity of rule activation instance-oriented, action execution interruptable, and event consumption local at consideration; then we show its translation into core format. Note that all the semantic choices indicated are hard coded in the behaviour of the Postgres system, and not shown in the rule syntax.

```
define rule Participants_list is
on append to PAYMENTS                              (* event part *)
    where NEW.name=REQUEST.name and               (* condition part *)
          NEW.conference=REQUEST.conference
do append to PARTICIPANTS (name = REQUEST.name,    (* action part *)
                   conference = REQUEST.conference,
                   address = REQUEST.address,
                   nation = REQUEST.nation)
```

Core Rule Participants_list
active(EID, "Participants_list") ∧
∃ TS *event (EID, "insert(payments)", (Name, Conf, Sum), TS);*
requests(Name, Addr, Nation, Conf) ∧ *payments(Name, Conf, Sum)*
⟶
delete(active (EID, "Participants_list")),   (* event consumption *)
delete(active (EID, "Participants_list_2")),   (* event consumption *)
insert(event (EID*, "insert(participants)", (Name, Address, Nation, Conf), TS*)),
insert(active (EID*, <activated rule>)),   (* action *)

Core Rule Participants_list_2
active(EID, "Participants_list") ∧
∃ *TS event(EID, "insert(payments)", (Name, Conf, Sum), TS);*
¬ *(requests(Name, Addr, Nation, Conf)* ∧ *payments(Name, Conf, Sum))*
⟶
delete(active (EID, "Participants_list")),   (* event consumption *)
delete(active (EID, "Participants_list_2"))   (* event consumption *)

EID, *Name, Addr, Nation* and *Conf* are variables used in the event-condition part and whose bindings are transferred to the action part; variable *Sum* is used only in the event-condition part; variables $EID*$ and $TS*$ appear only in the action part, whose (invented) values are generated by the system.

3.4 Execution Semantics

Active rules are executed within a user transaction: w.r.t. our model [11] a user transaction is composed by a sequence of *transaction units* $T = TU_1, \ldots, TU_n$. A transaction unit contains a sequence of *elementary updates*, which can affect both the database and the eventbase (e.g. update commands, like insertions and deletions, which can affect both parts of the active database, or transactional commands, like *commit, rollback* and *begin transaction*, which can affect only the eventbase) and must be executed atomically: only at its end the active rules triggered by the elementary updates are executed (if the E-C coupling mode is immediate, otherwise the rules are executed at the end of the whole transaction). The execution of the user transaction and of the active rules has been defined [12] by means of an algorithm composed of two procedures: procedure **execute_TU** and procedure **execute_rules**. Pocedure **execute_TU** processes the sequence of m transaction units $TU_i(\vec{x}_i)$. After the execution of the first transaction unit TU_1, the first *rule starting point* is reached, from which the reactive processing of the core rules, defined by procedure **execute_rules**, may start. The execution of the rules may lead the database to a state where no other rule is eligible to fire: this state is called *quiescent state*. From this state the next transaction unit is initiated and so on until the last transaction unit and the last rule processing session are performed or until an error arises.

Rule processing, defined by procedure **execute_rules**, starts rule execution from the rule starting point and returns, upon termination, the quiescent state. It consists of the iteration of the triggering, the consideration and the action execution phase.

If a *rollback* event arises, the database state is reset to the pre-transactional state, and the execution is halted.

In the *triggering phase*, the ebq part of every rule of R is evaluated and the set of substitutions Θ_1 of the triggering events is determined: if the rule is triggered, it is inserted in the *conflict set* τ.

In the *consideration phase* a rule is chosen from the *conflict set* to be considered (taking into account the priorities among rules): its *db/ebq* part is evaluated and the set of substitutions Θ_2 of the variables that satisfy the formula is determined. On the basis of Θ_1 and Θ_2 the set of substitutions Θ_3 to be passed to the action part and the effect on the database and eventbase due to the execution of the rule are computed. These operations are repeated until no rule is in the *conflict set* or a rule is found whose action can modify the active database state.

Finally the *action execution phase* calls procedure **execute_TU** to perform the action part of the chosen rule, which consists of a sequence of updating operations, expressed as n transaction units. The execution of the rule actions can generate new events which can trigger or detrigger other rules: thus, **execute_TU** is recursively repeated until a quiescent state is reached, i.e. until no rules can change the state of the active database.

The sequential execution of the three phases of *triggering, consideration* and *execution* of procedure **execute_rules** is called *Elementary Production Step (EPS)* and is modelled by a binary relation EPS_{R_A}, analogous to the relation defined by the *Immediate Consequences Operator* used to describe the fixpoint semantics of deductive databases. Given an active database with set of rules R_A, EPS_{R_A} associates an active database state to a (possibly empty) set of active database states, which represent *all* the possible states produced by the process of firing a single rule and executing the three computational phases (thus possibly all the rules recursively triggered by it). A possible execution trace of the reactive system is represented in EPS_{R_A} as an ordered set of tuples, such that the second value of one tuple equals the first value of the subsequent one. Then, a terminating computation is represented by a finite such chain, whose last element has no possible successors in EPS_{R_A}.

A state s of an active database $\langle s, R_A \rangle$ is said to be an *active fixpoint* if $\not\exists$ s' such that $\langle s, s' \rangle \in EPS_{R_A}$. Thus, no further rule execution is possible, when the rule processing system enters a state corresponding to a fixpoint. Based on the EPS_{R_A}, the semantics of the execution of a set of rules is given by the *rule processing* relation, defined as follows:

Definition 1: (Rule processing) Given an active database, the *rule processing* relation Γ^{Att} is defined as follows:

$$((s_i, R_A), s_f) \in \Gamma^{Att} \Leftrightarrow (\langle s_i, s_f \rangle \in \overline{EPS_{R_A}} \wedge s_f \text{ is an active fixpoint of } EPS_{R_A})$$

where s_i and s_f are the initial and the final quiescent active database states respectively, R_A is a set of active rules and $\overline{EPS_{R_A}}$ is the (possibly infinite) transitive closure of EPS_{R_A}.

Γ^{Att} is a relation because we can obtain more than one final state, since the process is generally non-deterministic.

4 Termination and Confluence

We study the properties of termination and confluence of the execution of *core active rules*, defined by relation Γ^{Att}. The proofs of all the theorems listed in this Section can be found in [11].

Definition 2: (Termination) Let s_i be a rule starting point and $\mathcal{R}_A$ a set of core rules: then, rule processing from the database state s_i *terminates* iff both the following conditions hold:

1. $| \sigma_{1=s_i} \overline{EPS_{R_A}} | < \infty$
2. $(\not\exists i, j \text{ such that} \langle s_j, s_j \rangle \in \overline{EPS_{R_A}} \wedge \langle s_i, s_j \rangle \in \sigma_{1=s_i} \overline{EPS_{R_A}})$

where $\sigma_{1=s_i} \overline{EPS_{R_A}}$ is the set of pairs in the transitive closure of EPS_{R_A} starting from s_i.

Thus, rule processing terminates if (1) every chain beginning from the state s_i and determined by the execution of the active rules is finite, and (2) and there are no cycles in these chains.

In order to give an appropriate definition for the property of confluence we have to take into account the invented values generated by the system:

Definition 3: (State equivalence) Let $s = (DB, EB)$ and $s' = (DB', EB')$ be two states; we say that s is *equivalent* to s' (i.e. $s \simeq s'$) if there exists a substitution of eids and time-stamps $\xi = (eid_1/eid'_1, ts_1/ts'_1 \ldots eid_n/eid'_n, ts_n/ts'_n)$, such that $DB\xi = DB'$ and $EB\xi = EB'$, i.e. $s\xi = s'$.

If different states are equivalent according to Def. 3 this corresponds to the fact that two databases are the same *up to eid and timestamps isomorphism* [9].

Definition 4: (Confluence) Let s_i be a rule starting point, $\mathcal{R}_A$ a set of core rules, and Γ^{Att} the rule processing relation: then, rule processing (starting from s_i) is *confluent* iff it terminates and all s_f such that $((s_i, \mathcal{R}_A), s_f) \in \Gamma^{Att}$, are equivalent class w.r.t. state equivalence.

The process from s_i is therefore confluent iff it terminates and, indipendently of the rule execution order, only equivalent final states are reached.

4.1 A language based on deductive rules: Datalog and its extensions

In the following analysis we consider *Datalog* [10], a database query language based on deductive rules. A Datalog program is a logic program [19], consisting of *rules* and *facts*: rules and facts of a Datalog program are Horn clauses [10], and have the general form $L_0 : -L_1, \ldots, L_n$ where each L_i $(i = 0..n)$ is a literal of the form $p_i(t_1, \ldots, t_k)$: p_i is a *predicate* symbol and each t_j $(j = 1..k)$ is a variable or a constant.

In pure Datalog, all literals $L_0, \ldots, L_n$ do not contain a negation symbol. Pure Datalog has been extended with the introduction of negated predicates (preceded by the symbol "¬") both in the body and in the head of the rules [2, 10]. In the literature, Datalog with negation in the body is denoted as Datalog¬ and with negation both in the body and in the head as Datalog¬*. The semantics of rules with negated predicates are not immediate, so we refer to semantics which interpret the negation as follows: if a negated predicate is in the body, the rule checks for the absence of a fact; if a negated predicate is in the head, it is considered as the deletion of a fact. Datalog and Extended Datalog semantics execute all the rules in parallel until no new facts can be inferred. The execution of a set of Datalog rules (and all the extensions of Datalog that we shall consider) can be defined as an application Γ^D from an initial pair formed by facts and Datalog rules $(F_i, \mathcal{R}_D)$ to a final set of resulting facts F_f, i.e. $\Gamma^D : ((F_i, \mathcal{R}_D), F_f)$ (written as a relation in analogy with the active rule relation defined in 3.4). In [2] the authors show which processes of Datalog and its extensions are deterministic: our analysis is principally based on these results.

4.2 Translation of core rules into logical rules

In order to transfer the results about termination and determinism available for Datalog and its extensions to active rule processing, core active rules must be transformed into logical clauses.

Some restrictions are needed: 1) we consider only operations of insertion and deletion in the action part of an active rule; these will be represented respectively by positive and negated predicates; if the action part of an active rule queries the database or the eventbase, the query must be moved to the condition part[4]; 2) we focus only on a subset of active rules, which present no function symbols.

With these assumptions the core rule can be seen as a f.o. formula

$$ebq(\vec{y_1}) \wedge db/ebq(\vec{x_2}, \vec{y_2}) \rightarrow TU_1(\vec{x}_{31}, \vec{y}_{31}*) \wedge \ldots \wedge TU_n(\vec{x}_{3n}, \vec{y}_{3n}*)$$

where $ebq(\vec{y_1})$ and $db/ebq(\vec{x_2}, \vec{y_2})$ are f.o. formulas "$\rightarrow$" is interpreted as logical implication ($\Rightarrow$) and $TU(\vec{x_3}, \vec{y_3}*)$ is a conjunction of positive and negated literals. This formula can be transformed into a set of clauses [19], as shown in [11].

For example the core rule *Participants_list* is transformed into a clause as follows:

active(EID, "Participants_list") $\wedge$
event (EID, "insert(payments)", (Name, Conf, Sum), TS)$\wedge$
requests(Name, Addr, Nation, Conf) $\wedge$ *payments(Name, Conf, Sum)*
$\Rightarrow$
$\neg$ *active(EID, "Participants_list")* $\wedge$ $\neg$ *active(EID, "Participants_list_2")* $\wedge$
event(f_{eid}(Name, Addr, Nation, Conf), "insert(participants)", (Name, Addr, Nation, Conf),f_{ts}(Name, Addr, Nation, Conf)) $\wedge$
active (f_{eid}(Name, Addr, Nation, Conf), <activated rule>) $\wedge$
participants(Name, Addr, Nation, Conf)

where $f_{eid}()$ and $f_{ts}()$ are Skolem functors.

If the active rule has multiple operations in its action part it is transformed into a set of active rules with just one operation in their action part. This transformation is possible because bindings needed in the action part are passed only from the event-condition part of the rule, and not from other operations of the action part, since queries are all in the event/condition part.

When applying a deductive process to the logical rules we have derived, the semantics of the literals in their heads is that of the theory of relational systems: a tuple is inserted in the database, only if there is no other tuple with the same attribute values and it is deleted only if it actually exists in the database; the corresponding event is recorded in the eventbase only if the tuple is actually inserted or deleted: insertions (deletions) of tuples previously inserted (deleted) are handled as "no operation".

To refer to the different types of ECA rules, for which properties of termination and confluence are studied separately, we introduce the following classification: by ECA$^+$ we denote ECA rules with only positive predicates (in particular, with only insertions in the action part); by ECA$^\neg$ we denote rules with negated

---

[4] This imposes a limit in the expressive power of the rule language, since this operation can be done only for rules whose semantics is not affected by it.

predicates in the event/condition part and only insertions in the action part; by ECA⁻*, rules which presents deletions and insertions in the action part and negated predicates in the condition part.

4.3 Transformation Diagram

For each given relational database schema S, on the basis of the translation of the core rules into logical rules, we define the correspondence between an active database state and the set of Datalog facts (function γ_1), and between the active rules and the Datalog rules (functions γ_2 and $\gamma_2\prime$) :

Relation γ_1: let S be the domain of the active database states on S, and $\mathcal{F}$ be the set of possible Datalog facts that can be built from the relation schema S, i.e. the Herbrand Base, then:

$$\gamma_1 : S \longrightarrow 2^{\mathcal{F}}$$

is an invertible application, which associates to a database state s, a set of Datalog facts F.

Relation γ_1 is trivially bijective: for every Datalog fact there is also a tuple in the active database.

By transforming the core rules into logical rules, as seen in the previous subsection, we can obtain a set of clauses, beginning from any set of core rules; the following relation is defined:

Relation γ_2: let $\mathcal{R}_A$ be the set of possible active rules on S and $\mathcal{R}_D$ be the set of possible Datalog rules on S. Then:

$$\gamma_2 : 2^{\mathcal{R}_A} \longrightarrow 2^{\mathcal{R}_D}$$

associates to a set of active rules R_A, a set of Datalog rules R_D.

Relation $\gamma_2\prime$: Relation γ_2 is not invertible, but a kind of inverse transformation can be obtained straightforwardly:

$$\gamma_2\prime : 2^{\mathcal{R}_D} \longrightarrow 2^{\mathcal{R}_A}$$

associates to a set of Datalog rules R_D, a set of active rules R_A. Indeed, given a Datalog rule, its body can be transformed into the condition of an active rule and its head into the action part; the event part is substituted by *true*.

Up to this point, we have defined a *syntactic* correspondence between core and Datalog rules. Since the aim of this paper is to transfer the results of the properties of Datalog to the active rules execution process, we need to verify the *semantic* correspondence between the rule execution processes too. For this reason we introduce the *transformation diagram* of Figure 1.

The upper part of the diagram represents the behaviour of a Datalog program (or of its extensions) while the lower part represents the rule execution process of an active database. The execution process Γ^{Att} applied to an initial active database state s_i and to a set of rules R_A produces a final state s_f; we can check if, by transforming the initial state of an active database (s_i, R_A) into the initial Datalog state (F_i, R_D) (via γ_1, γ_2), then processing by Γ^D the Datalog rules R_D with initial set of facts F_i and transforming the final set of facts F_f into the

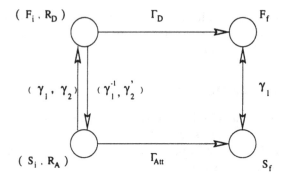

Fig. 1. Transformation diagram between Datalog and the active rule processing.

corresponding database state (via γ_1^{-1}), we obtain the same result s_f achieved by Γ^{Att}. If this operation is possible, the diagram is *commutative*.

Remark 1: Note that in order to compare the results on active rule processing to the execution of a Datalog program, we consider a single execution process of active rules, from a rule starting point to the next quiescent state.

Remark 2: Note that we obtain our results by simulating the serial execution order of active rules by the execution of the corresponding set of Datalog rules, which run in parallel. Thus, in the parallel evaluation of the Datalog rules the concept of action atomicity becomes useless, and useless will be the test for the "BeginAction" event in the left hand side of the Datalog rules. Therefore, we can eliminate such test, together with the insertion and deletion of the same event in the core rule action *without affecting the generality of our results*.

The diagram can be defined for every Datalog (and its extensions) semantics and for each type of ECA rules: for each diagram we can determine sufficient conditions for guaranteeing the commutativity. In the sequel we analyze the cases of ECA^+, ECA^- and ECA^{-*} rules. All these rules are characterized by the following common semantic dimensions: granularity of rule activation instance-oriented or set-oriented, E-C coupling mode immediate or deferred, action execution interruptable or atomic (which do not differ if evaluated in parallel).

4.4 Mapping between ECA^+ rules and Datalog rules

ECA^+ rules can only query the presence of tuples and insert new tuples in the database or in the eventbase, thus they do not consume events.

Theorem 1: (Properties of the ECA^+ rules execution process) Let R_A be a set of ECA^+ rules and s_i be a rule starting point: the execution process of Γ^{Att} applied to (s_i, R_A), terminates and is confluent.

Indeed, for each set R_A of active rules ECA^+ and for each initial database state s_i, it can be shown that there exist a set of Datalog rules R_D and a set of Datalog facts F_i such that $(F_i, R_D) = (\gamma_1(s_i), \gamma_2(R_A))$, thus the diagram is commutative. Since the execution process of a Datalog program terminates and is confluent, the execution process of ECA^+ rules also terminates and is confluent.

Notice that the self-triggering ECA^+ rules are taken into account. Indeed, as remarked in Section 4.2, our hypothesis is that a tuple is never inserted twice, thus the system terminates when a fixpoint is reached.

4.5 Mapping between ECA⁻ rules and Datalog⁻ rules

ECA^- rules extend ECA^+ rules with the possibility of querying the absence of tuples from the database. In this paper we do not consider negated predicates on the eventbase (remind that we have eliminated the test for the absence of the "BeginAction" event).

We distinguish the cases of stratified and inflationary semantics [10].

Stratified Semantics: Given a set of active rules, we can guarantee termination and confluence if their corresponding set of Datalog rules (via γ_2) is stratified. Indeed, we can impose priorities to the active rules in such a way that all rules with the same priority belong to the same stratum. The initial set of rules, thus "prioritized", will satisfy the properties of termination and confluence if the corresponding transformation diagram is commutative.

Definition 5: (First priority assignment rule) We call *first priority assignment rule* the partitioning of the set of rules R_A in n subsets of active rules $R^1, \ldots, R^i, \ldots, R^n$, each having priority i, such that negated predicates of the condition part of the rules of the layer R^i do not appear in the action part of the rules belonging to R^j, with $j > i$.

The priority assignment rule assigns a higher priority to rules which insert a tuple in a relation and a lower priority to rules which query the absence of a tuple in the same relation. Any stratification algorithm of Datalog⁻ [10], extended to take into account that active rules can contain more than one operation in their action part, can be applied to obtain the prioritization of the active rules.

Theorem 2: (Properties of the ECA⁻ rules execution process) Let R_A be a set of ECA^- rules, prioritized on the basis of the first priority assignment rule, and s_i be a rule starting point: the execution process of Γ^{Att} applied to (s_i, R_A), terminates and is confluent.

Indeed, by assigning the priorities to the active rules on the basis of the first priority assignment rule, the transformation diagram is commutative, i.e. $(F_i, R_D) = (\gamma_1(s_i), \gamma_2(R_A))$. Since the execution of Datalog⁻ rules terminates and is confluent, the same results apply to ECA^- rules.

Inflationary Semantics: In some cases we can assign priorities to the ECA^- rules in order to simulate the evaluation strategy of inflationary Datalog⁻.

Definition 6: (Second priority assignment rule) We call *second priority assignment rule* the partitioning of the set of R_A rules in n subsets of active rules

$R^1, \ldots, R^i, \ldots, R^n$, each having priority i, such that the predicates that appear negated in the condition part of rules of R^i do not appear in the action part of the rules of partitions R^j, with $j \leq i$.

To assign the priority to the active rules, we can adopt the same criteria of the first priority assignment rule, but inverting the order of rule priority assignment. Notice that this does not correspond to a *stratification* of the rules, since rules of a layer with higher priority can be executed again after other rules of lower layers are computed. As in the previous case, we have:

Theorem 3: (Properties of the ECA¬ rules execution process) Let R_A be a set of ECA¬ rules, prioritized on the basis of the second priority assignment rule, and s_i be a rule starting point: the execution process of Γ^{Att} applied to (s_i, R_A), terminates and is confluent.

Notice that, in the case in which no conflict among the event-condition and the action part of the rules arise, the rules can have the same priority.

4.6 Mapping between ECA¬* rules and Datalog¬* rules

In the ECA¬* rules deletions in the action part are allowed: tuples can be deleted from the database, or from the eventbase for event consumption.

With the insertion of the negated predicates in the action part of the core rule, new problems arise for the study of the properties of termination and confluence in an active database, where rule execution is sequential: 1) a fireable rule can query the presence of a tuple/fact which is deleted in the action part of another fireable rule, 2) a triggering event may be consumed, which can disactivate a rule whose condition part may become true after the execution of other fireable rules, and 3) two or more rules which try to insert and to delete the same tuple in the database may be simultaneously triggered.

The first problem does not arise in Datalog¬*, since rules are executed in parallel: if a rule queries the presence of a tuple which is deleted by a second rule in the same execution step, their executions do not influence each other.

The second problem is very similar to the first one, except that it concerns the eventbase relation ACTIVE: if the events are deleted at each consideration of the rule, in Datalog they remain triggered at most for one step and cannot influence each other, whereas in an active database with sequential execution they can behave differently, depending on the rule execution order. Consider, for example, two triggered rules and suppose that the condition of the first one is false but may become true after the execution of the second rule. The execution order is relevant: if the first rule is considered before the second one, its events are consumed and it is not executed; instead, if the order is inverted, it is executed for the values updated by the second rule.

These two problems are solved in our framework by assigning rule priorities that allow ECA¬* rules to simulate Datalog¬*.

Finally, the third problem is generally solved in Datalog¬*, by handling the pair insertion-deletion as no operation. We do not consider it in this paper.

Definition 7: (Third priority assignment rule) We call *third priority assignment rule* the partitioning of the set of R_A rules in n subsets of active rules $R^1, \ldots, R^i, \ldots, R^n$ having priority i, such that 1) the positive predicates of the condition part of rules of R^i are not negated in the action part of rules of partitions R^j, with $j \geq i$; 2) if events are consumed, the predicates of the action part of rules of R^i do not appear in the condition part of rules of partitions R^j, with $j \geq i$, unless the update done in the action part triggers those rules.

Theorem 4: (Properties of the ECA⁻* rules execution process) Let R_A be a set of ECA⁻* rules, prioritized on the basis of the second and on the third priority assignment rules, and let s_i be a rule starting point: the execution process of Γ^{Att} applied to (s_i, R_A), terminates and is confluent.

Indeed, if R_A can be partitioned according to the second and the third priority assignment rule, then $\Gamma^D(F_i, R_D) = \gamma_1(\Gamma^{Att}(s_i, R_A))$, i.e. the transformation diagram is commutative. Thus, the results of Datalog⁻* rules can be transferred to the ECA⁻* rules.

If the single layers are considered, each layer can guarantee both properties: thus, the inverted order of execution of the layers which leads to a stratification of the rules is possible. However different results from those of Datalog⁻* rules can be obtained.

5 Conclusions and Future Work

In this paper we have presented a model based on Logic Programming for the analysis of termination and confluence of a set of active rules: the known results about these properties in the field of deductive databases are transferred to the active ECA rules, so that sufficient conditions for the active rules are provided. Negated predicates in rule conditions have been taken into account: the positive and the negated predicates are handled in different ways because they influence the execution process differently w.r.t. the properties of termination and confluence. We plan to use the results of this paper to indicate guidelines for assigning priorities to the original system's rules in order to guarantee termination and confluence.

The most relevant contribution of our approach, that makes it more general than other analogous efforts, is that we have considered the most important semantic dimensions of the active rules, so the results can be applied to systems having different semantics. Other objectives of future work are the treatment of other semantic dimensions and the extension of the action language dealt with by our analysis.

Acknoledgements. We would like to thank Piero Fraternali, Giuseppe Psaila and Ernest Teniente for the helpful comments and advice on this work.

References

1. S. Abiteboul, P.C. Kanellakis, "Object Identity as a Query Language Primitive", Proc. ACM SIGMOD, June 1989.

2. S. Abiteboul, E. Simon, "Fundamental Properties of Deterministic and Nondeterministic Extensions of Datalog", J. Bases de Données Avancés, Sept. 1989.
3. A. Aiken, J. Widom, J. M. Hellerstein, "Behaviour of Database Production Rules: Termination, Confluence and Observable Determinism", Proc. ACM-SIGMOD, Int. Conference, San Diego, California, May 1992, pp.59-68.
4. E. Baralis, S. Ceri, S. Paraboschi, "Improved Rule Analysis by Means of Triggering and Activation Graphs", RIDS'93, Edinburgo, August 1993.
5. E. Baralis, S. Ceri, J. Widom, "Better Termination Analysis for Active Databases", RIDS'93, Edinburgo, Scozia, Springer-Verlag Berlin, August 1993, pp. 163-175.
6. E. Baralis, S. Ceri, S. Paraboschi, "Modularization Techniques for Active Rules Design", Transaction on Database Systems, Volume 21 (1), pp.1-29 (1996).
7. E. Baralis, J. Widom, "An Algebraic Approach to Rule Analysis in Expert Database Systems", VLDB'94, Santiago, Cile, September 1994, pp. 475-485.
8. J. Bailey, L. Crnogorac, K. Ramamohanarao, "Abstract Interpretation of Active Rules and Its Use in Termination Analysis", ICDT '97.
9. L. Cabibbo, "Expressiveness of Semipositive Logic Programs with Value Invention", LID'96, San Miniato (PI), Italy, July 1-2 1996, pp. 467-484.
10. S. Ceri, G. Gottlob, L. Tanca, "Logic Programming and Databases", New York: Springer Verlag, 1990.
11. S. Comai, L. Tanca, "Using the Properties of Datalog to prove Termination and Confluence in Active Databases", Tech. Rep. Politecnico di Milano n. 97-015, 1997.
12. P. Fraternali, L. Tanca, "A Structured Approach for the Definition of the Semantics of Active Databases", ACM-TODS, Volume 20, n. 4, pp. 414-471.
13. G. Gottlob, G Moerkotte, V.S. Subrahmian, "The PARK semantics for Active Rules", EDBT'96, Avignon, France.
14. E. Hanson, "Rule Condition Testing and Execution in Ariel", rpc, ACM-SIGMOD Int. Conference, San Diego, Maggio 1992.
15. R. Hull, M. Yoshikawa, "ILOG: Declarative Creation and Manipulation of Object Identifiers", VLDB'90, Brisbane 1990, pp. 455-468.
16. Illustra User's Guide, Release 3.2, Ottobre 1995.
17. A. P. Karadimce, S. D. Urban, "Conditional Term Rewriting as a Formal Basis for Analysis of Active Database Rules",RIDE-ADS '94, Houston, February 1994.
18. A. P. Karadimce, S. D. Urban, "Refined Triggering Graphs: A Logic-Based Approach to Termination Analysis in an Active OO Database", ICDE'96, pp. 384-391.
19. J. W. Lloyd, "Foudations of Logic Programming", Springer, 1987.
20. B. Ludäscher, U. Hamann, G. Lausen, "A Logical Framework for Active Rules", COMAD'95, Pune, India, December 1995, TataMcGraw Hill.
21. ORACLE7 Server Concepts Manual, Part No 6693-70, Dicembre 1992.
22. SQL3 Document X3H2-94-080 e SOU-003, ISO-ANSI Working Draft, Database Language SQL, 1994.
23. M. Stonebraker, "The Integration of Rule System and Database Systems", IEEE Trans. on Knowledge on Data Engeneering, Vol. 4, N. 5, Ottobre 1992.
24. L. van der Voort, A. Siebes, "Termination and Confluence of Rule Execution", CIKM'93, Washington DC, November 1993.
25. T. Weik, A. Heuer, "An Algorithm for the Analysis of Termination of Large Trigger Sets in an OODBMS", ARTDB'95, Skövde, Svezia, June 1995, pp. 170-189.
26. C. Zaniolo, "Active Database Rules with Transaction-Conscious Stable-Model Semantics", DOOD'95, Singapore, 1995, pp. 55-72.
27. Y. Zhou, M. Hsu, "A Theory for Rule Triggering Systems", in Advances in Database Technology: EDBT '90, LNCS 416, 1990, pp. 407-422.

On Confluence Property of Active Databases with Meta-Rules

Xianchang Wang, Jia-Huai You, Li Yan Yuan

Department of Computing Science, University of Alberta
Edmonton, Alberta, Canada T6G 2H1
{xcwang, you, yuan}@cs.ualberta.ca

Abstract. An active database consists of a collection of event-condition-action rules (or ECA-rules), some meta rules that specify the desired interactions and constraints for the execution of firable rules, and a traditional database. The main goal of an active database is to automatically manage database operations. In general, the occurrence of an event can cause several rules to be firable nondeterministically and the execution of a firable rule may dynamically cause some other rules to be firable. It is this nondeterministic and dynamical behavior that may result in more than one valid sequence of possible rule executions. In this paper we address the following problem in active database with meta-rules: Upon the occurrence of an event, whether, or under what conditions, one is guaranteed with a unique final database state when the rule execution terminates. This property is called the *confluence property*. The main result is a sufficient condition for an active database to be confluent. We show that under some reasonable assumptions this condition is also necessary for the confluence property.

1 Introduction

Recent development in information systems has seen the use of active rules to manipulate database content. An active rule is of the form

$$Action \leftarrow Event, Condition$$

Intuitively, it specifies that upon the occurrence of *Event*, if *Condition* is satisfied, then perform *Action*.

An event is usually a database operation such as *insert, delete, update*, etc., or a point of time that requires the database management to react. A condition in an active rule is specified and checked against a database state (situation), e.g. any query that can be answered true or false by using SQL commands. An action is usually a database operation, or some predefined actions.

When an event occurs, a rule with the event specified in its body becomes *firable* and may be performed. If the condition in the body is satisfied at the performing point, the action is then performed. In general, multiple rules may be firable when an event occurs. In this case, rule interactions may be specified in a meta language to constrain their execution [4]. For example, one may specify that rule r_1 must be executed before that of rule r_2; or only one of the two rules r_1 and r_2 may be executed. Thus, an active database is a database with an active rule system built on top of it. Such an active rule system consists of ECA rules and some meta rules that specify the desired interactions among them. Nondeterminism arises when there are several rules that can be executed in any order without violating the rule interactions.

In general, different orders of execution may lead to different system states. In many situations this is undesirable since the choice of which state to continue becomes arbitrary, and any such choice becomes implementation dependent. Sometimes the problem can make a system unsafe to use, e.g. in a banking system. On the other hand, active rules are often used to achieve automatic database management. The possibility that a database transaction may lead to different database states is in general unacceptable in the present practice of database management. Thus, any active database developer would have the following question: *Is there a criterion by which the confluence property can be guaranteed?*

Note that the execution of a rule may cause other rules to be firable. Thus, the confluence property subscribes to a *dynamic* behavior of the underlying rule system. This is the key difference with the recent study by Jagadish *et al.* [4] where they are concerned with static properties, namely, given a set of firable rules, which rules should be executed so that the rule interactions are satisfied. In particular, they do not consider the situation where the execution of a rule may cause others to be firable. Our work can be seen as an extension of that of Jagadish *et al.* to a dynamic context.

A sufficient condition for confluence of active databases has been developed in [9]. It however only focuses on a single condition-action rule language and the restriction about confluence is too strong; namely, only monotonic accumulation of the database is allowed. This is unrealistic for most database applications, since it does not allow any modification to existing information. The solution proposed in this paper does not require that a database be changed only monotonicly. In [1], confluence is analyzed in a simpler context where the impact of events and database states is not considered. Etzion's work [3] focuses on the issue of predicating an application's behavior based on a special mete-data model which provides a low level implementation of an active database. However, since this model only considers the scheduled priority, more interactions between active rules need to be integrated.

This paper is organized as follows. In section 2, we provide notations and a formalization of active database systems with meta-rules. The meta-rules in this paper are adopted from Jagadish *et al's* work [4]. In section 3, we first give a static description of an active database, which is essentially borrowed from [4]. Since a performing rule may trigger other rules, which is not discussed by Jagadish *et al*, we further provide a dynamic characterization of an active database. In section 4, we show how to guarantee the confluence property of an active database with meta rules and develop an algorithm to check the confluence property. We also show that under some reasonable assumptions, this sufficient condition is also a necessary condition. We further show that under these assumptions, the confluence property coincides with the notion of *dynamic determinism*. That is, an active database with meta-rules is confluence if and only if for any event and database state, all the possible dynamic performing rule sequences contain the same rules. We show how to use this result to design a confluent active database. Finally, we discuss the complexity of the algorithm.

Proofs of the results stated in this paper have been removed because of the space limit.

2 Active Rules and Active Databases

An active rule system is built on top of a system with *system states* to control system changes. In many applications, such a system is usually a database system (though it does not have to be). When an active rule system is built on top of a database system, it is usually called an *active database*.

There are many *representation models* for active database [6]. In this paper, we choose a model general enough to cover a wide range of active databases.

We assume three sets of predicates E (events), C (conditions), and A (actions).

An *active rule* is of the form $l : a \leftarrow e, c$ where l is the rule label (for the purpose of reference), $e \in E$, $c \in C$, and $a \in A$. We may omit the label l if it is irrelevant to the discussion. If c is always satisfied, then we simply denote the rule by $l : a \leftarrow e$.

There have been a number of attempts to define what an event is and when an active rule becomes triggered and performed (called the *execution model* of active database in [7]). But for the purpose of fixing the notation, we select the following *deferred* model:

> An active rule $a \leftarrow e, c$ becomes triggered at the state s when event e occurs and if it is to be performed according to the meta-rules, its action 'a' will be performed when the transaction of event e reaches a commit point.

That is, when an event occurs, we first consider which rules are triggered, and among these rules which rules are to be performed and in which order. The action in a triggered rule is performed only after the event reaches its commit point. More details can be found in the next section.

We note that the above choice of the execution model is for the purpose of fixing the notion. That is, the main results of this paper do not depend on the execution model we select. It can be an *immediate* model where a rule must be evaluated when the triggering event occurs or a *deferred* model where a rule will be evaluated when the transaction reaches a commit point or some mixed models.

The execution of an action may cause an event to occur. For simplicity, we do not distinguish actions from events. For example, with the following active rules: $a \leftarrow e, c$ and $a' \leftarrow a, c'$, it is understood that performing a (in the first rule) also means that event a (in the second rule) occurs.

Meta-rules are used to specify active rule interactions. A meta-rule is of the form $l \otimes l'$ where l and l' are rule labels and $\otimes \in \Phi$ where Φ is a set of rule interaction operators. In this paper, we introduce four rule interaction operators proposed by Jagadish *et al.* [4], which are as follows:

- *Positive requirement:* $l \subset l'$ means that if l is executed, then l' should be also executed.
- *Disable:* $\overline{l, l'}$ means that if l and l' are firable, then only one of them may be executed.
- *Preference:* $l < l'$ means that in case both l and l' are triggered, if only one of them can be executed, then preferably perform l'.
- *Schedule:* $l \prec l'$ specifies that if both l and l' are executed, then l should be executed before l'.

An *active rule system* is then a tuple $\Pi = \langle R, Q \rangle$ where R is a finite set of active rules and Q a finite set of meta-rules.

Note that since we assume that an active rule system Π is built on top of a database system, associating with it is a database $\mathcal{D}$, we also use $\Pi = \langle R, Q \rangle$ to refer to an active database system.

In general, a database $\mathcal{D}$ can be regarded as a state transition function: $\mathcal{D} : \mathcal{A} \times \mathcal{S} \rightarrow \mathcal{S}$ where $\mathcal{A}$ is a set of database operations or actions (usually determined by a data manipulation language), and $\mathcal{S}$ is a set of database states. Function $\mathcal{D}$ can be extended to apply to a sequence of operations $\langle a_1...a_n \rangle$ (n ≥ 0), $\mathcal{D}: \mathcal{A}^* \times \mathcal{S} \rightarrow \mathcal{S}$, which is defined as:
$$\mathcal{D}(nil, s) = s,$$
$$\mathcal{D}(a_1.a_2...a_{i+1}, s) = \mathcal{D}(a_1...a_i, \mathcal{D}(a_{i+1}, s)).$$
Given an active database $\Pi = \langle R, Q \rangle$ and event e, we use $\mathcal{P}_\Pi(e)$ to denote the set of active rules with e in the body, that is, $\mathcal{P}_\Pi(e) = \{l : a \leftarrow c \mid l : a \leftarrow e, c \in R\}$. In the literature $\mathcal{P}_\Pi(e)$ is usually regarded as the set of rules that are triggered under the event e. Give a condition c and a database state s, we use $s \models c$ to denote that c is satisfied under s. Since our discussion is always with respect to a particular active rule system, we may omit Π in subscript when no confusion arises.

3 Static and Dynamic Characterizations

Given an event e and database state s, we are interested in which active rules should be executed so that the meta rules are satisfied. In general, an event can cause a chain of actions to be performed.

3.1 Static characterization

We first deal with static situations, the situations where action-causing-an-event propagation is not taken into consideration. First, we need to define, when an event e occurs at database state s, which rules should be triggered (or called *input rule* in [4]). Obviously it should be a function of the event e and database state s, denoted by $\mathcal{I}(e, s)$. There are different opinions on which rules should be selected as triggered rules. In this paper, we select $\mathcal{I}(e, s) = \mathcal{P}(e)$ as the triggered rule set[1]. Because of the interactions between triggered rules, not every triggered rule is chosen to be performed. The following definition tells us which rules should be performed and in which order.

Definition 1. (*Static sequence*)

Suppose e is an event, s is a database state. A sequence $O = \langle l_1, ..., l_n \rangle$ is said to be a *static sequence* from event e and database state s if $\{l_1, ..., l_n\} \subseteq \mathcal{I}(e, s)$ is a maximal set that satisfies the following conditions:

1. For every $l \supset l' \in Q$, if $l \in O$, then $l' \in O$;
2. For every $\overline{l, l'} \in Q$, either $l \notin O$ or $l' \notin O$;
3. For every $l < l' \in Q$, if $l, l' \in \mathcal{I}(e, s)$ and either $l \in O$ or $l' \in O$, then $l' \in O$;
4. For every $l \prec l' \in Q$, if $l, l' \in O$, then there are two integers $1 \leq i < j \leq n$, such that $l = l_i$ and $l' = l_j$;

The set of all static sequences induced from $\mathcal{I}(e, s)$ is denoted by $\mathcal{M}(e, s)$.

Without confusion, we use the set notation to describe a sequence, e.g. O by the set $\{l_1, ..., l_n\}$. Further, since $\mathcal{M}(e, s)$ does not depend upon the state s, we may simply denote it by $\mathcal{M}(e)$.

This definition is the same as the *model definition* given by Jagadish *et al* except that here O is required to be maximal. This means that as many rules as possible should be performed in our model. If O is not required to be maximal, then O is the *model* under Jagadish *et al*'s definition.

Definition 2. Suppose $\Pi = \langle R, Q \rangle$ is an active database. For any event e and database state s, suppose $\mathcal{I}(e, s)$ is the triggered rule set, we say a meta-rule $l \otimes l'$ is implied in Π under event e and state s, denoted by $\Pi, e, s, \models l \otimes l'$, if for any model O of $\mathcal{M}(e, s)$, $l \otimes l'$ is satisfied in O.

Example 1. Let $+\phi$ and $-\phi$ denote some actions (database operations), e_i (i=1, 2, 3, 4) be events. Suppose the active database is:

$$R = \{1 : +p \leftarrow e_1, 2 : +q \leftarrow e_1, 3 : +p \leftarrow e_2, 4 : -q \leftarrow e_2,$$
$$5 : -p \leftarrow e_3, 6 : +q \leftarrow e_3, 7 : -p \leftarrow e_4, 8 : +q \leftarrow e_4\}$$

$$Q = \{\overline{1, 2}, 1 < 2, 3 \prec 4, \overline{5, 6}\}$$

When event e_1 occurs, either $+p$ or $+q$ may be performed, but $\overline{1, 2}$ constrains that only one of them can be performed.

---

[1] If we require that a rule's condition be satisfied under current database state, then the subset $\{l : a \leftarrow c \mid l \in \mathcal{P}(e), s \models c\}$ of $\mathcal{P}(e)$ should be taken as the triggered rule set.

Intuitively, this rule specification says that, when event e_1 occurs exactly one of $+p$ and $+q$ should be performed. $1 < 2$ further says if only one of them can be performed, we prefer performing action $+q$. So when event e_1 occurs, we perform action $+q$. When event e_2 occurs, we perform action $+p$ and then action $-q$. When event e_3 occurs, we perform only one of the actions $-p$ and $+q$. Thus we have

$$\mathcal{P}(e_1) = \{1,2\}, \mathcal{P}(e_2) = \{3,4\}, \mathcal{P}(e_3) = \{5,6\}, \mathcal{P}(e_4) = \{7,8\}, \text{ and}$$
$$\mathcal{M}(e_1) = \{2\}, \mathcal{M}(e_2) = \{34\}, \mathcal{M}(e_3) = \{5,6\}, \mathcal{M}(e_4) = \{78,87\}.$$

The first requirement for the confluence property is that the set of execution rules remains the same for all static sequences. This is called *static determinism* in [4] and is defined as follows:

Definition 3. (*Static determinism*)

An active rule system is said to be *statically deterministic* if for any event e and database state s, all the static sequences of $\mathcal{M}(e, s)$ contain the same set of rules.

That is suppose $\langle q_1...q_n \rangle$ and $\langle p_1...p_m \rangle$ are two static sequences of $\mathcal{M}(e, s)$, then we have $n = m$ and $\{q_1, ..., q_n\} = \{p_1, ..., p_m\}$. Under this definition, the active database in Example 1 is not statically deterministic because there are two static sequences $\langle 5 \rangle$ and $\langle 6 \rangle$ that contain different rules at event e_3. Note that above definition only gives a static property in the sense that action-event propagation is not taken into consideration. In order to ensure a unique final database state, Jagadish *et al* require that the active database be *well ordered*; that is, at any event e, there is only one static-sequence.

By Jagadish *et al*'s result, the following two decision problems can be answered in polynomial time:

1. Given an active database $\langle R, Q \rangle$, is it statically deterministic under database state s and event e?

2. Given a meta rule $l \otimes l'$, event e and database state s, $\Pi, e, s \models l \otimes l'$?

We apply these results in our algorithm to check if an active database with meta-rules is confluent when a performing rule may trigger other rules and thus lead to new actions. This topic is not discussed in Jagadish *et al*'s paper.

3.2 Dynamic characterization

A performing action may cause an event to occur, and thus may trigger a chain of new actions. However, different sequences may result in different database states, and thus possibly different sets of firable rules (since conditions in rules are checked at different states).

To characerize the possible sequences of actions from an event we use the following transformation as a *deferred execution model*. Suppose we have a triple $\langle A, s, B \rangle$, where A is a sequence of rules that have already been executed, s is the current database state and B is the sequence of rules to be executed.

Definition 4. Given an active database, we define

$\langle A, s, (a \leftarrow c)C \rangle \implies \langle A(a \leftarrow c), s, C \rangle$ if $s \not\models c$;

$\langle A, s, (a \leftarrow c)C \rangle \implies \langle A(a \leftarrow c), s', C \rangle$ if $s \models c$, $s' = \mathcal{D}(a, s)$ and $\mathcal{M}(a) = \{\}$.

$\langle A, s, (a \leftarrow c)C \rangle \implies \langle A(a \leftarrow c), s', BC \rangle$ if $s \models c$, $s' = \mathcal{D}(a, s)$ and $B \in \mathcal{M}(a)$.

For any e, G is said to be a *dynamic sequence* from event e and state s if ε is an empty sequence and

$$\langle \varepsilon, s, e \leftarrow \rangle \implies^* \langle (e \leftarrow)G, s', \varepsilon \rangle.$$

s' is defined to be *the final state* of event e under state s.

The first transaction means that if a rule's condition is not satisfied under current database state, then we can not perform the action. The second transaction means that if a rule's condition is satisfied and the performance of the action does not trigger new rules, then simply perform the action. The third transaction means that if a rule's condition is satisfied and the performance of the action may trigger a sequence of new rules B, then perform the action and then immediately perform the triggered rules.

Since a rule may be triggered and performed more than once, for the purpose of referring to all rule executions, we assume that each time when a rule becomes triggered and performed it has a different label. Thus, we can extend the static determinism into a dynamic one and talk about the set of rules to be executed in a sequence.

Definition 5. (*Dynamic determinism*)

An active database is dynamically deterministic if for any event e and database state s, all of the dynamic sequences from e and s contain the same set of rules. We denote the set of rules from event e and state s by $W(e, s)$.

Definition 6. (*Confluence*)

We say an active database $\langle R, Q \rangle$ is *confluent* for database state s and event e, if it has only one final state. We say an active database $\langle R, Q \rangle$ is *confluent*, if for any database state s and event e, it has only one final state.

Generally, dynamic determinism and confluence are two unrelated concepts. That a system is dynamically deterministic does not mean it is confluent, and vice versa. For example,

Example 2. Let $+\phi$ and $-\phi$ denote some insert and delete actions (database operations). A database state is a set of propositions. Suppose the active database under consideration is:

$1 : +q \leftarrow +p,$
$2 : +r \leftarrow +q,$
$3 : +s \leftarrow +q,$
$4 : -s \leftarrow +r,$
$5 : -r \leftarrow +s,$

where the meta rule set is empty. Then we have

$\mathcal{M}(+p) = \{1\}; \mathcal{M}(+q) = \{23, 32\}; \mathcal{M}(+r) = \{4\}; \mathcal{M}(+s) = \{5\}.$

For event $+p$ (we denote 0 for $+p \leftarrow$) and initial state $s = \{\}$, we have

$$\langle \varepsilon, \{\}, 0 \rangle \Longrightarrow \langle 0, \{p\}, 1 \rangle \Longrightarrow \langle 01, \{p, q\}, 23 \rangle \Longrightarrow \langle 012, \{p, q, r\}, 43 \rangle \Longrightarrow$$
$$\langle 0124, \{p, q, r\}, 3 \rangle \Longrightarrow \langle 01243, \{p, q, r, s\}, 5 \rangle \Longrightarrow \langle 012435, \{p, q, s\}, \varepsilon \rangle$$

So event $+p$ has one dynamic sequence 012435 under state $\{\}$ and the corresponding final state is $\{p, q, s\}$. Similarly, event $+p$ has another dynamic sequence 013524 and the final state is $\{p, q, r\}$. Obviously, this active database is dynamically deterministic but it is not confluent at event $+p$ and state $\{\}$.

The execution model becomes clearer if we use a tree representation for the relationship between events: a node is an event and its children (from left to right) are the actions of the triggered rules. Thus, different levels of the tree represent the different levels of triggered events. The performing rule sequences are sequences generated by the depth first traversals of all such trees. The above two performing sequences can be drawn as:

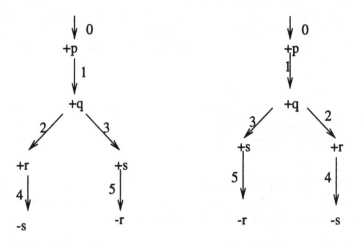

Preorder traversal: 012435   Preorder traversal: 013524

Example 2 shows the fact that a system is deterministic (either statically or dynamically) does not guarantee a unique final database state. Dynamic determinism requires that all valid execution sequences contain the same set of actions and does not guarantee the confluence because in the general case different performing sequences of the same actions may lead in different database states. For example, suppose there are two operations $x := 2x$ (double x) and $x := x + 20$ (add 20 to x). Different orders of executions would give us different results. However, dynamic determinism has a close relationship with confluence property. In next section, we prove that under some reasonable assumptions, these two concepts coincide.

4 Confluence

4.1 Previous work

In the past *commutativity* was studied (cf. [1]) to ensure the confluence in a much simpler context; namely, operations are not determined by events and database states.

Definition 7. (*Commutativity under constraint* [1])
Two actions a_1 and a_2 are said to be *commutative under constraint condition* c, if for every database state s that satisfies c, we have,
$$\mathcal{D}(a_1, \mathcal{D}(a_2, s)) = \mathcal{D}(a_2, \mathcal{D}(a_1, s))$$
If a_1 and a_2 are commutative under a tautology, we simply say a_1 and a_2 are commutative.

There is a simple case where two actions are commutative: when they operate on different parts of the database. For example, actions *insert employee* and *insert student* are commutative. When two actions operate on the same part of the database, they may also be commutative. For example, actions $x := x + 100$ and $x := x + 200$ are commutative. Two actions may be commutative under some constraint conditions. For example, actions $x := 2 \times x$ and $x := x \times x$ are not commutative in general, but they are commutative if $x = 0$. Commutativity needs only to be applied to those rules whose exchange of positions does not violate any meta rule.

Definition 8. (*Commutativity between two rules*)
Given an active database, suppose S is a set of rule sequences. Two rules r and r' are *commutativity* in S if S contains two rule sequences such that in one r appears before r' and in the other r' appears before r.

We say an active database is *terminating*, if for any event e and database state s, the active database terminates at a state when event e occurs under state s. In this paper termination is a basic assumption and not a subject of investigation (cf. [2]). We are now ready to describe a sufficient condition directly from [1] for confluence of a very restricted active database where each rule's condition is always satisfied:

Theorem 9. *Let $\langle R, Q \rangle$ be a dynamically deterministic and terminating active database such that each condition of its rule is always satisfied. If for any commutativity rules $a \leftarrow, a' \leftarrow \in W(e, s)$, a and a' are commutative, then the active database terminates at a unique final state when event e occurs at state s.*

If some of the rule's condition are not always satisfied, then this theorem is not applicable. For example, suppose $W(e, s_0) = \{12, 21\}$ where 1 is $x := x + 100 \leftarrow x > 100$ and 2 is $x := x + 200 \leftarrow$, s_0 is the initial state such that under $\mathcal{D}(e, s_0)$, $x = 0$ is true, then we can see that there are two final states such that one makes x be 200 and another makes x be 300 although two actions $x := x + 100$ and $x := x + 200$ are commutative.

4.2 Checking confluence

We are interested in this question: From $\mathcal{M}(e,s)$, how can we check that the active database is confluent?

There are two aspects of Theorem 9 that makes it difficult to be used for checking confluence. First, it requires that the conditions of all the rules to be always satisfied; Second, it requires the computation of all the dynamic sequences $W(e,s)$ under event e and database state s.

In this section we give a result that describes a condition that guarantees the property of confluence. Essentially, it identifies syntactically a set of actions and conditions whose commutativity needs to be checked.

We first calculate the set of all the possible triggered rules caused by a performing rule $a \leftarrow c$. We denote it by $\mathcal{P}^*(a \leftarrow c)$ which is a minimal set satisfying the following two conditions:

1. $a \leftarrow c \in \mathcal{P}^*(a \leftarrow c)$, and
2. for any $a' \leftarrow c' \in \mathcal{P}^*(a \leftarrow c)$, we have $\mathcal{P}(a') \subseteq \mathcal{P}^*(a \leftarrow c)$.

Given an active database $\langle R, Q \rangle$, if its event set and rule set are both finite, then the problem of computing all the possible triggered rule set is tractable.

Definition 10. (*Invariance condition*)

A condition c' is defined to be *invariable* for the active rule $l = a \leftarrow c$, denoted by $l \vdash_d c'$, if for any state s that satisfies c, we have $s \models c'$ iff $\mathcal{D}(a,s) \models c'$.

When c is always satisfied, we simply say c' is invariable for action a.

For example, condition $y > x$ is invariable for the rule $x := x + 1 \leftarrow y > (x + 1)$; condition $x > 100$ is invariable for action *update y*. Now we are ready to relate the confluence of an active database with checking of the commutative rules of $\mathcal{M}(e)$ instead of $W(e,s)$.

Theorem 11. Let $\Pi = \langle R, Q \rangle$ be a statically deterministic and terminating active database. If for any event e, any two commutative rules $r_1 : a_1 \leftarrow c_1$ and $r_2 : a_2 \leftarrow c_2$ of $\mathcal{M}(e,s)$, such that for any two rules $r = a \leftarrow c \in \mathcal{P}^*(r_1)$, $r' = a' \leftarrow c' \in \mathcal{P}^*(r_2)$, we have

1. a and a' are commutative under constraint condition $c \wedge c'$ and
2. $r \vdash_d c'$ and $r' \vdash_d c$,

then Π is confluent.

Example 3. Let's check the active database in Example 2. Obviously, only rules 2 and 3 are commutative in $\mathcal{M}(+q)$, and

$$\mathcal{P}^*(2 : +r \leftarrow +q) = \{2 : +r \leftarrow +q, 4 : -s \leftarrow +r\}$$
$$\mathcal{P}^*(3 : +s \leftarrow +q) = \{3 : +s \leftarrow +q, 5 : -r \leftarrow +s\}.$$

We can see that $+r$ and $-r$ are not commutative, and $+s$ and $-s$ are not commutative either. This is why the active database is not confluent.

The following proposition tells us how we use Jagadish *et al*'s framework to deduce that two rules are commutative.

Proposition 12. *For any statically deterministic active database $\Pi = \langle R, Q \rangle$, any event e and database s, two rules l and l' of $\mathcal{I}(e, s)$ are commutative in $\mathcal{M}(e)$ iff $\Pi, e, s \not\models c$ where $c \in \{\overline{l, l'}, l \prec l', l' \prec l\}$ iff $Q \cup \{\overline{l, l} \mid l \in R, l \notin \mathcal{I}(e, s)\}$ does not imply[2] any meta-rule of $\{\overline{l, l'}, l \prec l', l' \prec l\}$.*

By Theorem 11 and Proposition 12 we can use the following algorithm to decide if a statically deterministic and terminating active database $\langle R, Q \rangle$ is confluent:

Algorithm

1	First, compute the function $\mathcal{P}^*$
2	**For each** event $e \in E$ **do**
3	**For each** rule couple $l_1 = a_1 \leftarrow c_1$ and $l_2 = a_2 \leftarrow c_2$ of $\mathcal{P}(e)$ **do**
4	**If** Not $(Q \cup \{\overline{l, l} \mid l \notin \mathcal{P}(e)\}$ implies $\overline{l_1, l_2}, l_1 \prec l_2$ or $l_2 \prec l_1)$ **then**
5	**If** For all $a \leftarrow c \in \mathcal{P}^*(l_1)$, $a' \leftarrow c' \in \mathcal{P}^*(l_2)$ such that
6	1. a and a' are commutative under $c \wedge c'$, and
7	2. $a \leftarrow c \vdash_d c'$ and $a' \leftarrow c' \vdash_d c$
8	**then** *success* $= 1$ **else begin** *success* $:= -1$, exist end
9	**end if**
10	**end if**
11	**end do**
12	**end do**

In this algorithm, we can see that Q, the meta rule set, plays an important role in reducing the complexity of deciding confluence of an active database $\langle R, Q \rangle$. In a simple case, if for any two rules, $l_1 = a_1 \leftarrow e, c_1$ and $l_2 = a_2 \leftarrow e, c_2$ of P, Q has at least one of the meta-relations $\{\overline{l_1, l_2}, l_1 \prec l_2, l_2 \prec l_1\}$ in Q, then the active database must be confluent.

4.3 Necessary condition?

The condition of Theorem 11 becomes a necessary condition under certain assumptions.

Theorem 13. *Suppose $\langle R, Q \rangle$ is an active database under the database $\mathcal{D}$. If*
   1. for any database state s and action a that appear in $\langle R, Q \rangle$, there exists a unique s' such that $\mathcal{D}(a, s') = s$ and $s' \neq s$, and
   2. for any state s, s', and action a that appear in $\langle R, Q \rangle$, if $s \neq s'$, then $\mathcal{D}(a, s) \neq \mathcal{D}(a, s')$,
then the sufficient condition of Theorem 11 is also a necessary condition.

---

[2] Refer to the more detailed definition of implication in Definition 4.1 of [4].

Assumption 1 says that actions of an active database should be powerful enough to be able to reach any state. In addition, an action should not be included in an active database rule if it does not change the database state. Assumption 2 says that the performance of an action should not result in the same final state with two different initial states.

These two assumptions do not hold in general. For example, assumption 2 may fail for some update operations, since they can overwrite previous operations. For example, suppose a is $x := 100$, s and s' are the same except that at s, $x = 30$ and at s', $x = 50$. Then, it is straightforward to see that after performing a at either s or s', the resulting state is the same.

Under these two assumptions we conclude that the confluence and the dynamic determinism coincide.

Theorem 14. *Suppose $\langle R, Q \rangle$ is an active database that satisfies the assumptions of Theorem 13, then the active database is confluent if and only if it is dynamically deterministic.*

This result has important implications in active database. First, a system developer can use this result to prove the confluence property of the system being developed which may be targeted to a particular application domain. Since the condition is also necessary under some reasonable assumptions, that the condition is not satisfied implies that there is a good chance that there are unintended behavior in active rules. In this case, the system developer can focus on revising these rules. Furthermore, requiring that a system be confluent makes implementation flexible, since any particular execution strategy, say adopting different execution models, would not change the result of rule executions. If some applications allow nondeterminism, the set of events can be divided into two subsets, those that should always result in a unique final state and those that are not required to result in a unique final state.

4.4 A case study

In this section, we show how theorem 11 and theorem 13 can be applied to analyze the confluence of an active database. Suppose we have four actions x^+, x^-, y^+ and y^- which respectively express increasing x by 1, decreasing x by 1, increasing y by 1, and decreasing y by 1. Here x and y are two integer variables. We also suppose that a database state is a tuple $(x = m, y = n)$ where x and y are assigned by two integers. Our goal is to design an active database $\Pi = \langle R, Q \rangle$ such that:

1. If x^+ or y^- occurs and the current state satisfies $x < y$, then the final state would make $x = y$, which is the mean value of x and y;

2. If x^- or y^+ occurs and the current state satisfies $y < x$, then the final state would make $x = y$, which is the mean value of x and y.

R contains:

$1 : x^+ \leftarrow y^-, x < y$

$2 : y^- \leftarrow x^+, x < y$

$3 : x^- \leftarrow y^+, x > y$

$4 : y^+ \leftarrow x^-, x > y$

and $Q = \{\}$.

Let us verify that this active database is confluent.

First, we can determine that it is statically deterministic because $\mathcal{M}(x^+) = \{2\}, \mathcal{M}(x^-) = \{4\}, \mathcal{M}(y^+) = \{3\}$ and $\mathcal{M}(y^-) = \{1\}$. Since there are no commutative rules in any $\mathcal{M}(e)$ of event e, by Theorem 11, the above active database is confluent.

The reader can check, for example, that if the initial state is $(x = 2, y = 7)$, then the event x^+ would lead to a unique final state $(x = 5, y = 5)$.

Now we add the following active rules to the above active database:

$5 : x^+ \leftarrow x^+, x < y;$

$6 : y^- \leftarrow y^-, x < y;$

$7 : x^- \leftarrow x^-, x > y;$

$8 : y^+ \leftarrow y^+, x > y;$

Is this extended active database confluent? As this active database satisfies the assumptions of theorem 13, we can check its confluence by just checking if it satisfies the condition of theorem 11.

First, we can prove that this active database is statically deterministic because $\mathcal{M}(x^+) = \{25, 52\}, \mathcal{M}(x^-) = \{47, 74\}, \mathcal{M}(y^+) = \{38, 83\}$ and $\mathcal{M}(y^-) = \{16, 61\}$. There are four couples of commutative rules: 2 and 5, 4 and 7, 3 and 8, and 1 and 6. Let's check $\mathcal{P}^*(2)$ and $\mathcal{P}^*(5)$. We can see: $\mathcal{P}^*(2) = \{1, 2, 5, 6\}$, $\mathcal{P}^*(5) = \{1, 2, 5, 6\}$.

Obviously, for any two rules respectively from above two sets, say 1 and 2, we do not have:

$$x^+ \leftarrow x < y \vdash_d x < y$$

For example, suppose $x = 3, y = 4$, then after x^+, $x < y$ is no longer true.

So the condition of theorem 11 does not hold. Since this condition is also a necessary condition, the above active database is neither dynamically deterministic nor confluent.

The reader can check, for example, that in this new active database rule set, if the initial state is $(x = 2, y = 7)$, then the event x^+ would lead to a final state $(x = c, y = c)$ such that c can be any number between 3 and 7.

5 Complexity Analysis

In this section we discuss the complexity of the algorithm given in Subsection 4.3. Given an active database $\langle R, Q \rangle$, let $|E| = m, |R| = n$ and $|Q| = k$. First we can determine if it is statically deterministic in polynomial time. If it is not statically deterministic, then the database is not well-behaved. Suppose it is statically deterministic, it is known that performing 4 of the algorithm takes polynomial time (cf. [4]). Suppose it is $\mathcal{O}((n + k)^t)$. Suppose further that computing lines 6 and 7 of the algorithm respectively takes δ_1 and δ_2 in the worst case. Then we have the following result:

Proposition 15. *The complexity of the above algorithm is bounded by* $\mathcal{O}(m \times (n + k)^{t+4} \times (\delta_1 + \delta_2))$.

Since the database state space is so large, there is no general and practical method to check if two actions are commutative for a given constraint and/or if one condition is invariable for a given active rule . However, there are some special cases that are easy to decider if two actions are commutative under certain constraint. We also find some methods to divide the problem of decisiding if a condition is invariable for a rule into small problems.

A note on commutativity

Suppose a and a' are two actions, c is a constraint condition, we are interested in when a and a' are commutative under c. When c is not satisfiable, a and a' are obviously commutative under c.

When c is satisfied, we constrain the actions to the following types: *insert, update, remove* on certain tables of a relational database [5].

If a and a' operate on different tables, then they are commutative; If a and a' operate on the same table, but with different keys, then they are commutative too; If both a and a' are *remove* operations, then they are commutative; If one of a and a' is *update* operation, another is *remove* operation, then they are commutative; If a and a' are the same operation, then they are commutative.

In other cases, if a and a' operates on the same table and with the same key, then they are not generally commutative. However, this also depends on the more details of the actions and the constraint condition.

A note on invariance condition

How can we decide that a condition 'c' is invariable for a given rule $a \leftarrow c$? Suppose c and c' are regarded as a composition of some basic propositions, then we reduce a composition condition to simple ones.

Theorem 16. *For any action a, conditions c, c', c_1 and c_2, we have:*

$a \leftarrow c \vdash_d T$; $a \leftarrow c \vdash_d F$ *and* $a \leftarrow F \vdash_d c'$, *where T is a tautology, F is a false statement;*

$a \leftarrow c \vdash_d c'$ *if and only if* $a \leftarrow c \vdash_d \neg c'$;

$a \leftarrow c \vdash_d c_1$ *and* $a \leftarrow c \vdash_d c_2$ *implies* $a \leftarrow c \vdash_d c_1 \wedge c_2$;

$a \leftarrow c \vdash_d c_1 \vee c_2$ *and* $a \leftarrow c \vdash_d c_1$ *implies* $a \leftarrow c \vdash_d c_2$;

$a \leftarrow c_1 \vdash_d c'$ *and* $a \leftarrow c_2 \vdash_d c'$ *if and only if* $a \leftarrow c_1 \vee c_2 \vdash_d c'$.

These results show that analyzing if a condition is invariable for a given rule can be divided into the questions of analyzing if a basic condition is invariable for a more basic rule. However, answer of this final question does really depend upon the given action (a), the given condition (c) and the given constraint condition (c') of active database.

6 Summary

In this paper we have given a dynamic characterization of an active database, and shown how one can check the confluence property of an active database with meta rules. An algorithm to check the satisfiability of the condition of confluence has been provided. We have also shown that under some reasonable assumptions, this sufficient condition is also a necessary condition. Finally, we discussed the complexity of our algorithm.

In the future we would like to consider extending our results to active database models which permit more complex operations, such as composition events and actions, and concurrent actions.

References

1. A. Aiken, J. Widom, and J.M. Hellerstein. Behavior of database production rules: termination, confluence, and observable determinism. In *Proc. of the ACM SIG-MOD Int. Conf. on Management of Data*, pages 59–68, 1992.

2. E. Baralis, S. Ceri, and J. Widom. Better termination analysis for active databases. In *Rules in Database Systems: The workshop in computing*, pages 163–179, 1993.

3. O. Etzion. Reasoning about the behavior of active database applications. In *Rules in Database Systems, LNCS 985*, pages 86–100, 1995.

4. H. V. Jagadish, A. O. Mendelzon, and I. S. Mumick. Managing conflicts between rules. In *Proc. of PODS*. Montreal Quebec, Canada, 1996.

5. Philip J. Pratt, Joseph J. Adamski. Database Systems Management and Design. *Boyd & Fraser Publishing Company*, 1987.

6. N. W. Paton, J. Campin, A.A. A. Fernandes, and M.H. Williams. Rules in database. In Timos Sellis, editor, *Formal Specification of Active Database Functionality: A Survey*, pages 221–35. Lecture Notes in Computer Science, 985, Springer, 1995.

7. C. Tawbi, G. Jaber, and M. Dalmau. Activity specification using rendezvous. In *Rules in Database Systems, LNCS 985*, pages 51–65, 1995.

8. L. van der Voort and A. Siebes. Enforcing confluence of rule execution. In *Proceedings of the first Int. Workshop on Rules In Databases Systems*, pages 194–207. Springer-Verlag, 1994.

9. Y. Zhou and M. Hsu. A theory for rule triggering systems. In *Proc. Extending Database Technology (EDBI)*, pages 407–421. Springer-Verlag, 1990.

An Implementation and Evaluation of the Refined Triggering Graph Method for Active Rule Termination Analysis[1]

Michael K. Tschudi, Susan D. Urban, Suzanne W. Dietrich, Anton P. Karadimce

Department of Computer Science and Engineering
Arizona State University, Tempe, AZ 85287-5406
602-965-2874
s.urban@asu.edu

Abstract. This paper describes the implementation of the Refined Triggering Graph (RTG) method for active rule termination analysis. The RTG method has been defined in the context of an active, deductive, object-oriented database language known as CDOL (Comprehensive, Declarative, Object Language). The RTG method studies the contents of rule pairs and rule cycles in a triggering graph and tests for: 1) the successful unification of one rule's action with another rule's triggering event, and 2) the satisfiability of active rule conditions, asking if it is possible for the condition of a triggered rule to evaluate to true in the context of the triggering rule's condition. If the analysis can provably demonstrate that one rule cannot trigger another rule, the directed vector connecting the two rules in a basic triggering graph can be removed, thus refining the triggering graph. Two important aspects in the implementation of the method include the development of a satisfiability algorithm for CDOL conditions and the extension of the RTG method with knowledge of the rule execution semantics. The effectiveness of the approach within the context of the sample application is also addressed.

1 Introduction

In the past few years, several techniques have been developed to support termination analysis of active database rules. These techniques range from the conservative construction of basic triggering graphs, showing how the action of one rule relates to the event of another rule (e.g., [Aiken et al. 1992]), to more semantic methods that examine the conditions of rules (e.g., [Baralis et al. 1993, 1995a]). One such semantic approach is the *refined triggering graph method (RTG)* of Karadimce and Urban [1996a, 1996b]. The RTG method studies the contents of active rules and tests for: 1) the successful unification of one rule's action with another rule's triggering event, and 2) the satisfiability of active rule conditions, asking if it is possible for the condition of a triggered rule to evaluate to true in the context of the triggering rule's condition. If the analysis can provably demonstrate that one rule cannot trigger another rule, the directed vector connecting the two rules in the basic triggering graph can be removed, thus refining the triggering graph. One can continue the refinement until no cycles remain in the graph or until the remaining cycles of the graph cannot be eliminated. In the former case, termination is assured. In the latter

---

[1] This research was sponsored by NSF Grant No. IRI-9410983.

case, the refined triggering graph can serve other termination analysis methods, such as the static and run-time analysis tools of [Baralis et al. 1995a, 1995b].

The RTG method was defined in the context of *CDOL* (*C*omprehensive, *D*eclarative, *O*bject *L*anguage), an active, deductive, object-oriented language [Urban et al. 1997]. The method defines the use of *triggering formulae* within three different levels of termination analysis, where each level of analysis provides an increasing degree of semantic analysis of rule connectivity. Triggering formulae are based on concepts borrowed from constraint logic programming. In particular, triggering formulae in the RTG method use the order-sorted, algebraic definition of CDOL to test for the satisfiability of constraint conditions that are formed by a sequence of rules within a triggering graph. Simplification rules are applied to CDOL rule conditions within triggering formulae, some of which transform rule conditions into a more efficient form for data retrieval and some of which help to identify unsatisfiable triggering relationships between rules.

The primary objective of the research described in this paper has been to implement and evaluate the RTG method [Tschudi 1997]. The goal of the implementation was to: 1) demonstrate the utility of triggering formulae to support the satisfiability analysis of rule connectivity, and 2) extend the original, theoretical definition of the RTG approach with practical implementation considerations. In particular, the implementation incorporates rule processing semantics, such as immediate and deferred coupling modes, rule priorities, and before/after triggering events into the implementation of the RTG method. The implementation also integrates the use of constraint simplification rules with the satisfiability algorithm of Rosenkrantz and Hunt [1980] to provide a more complete approach to testing for the satisfiability of rule triggering relationships.

The goal of the evaluation aspect of the research was to determine the effectiveness of the RTG method in the refinement of a basic triggering graph. Analyzing a sample active application, this implementation discovered 744 potential cycles of rule triggering among ten active rules. Using the RTG method, the implementation was able to determine that 739 of these cycles contain unsatisfiable triggering connections and thus will not actually cycle. This represents a tremendous savings in effort for an active rule designer. The evaluation process also allowed us to make several observations about the different types of triggering formulae and the conditions under which the different levels of termination analysis are the most effective. Although some levels of analysis are more effective than others for refining a triggering graph without user intervention, all three methods together form a useful semantic analysis of rule connectivity.

The remainder of this paper is structured as follows. Section 2 describes related work that has been done in the area of termination analysis. Section 3 then provides an overview of the RTG method on which this paper is based. Section 4 describes the static termination analysis tool developed using the refined triggering graph method. Section 5 contains an evaluation of the static analysis tool as applied to a sample application involving vehicle engine control. Lastly, Section 6 summarizes the research performed and describes directions for future research.

2   Related Work

To address the problem of rule termination, static rule analysis techniques have been developed by several research groups. The techniques are generally based on the use of triggering graphs [Aiken et al 1992], where a collection of rules can be visualized as a graph with the nodes symbolizing rules and directed vectors connecting nodes symbolizing the triggering of one rule by another. Cycles in a triggering graph indicate possible infinite sequences of rule triggering; the lack of cycles guarantees a terminating rule set.

The work in [Baralis et al. 1993, Baralis and Widom 1994] builds an "activation graph", where nodes are rules and directed edges in the graph indicate that a rule supplies data to another rule. In [Baralis et al. 1995a], both a triggering graph and an activation graph are used. In this approach, the nodes of an activation graph still represent rules, but directed edges connect rules only if the action of the triggering rule can cause the condition of the triggered rule to evaluate to true. The value of an activation graph lies in its ability to help predict the possible value of a triggered rule's condition: nodes that don't have edges leading into them in the activation graph don't have rules—including themselves—that set their condition to true. Without such rules, the node cannot participate in infinite rule triggering. The static termination analysis tool called Arachne described in [Ceri et al. 1995] implements this approach. In this tool, the results of the software analysis are used to remove edges from the triggering graph.

Other researchers have tried different approaches to managing termination. Aiken et al. [1992] use the "execution graph" wherein nodes are database states and the directed arcs connecting nodes represent different rules that may be executed from a database state. A non-terminating set of rules is an infinite path through this graph. Fraternali et al. [1992] build a "triggering hypergraph". In this graph, nodes are constraints and arcs are rules that travel from a constraint to a set of constraints that the rule execution may violate. Cycles in the graph are conservatively interpreted to mean infinite rule sequences. Montesi and Torlone [1995] do not permit the rule set to have cycles. Weik and Heuer [1995] consider the case of rules whose action part performs an "increase" or "decrease" operation on some value in the database. If the value domain is bounded from above/below, then the repeated monotonic increases/decreases eventually reach the boundary value. As the database state does not change for the boundary point, the repeated triggering of the active rule stops.

The RTG method implemented as part of this work is complementary to many of the approaches described above. Unlike the approach of Baralis et al. [1995a], the RTG method simplifies the triggering graph by studying the satisfiability of triggering relationships between rules. The RTG method can therefore be used to simplify a triggering graph before applying a technique such as the activation graph approach of Baralis et al. [1995] or the approach of Weik and Heuer [1995]. The next section provides an overview of the RTG method as originally defined in Karadimce and Urban [1996], together with several examples from the active application studied as part of the research.

3 Overview of the Refined Triggering Graph Method

The RTG method, formally defined in [Karadimce and Urban 1996; Karadimce 1997], uses satisfiability of well-defined logic formulae, called *triggering formulae*, as a device for improving rule triggering analysis. The RTG method begins with the formation of a basic triggering graph, where nodes represent rules and a directed vector from node *r1* to node *r2* represents the fact that *r1* triggers *r2*. Informally, a triggering formula $T(r1,r2)$ is a finite conjunction of equational atoms formed from the condition of *r1*, the unification of *r1's* action with *r2's* event, and the condition of *r2*. If the formula $T(r1, r2)$ is satisfiable, then *r1* can trigger *r2*, otherwise the vector between *r1* and *r2* can be removed from the triggering graph (i.e., the condition of *r2* provably will never be satisfied based on the condition associated with *r1*). Within the RTG method, there are three different types of formulae: *unification formulae*, *connecting formulae*, and *qualified connecting formulae*. Connecting formulae can also be extended to the notion of *generalized connecting formulae*, which are used to test for the satisfiability of a sequence of three or more rules. Each formula type represents increasing levels of semantic analysis of triggering relationships.

This section presents an informal overview of the different types of triggering formulae through the use of a small sample active database application. The application is a vehicle engine-control database that uses ten active rules to enforce certain vehicle performance parameters. An entity-relationship diagram of the application is shown in Figure 1. As indicated in Figure 1, a vehicle has a current speed, a range of acceptable engine revolutions in revolutions per minute (rpm) for any engine installed in the vehicle, and an upper limit on the speed. A vehicle contains an engine for which the database stores the current oil pressure, engine speed, and engine revolutions. The database also contains a class for the manufacturer's specifications; this class contains a single attribute for minimum oil pressure.

The purpose of the database is to monitor changes to the vehicle speed, vehicle rpm range, engine speed, and oil pressure to catch excessive values. Active rules are used for this monitoring. In addition, a set of vehicle speed restrictions are implemented as active rules. The complete set of active rules can be found in the Appendix.

3.1 Basic Triggering Graph

In the RTG method, a basic triggering graph is first constructed from the set of active rules. Each method call in a CDOL rule action produces an event. This event triggers any other rules that are sensitive to that method's invocation, i.e., are triggered by that event. Each pairing of rules based on the production by one rule of an event and the consumption of the same event by another rule is represented as a pair of nodes connected by a vector. Affiliated with the vector are the parameters of the produced event as well as the signature of the consumed event. This information is used during the unification phase described in the next subsection.

The initial triggering graph for the engine-control database is shown in Figure 2. Each cycle represents a potential for infinite rule behavior. For example, the triggering graph for our sample database has 744 cycles that do not contain nested cycles. Each cycle has a unique collection and ordering of nodes (e.g., a cycle consisting of nodes 1-2-3-4-1 is considered the same as the cycle 3-4-1-2-3). Not all of these apparent rule-triggering cycles can really occur, but the basic triggering graph captures all such cycles.

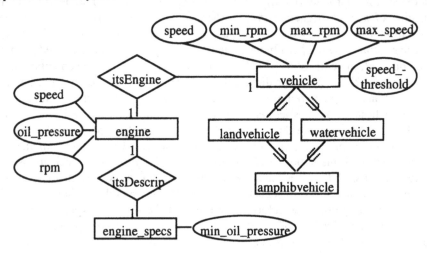

Fig. 1. Entity-Relationship Diagram for Sample Application

3.2 Unification Formulae

A rule event has a signature consisting of a method name and a list of parameters. An vent may be associated with multiple signatures, thus having different parameters or more constrained parameter types. A rule *r1* may produce an event named *n* with signature *s*, while another rule *r2* may be enabled by an event of the same name but with signature *t*. In the initial construction of the triggering graph, *r1* is shown as triggering *r2* in the triggering graph because of matching event names, but if signature *s* cannot be unified with signature *t*, then *r1* will not actually trigger *r2*.

As an example, consider the *landspeed_governor* rule and the *waterspeed_governor* rule. The *landspeed_governor* rule produces an event when method *set_speed* is invoked in its action. The *waterspeed_governor* rule is triggered by an event of the same name. Nominally, there exists a triggering connection from *landspeed_governor* to *waterspeed_governor*.

The development of a unification formula finds this triggering connection unsatisfiable for two reasons. The first source of a failure to unify comes from the type of the object to which the message *set_speed* is sent. The message is sent to an object of class *landvehicle*; the rule *waterspeed_governor* is triggered when *set_speed* is sent to an object of class *watervehicle*. Since *watervehicle* and *landvehicle* are different classes and *watervehicle* is not a superclass of *landvehicle*, we cannot equate the two classes. The second problem found during unification is that the triggering method has a signature with a single argument of the integer type, while the triggered rule's event has a signature with a single argument of the string type. These types are not compatible and unification fails.

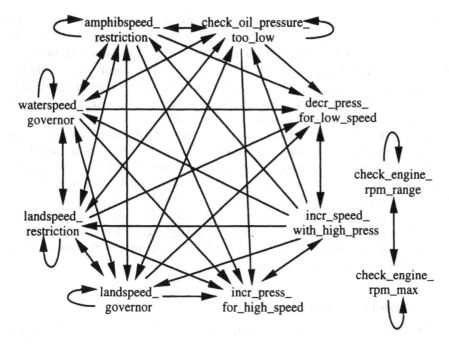

Fig. 2. Triggering Graph for Sample Application

3.3 Connecting Formulae

If the unification formula is satisfiable, then the unification formula can be extended to a connecting formula. In particular, the condition of *r1* can be combined with the condition of *r2* by way of the unification of the two rules. If the connecting formula is unsatisfiable, then *r2's* condition can never be satisfied, and thus the connection between the two rules in the triggering graph can be removed.

A constraint placed on the use of connecting formula is that the conditions involved in the test for satisfiability must be *database-independent*. A variable in a triggering formulae is database-independent if the value of the variable does not depend on the current database state; otherwise the variable is *database-dependent*. For example, if *r1* triggers *r2* and the connecting formula is unsatisfiable, then the vector between *r1* and *r2* is removed under the assumption that the condition associated with *r2* will not change between the execution of *r1* and the execution of *r2*. This condition be guaranteed under the connecting formulae method only if the variables in the connecting formula do not involve the retrieval of database values. Otherwise, there is no guarantee that a third rule will not execute in between *r1* and *r2* that will affect *r2's* condition. Thus, database-dependent conditions cannot be used for removing a directed vector from the refined triggering graph under the connecting formulae method. As described later in Section 3.4, qualified connecting formulae can be used to relax this restriction under certain conditions.

As an example of applying the connecting formulae method, consider the *landspeed_governor* rule from the Appendix. This rule produces an event when method *set_speed* is invoked in its action. This rule is also triggered by an event of the same name. Nominally, there exists a triggering connection from the rule to itself.

The unification formulae method finds this triggering connection satisfiable. When the unification formula is extended to a connecting formula, the condition to test for satisfiability reduces to 15 < 15 using the simplification rules described in the next section, which is obviously unsatisfiable. The vector in the triggering graph from *landspeed_governor* to itself can therefore be removed.

Note that connecting formulae can be extended to the notion of *generalized connecting formulae*. The extension involves developing a triggering formula for an entire cycle, as opposed to analyzing one vector at a time. If applied to the triggering graph in Figure 2, the generalized connecting formula will indicate that the potential cycle *check_engine_rpm_max* → *check_engine_rpm_range* → *check_engine_rpm_max* will not occur. Generalized connecting formulae, however, cannot be used to remove vectors from the triggering graph. A pair-wise analysis of the above rules indicates satisfiability. It is only when the entire cycle is analyzed that unsatisfiable conditions are discovered.

3.4 Qualified Connecting Formulae

The third level of the RTG method is a step beyond the connecting formulae method. This refinement seeks to use database-dependent rule conditions that enable us to eliminate a vector from the graph if we can be sure that the relevant database state does not change between the execution of the two rules. For example, assume that O and P are variables that contain object identifiers and that $O.l$ and $P.l$ refer to attribute values of O and P, respectively. If the condition of $r1$ asserts that $O.l = 5$ and if the condition of $r2$ asserts that $P.l = 10$, where O unifies with P, then this condition is unsatisfiable if we can be sure that the database state does not change between the evaluation of $r1$'s condition and the evaluation of $r2$'s condition. Otherwise, we cannot safely remove a vector from the triggering graph. The work described in this paper has enhanced the original definition of qualified connecting formulae in [Karadimce 1997] to consider characteristics of active rules that are related to the execution model. Any information that can be used to confirm database stability may help to eliminate a cycle that never truly occurs.

The active rule language of CDOL supports the use of *immediate* and *deferred* coupling modes in the specification of event-condition and condition-action coupling [Urban et al. 1997]. Furthermore, an event can be raised *before* the execution of a method or *after* the execution of a method. Rule priorities can also be specified, although they are not required. Examples of these rule features are demonstrated in the Appendix. Our extended version of qualified connecting formulae examines these rule attributes to determine if database-dependent conditions can be included in the analysis of triggering formulae [Tschudi 1997].

In particular, if $r1$ triggers $r2$ and the event e is raised after the execution of $r1$'s action, then database-dependent conditions cannot be included in the triggering formula, regardless of the coupling mode. Since the method executed by $r1$'s action can potentially change the database state, there is no guarantee of database stability (without further analysis of the implementation of the method) between the evaluation of *r1*'s condition and the evaluation of *r2*'s condition.

If *r1* triggers *r2*, where the event *e* is raised before the execution of *r1*'s action, then *r2* must have an immediate event-condition coupling mode according to the semantics of the CDOL rule execution model. If *r2* is the only rule triggered by *r1*, then database-dependent conditions from *r1* and *r2* can be included in the triggering formula since *r2*'s condition is guaranteed to execute immediately after *r1*'s condition. If, however, more than one rule is triggered by *r1*, then the inclusion of database-dependent conditions depends on rule priorities. As an example, consider the *set_speed* method of class *vehicle*, which triggers *decr_press_for_low_speed* and *incr_press_for_high_speed*. Notice that the event of each rule is raised before the execution of *set_speed* and that both rules have an immediate event-condition coupling mode. When examining a triggering connection involving one of these rules, one needs to consider the potential effect if the other rule triggered at the same time were to execute first. If priorities are specified between the two rules, then database-dependent conditions can be included to analyze the connection between the triggering rule and the triggered rule with the highest priority. If there are missing priorities, or if more than one rule has the highest priority, then we cannot guarantee the stability of the database for the analysis of the involved rules.

4 Implementation of the Refined Triggering Graph Method

An important aspect in the implementation of the RTG method for CDOL was to develop an algorithm for use in testing the satisfiability of triggering formulae. This section presents the approach that was taken in the development of a satisfiability algorithm for triggering formulae expressed as CDOL conditions. In particular, this section describes how the simplification rules described in [Karadimce 1997] were applied and integrated with the satisfiability algorithm of Rosenkrantz and Hunt [1980] to support rule analysis in the RTG method. Section 4.1 summarizes the resolution process for CDOL rules, which is based on concepts from constraint logic programming. Section 4.2 then presents an overview of the satisfiability algorithm. Section 4.3 summarizes the overall RTG algorithm.

4.1 Constrained Resolution

CDOL supports the use of active *and* deductive rules. As an example, the list below shows several deductive rules that are used to support derived values that are referenced in the active rules shown in the Appendix:

```
rule max_engine_rpm_rule
/* Specify the maximum engine rotational rate in rpm. */
{
    vehicle:TheVehicle[max_engine_rating_rpm=Rate_rpm] <-
        Rate_rpm = TheVehicle.rate_Hertz * TheVehicle.conv_fact;
};

rule conv_Hz_to_rpm_rule
```

```
/* Specify the factor used to convert Hertz units to rpm units. */
{
    vehicle:TheVehicle[conv_fact=Conv_factor] <- Conv_factor = 60;
};

rule max_engine_Hz_rule
/* Specify the maximum engine rotational rate in Hertz. */
{
    vehicle:TheVehicle[rate_Hertz=Rate_Hz] <- Rate_Hz = 40;
};
```

When a triggering formula is constructed, the formula must be reduced to a *resolved form*. A formal description of the process and its foundation on constraint logic programming can be found in [Karadimce 1997]. Informally, the process involves viewing a triggering formula as a conjunction of constraint terms (e.g., $A > B$, $O.1 = 10$) and predicates (e.g., derived attribute values such as those illustrated in the above rules). Predicates, as well as constraints that contain predicates, must be resolved through a process called *constrained resolution* [Burckert 1991] by replacing derived attributes in the triggering formula with the body of the rule that is used to derive the value. The goal of the resolution process is to reduce a triggering formula to a conjunction of constraints, with no predicates. The resolved form can then be tested for satisfiability. For example, a triggering formula constructed from the *check_engine_rpm_max* rule would contain the term *TheVehicle.max_engine_rating_rpm* $<$ *Max_rpm*. Since *TheVehicle.max_engine_rating_rpm* is a derived value, this term would be resolved to *TheVehicle.rate_Hertz * TheVehicle.conv_fact < Max_rpm*, which in turn would be resolved to $60 * 40 < Max\_rpm$.

The complete investigation of the constrained resolution process for CDOL requires further work to fully address all of the features of CDOL. To limit the scope of the process for the purpose of this research, we limited deductive rules to non-recursive rules. We also limited derived attributes to those that could be computed using one rule only (i.e., those values that are not based on unions).

4.2 Satisfiability of Triggering Formulae

After a triggering formula has been reduced to a conjunction of constraints, the constraints can be manipulated by simplification rules. The result of the simplification process is a simpler query that uses the database more efficiently. Simplification is also used to seek an inconsistency in the set of constraints studied.

Simplification Rules. Rather than describe each of the 14 simplification rules of the RTG method, this section presents a few examples of the types of rules that are used. The complete description can be found in [Karadimce 1997; Tschudi 1997].

The most basic simplification rules of the satisfiability algorithm are unification rules from the simple-equality generator algorithm described by Haridi and Sahlin [1984]. For example, suppose we have a constraint of the form $X = Y$. Haridi and Sahlin specify the creation of a new expression that equates the value bound to X with the value bound to Y (e.g., $5 = 6$, assuming X is bound to 5 and Y is bound to 6). There are two simplification rules that recognize a pattern of the form "number equals number." One tells us to ignore the constraint if the first number is the same as the second number; the other tells us to trigger a failure to satisfy if the first number is not the same as the second number.

Haridi and Sahlin also define rules for unifying terms; this is used for unifying the parameter list of the method producing the event with the parameter list of the event that triggers an active rule. Standard unification, however, does not address hierarchies of class types such as that found in CDOL. Karadimce [1997] extends the standard unification approach such as that of Haridi and Sahlin [1984] for the object-oriented nature of CDOL. For example, an object of type *landvehicle* from the triggering rule cannot be unified with an object of type *amphibvehicle* from the triggered rule, since a *landvehicle* is not necessarily an *amphibvehicle*.

An example of another object-oriented simplification rules involves an unbound variable L of type *landvehicle* set equal to W of type *watervehicle*, which is either a bound variable or another unbound variable; this type of expression might be the result of previous simplification rules. In this case, the types of L and W are compared. If the type of L is the same as or a superclass of the type of W, then L is bound using the type of W. Otherwise, as is the case in this model, the types of L and W may each be superclasses of a common subtype. In this case, a new variable A of that subtype (*amphibvehicle*) is created, L is bound using A, W is bound using A, and all other occurrences of L and W in expressions are replaced with A. This is done because a common subtype is the only way that this expression could potentially be satisfiable at runtime; if there isn't a common subtype, the expression is unsatisfiable.

As a final rule example, suppose an expression exists wherein a variable *NewAmphib* of type *amphibvehicle* is set equal to the value of a method call *copy(ModelVehicle:vehicle)->vehicle*, where *copy()* returns type *vehicle* and variable *ModelVehicle* is of type *vehicle*. This expression is not satisfiable because the type of *NewAmphib* must be the same as or a superclass of the return type of *copy()*. Before we declare this to be unsatisfiable, we must check if there is an overloaded signature of *copy()* that has a compatible return type and the same number of parameters. If such a signature is not found, then this expression cannot be satisfiable. If, on the other hand, such a signature (e.g., *copy(ModelVehicle:amphibvehicle)->amphibvehicle*) is found, then it is possible that this expression is valid and thus we cannot deem it unsatisfiable. The original expression is replaced with *NewAmphib = copy(ModelVehicle:amphibvehicle)->amphibvehicle*, and each of the arguments of *copy(ModelVehicle:vehicle)->vehicle* is set equal to each of the arguments of *copy(ModelVehicle:amphibvehicle)->amphibvehicle* to create a new set of constraints that stem from using this alternate signature: *ModelVehicle:vehicle = ModelVehicle:amphibvehicle* (note that the left-hand-side varable is not the same as the right-hand-side variable). Clearly, if the signature of *copy(ModelVehicle:amphibvehicle)->amphibvehicle* is what makes the original expression satisfiable, its parameters are significant and provide constraints for the parameters on the original expression.

Sets of Inequalities. As part of this implementation, we integrated the simplification rules of CDOL with the satisfiability algorithm of Rosenkrantz and

Hunt [1980], which takes a set of inequality expressions and attempts to determine if the set is satisfiable. The algorithm is limited to expressions involving integers or unbound integer variables. For example, consider the case where *check_engine_rpm_range* triggers itself. In this case, we get the inequality expressions: *Min_rpm > Max_rpm & Max_rpm > Min_rpm*. The Rosenkrantz and Hunt algorithm is applied to resolve any further issues regarding satisfiability.

The algorithm first converts inequality expressions to the *form X <= Y + b*. Since the algorithm is limited to integers, we can convert the operation "<" to the operation "<=" by subtracting one from the right-hand side of the expression. Our two inequality expressions become: *Max_rpm <= Min_rpm - 1 & Min_rpm <= Max_rpm - 1*. The two expressions are then inserted into a directed graph with each unique variable occupying a node. An edge is drawn from node *X* to node *Y*; the edge is given a weight equal to "b". Each cycle in the graph has its total path weight calculated. If any cycle has a weight less than zero, the set of inequality expressions represented in the graph is not satisfiable. In this example, the only cycle in the graph has a total path weight of -2. Therefore, our two inequality expressions are not satisfiable.

4.3   The RTG Method

The RTG method may be instructed as to what analysis methods may be used. As described in Section 3, the analysis is partitioned into 1) the unification formulae method, 2) the connecting formulae method, and 3) the qualified connecting formulae method. A fourth partition covers the Rosenkrantz & Hunt algorithm. Possible choices for analysis levels are 1) only use method 1, 2) use methods 1 & 2, 3) use methods 1 through 3, or 4) use methods 1 through 4. Furthermore, the RTG method can be applied to pairs of rules or to an entire cycle. At a high level, the algorithm can be summarized as consisting of the following major steps applied to triggering formulae:

1. Permit—if possible—database-dependent references within a single rule.
2. Expand derived attributes by applying constrained resolution.
3. Eliminate simple impossible and redundant expressions (e.g., $X < X$, $X = X$, respectively).
4. Match the triggering event signatures with the triggered rule's event signature.
5. Permit—if possible—database-dependent references between multiple rules.
6. Unify derived attributes or methods.
7. Reorder expressions to support the recognition of simplification rules (e.g., change $3 = X$ to $X = 3$).
8. Apply rules concerning the assignment of values to variables (e.g., if X is bound to 4 and we are evaluating the expression $X < Y$, construct an alternative constraint to test for satisfiability: $4 < Y$).
9. Evaluate numeric mathematical and logical expressions and string equality expressions (e.g., $3 < 10$ is satisfiable, while *"one-third"* = *"full speed"* is not).

10. Perform the Rosenkrantz and Hunt algorithm for satisfiability of sets of inequalities.

Figure 3 shows the refined triggering graph that resulted from the application of the RTG method to the triggering graph of Figure 2. The RTG method was able to break 39 vectors (shown as gray arrows in Figure 3) that represented triggering relationships that would not be successful at runtime. The refined triggering graph now shows 5 potential cycles. The actual number of potential cycles is 4 due to the generalized connecting formulae method described earlier, but the graph cannot show an unsatisfiable cycle composed of satisfiable vectors. It is possible that the 4 remaining cycles do not actually occur, but we cannot assert such a statement with the information and analysis we have so far. We have, however, greatly refined the triggering graph. Even if a rule designer had to step in at this point, the designer would have been saved a considerable amount of manual analysis.

During the analysis process, the largest reduction in the number of potential cycles occurred using the unification formulae, eliminating 736 cycles. Two additional cycles were removed by the connecting formulae method, one cycle was removed by the Rosenkrantz and Hunt algorithm, and one cycle was removed by the generalized connecting formulae method.

5 Evaluation of the RTG Method

This implementation allowed us to explore the practical use of the RTG method. Experimentation of the method with additional applications still needs to be examined. The sample application that we used in this research, however, allowed us to make several observations about different aspects of the RTG method.

In general, the combination of the different levels of analysis within the RTG method is quite effective at finding unsatisfiable cycles--almost all of the cycles in this active rule set were found to be unsatisfiable. Only a few cycles remain for the rule designer to study or to monitor via dynamic analysis. For this particular application, the unification formulae were the most effective at finding unsatisfiable triggering conditions. The unsatisfiable triggering connections frequently had unification failures such as mismatches in the number or types of parameters between the triggering and triggered events. The unification algorithm of the RTG method fully supports the overloading and overriding of method names common to CDOL.

The connecting formulae identified several unsatisfiable triggering connections. The success of connecting formulae, however, is highly dependent on whether constants are encoded within the rules. If the values that must be examined as part of rule conditions are stored in database variables, then the analysis must resort to the qualified connecting approach which deals with database-dependent terms. Connecting formulae, however, do provide a filter for eliminating some rule connectivity problems before having to apply the more difficult analysis that involves database-dependent terms.

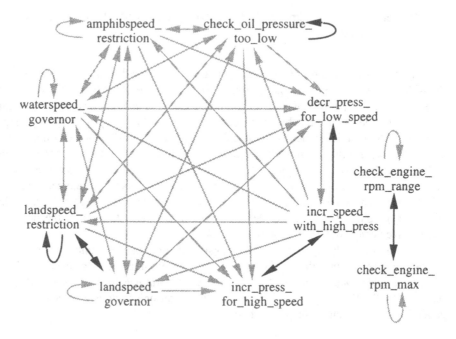

Fig. 3. Refined Triggering Graph after Unification, Connecting, and
Qualified Connecting Formulae and Rosenkrantz and Hunt Algorithm

In this particular application, the qualified connecting formulae were not successful at eliminating cycles, many of which had already been eliminated by the unification and connecting formulae. Analysis involving database-dependent terms is more difficult to apply due to the need to guarantee no change in the database state between the execution of the triggering rule and the execution of the triggered rule. The extensions that were applied to automatically determine database stability-- immediate coupling mode, before-method execution, and rule priorities--are quite restrictive, especially when working with smaller rule sets. This sample application's rules had database-dependent attributes, but these attributes were not susceptible to qualified connecting formulae analysis.

We envision three specific extensions to qualified connecting formulae to be investigated as part of future work. One extension involves an analysis of the method in the action of a triggering rule to determine read/write conflicts between the method and a triggered rule. The absence of conflicts would broaden the scope of the analysis to include rules with immediate event-condition coupling where the triggering event is raised after the execution of the action (rather than before the action as in the current approach). Another extension involves integration of refined triggering graphs with the activation graph approach described in [Baralis et al. 1995a]. The activation graph approach currently does not take advantage of the graph refinement that we currently apply with the use of unification and connecting formulae. Unification and connecting formulae can therefore be used to refine a triggering graph before the application of activation graphs. The RTG method, on the other hand, could be strengthened with the information about rule interference that is gained from activation graphs. Finally, Karadimce [1997] describes the need for possible user intervention for the specification of assertion points, where the user is involved in verifying database stability between rule executions.

6 Summary and Future Work

This paper has presented the results of our work on the implementation of the RTG method for rule termination analysis and the application of those results to a sample active database application. This approach is generalizable to any active database environment that is based on an object-oriented type system, with the use of qualified connecting formulae tailored to the specific rule execution semantics of the environment. In addition to the extensions described in Section 5, future refinements of the tool include: 1) extension of the constrained resolution algorithm to include all features of CDOL deductive rules, 2) extension of the simplification rules to include rules related to set-valued attributes, 3) extension of the Rosenkrantz and Hunt algorithm to include types other than integers as well as more complex arithmetic expressions, and 4) optimization of the satisfiability algorithm.

The development of the termination analysis tool described in this paper is part of a larger project, known as the A-DOOD (Active, Deductive, Object-Oriented Database) RANCH Project (http://www.eas.asu.edu/~adood). The objective of the project is to develop an environment that supports the static and dynamic analysis of active rules with respect to termination and confluence and to provide runtime support for rule testing and debugging [Jähne et al. 1996]. A companion paper describes our initial results with respect to the testing of active database rules [Chan et al. 1997]. We are currently experimenting with the development of an active rule environment that applies the notion of object deltas during runtime to support dynamic analysis of termination and confluence, as well as to support other testing and debugging activities.

References

AIKEN, A., WIDOM, J., AND HELLERSTEIN, J. M. 1992. Behavior of database production rules: Termination, confluence, and observable determinism. *SIGMOD 21*, 2 (Jun.), 59-68.

BARALIS, E., AND WIDOM, J. 1994. An algebraic approach to rule analysis in expert database systems. In *Proceedings of the Twentieth International Conference on Very Large Data Bases*, (Santiago, Chile, Sep.), 475-486.

BARALIS, E., CERI, S., AND PARABOSCHI, S. 1995a. Improved rule analysis by means of triggering and activation graphs. In *Rules in Database Systems: 2nd International Workshop, RIDS '95*, (Glyfada, Athens, Greece, Sep. 25-27), 165-181.

BARALIS, E., CERI, S., AND PARABOSCHI, S. 1995b. Run-time detection of non-terminating active rule systems. In *Deductive and Object-Oriented Databases*, T. W. Ling, A. O. Mendelzon, and L. Vieille (editors), *Proceedings of the Fourth International Conference on Deductive and Object-Oriented Databases DOOD '95*, (Singapore, Dec. 4-7), 38-54.

BARALIS, E., CERI, S., AND WIDOM, J. 1993. Better termination analysis for active databases. In *Proceedings of the First International Workshop on Rules in Database Systems*, (Sep.), 163-179.

BURKERT, H.-J. 1991. *A Resolution Principle for a Logic with Restricted Quantifiers.* Springer-Verlag (LNCS 568).

CERI, S., AND WIDOM, J. 1990. Deriving production rules for constraint maintenance. In *IBM Research Report RJ 7348 (68829)*, IBM Research Division, Yorktown Heights, NY, (Mar. 1).

CERI, S., BARALIS, E., FRATERNALI, P., AND PARABOSCHI, S. 1995. Design of active rule applications: Issues and approaches. In *Proceedings of the Fourth International Conference on Deductive and Object-Oriented Databases DOOD '95*, (Singapore (Dec. 4-7), 1-18.

CERI, S., FRATERNALI, P., PARABOSCHI, S., AND TANCA, L. 1996. Active rule management in Chimera. In *Active Database Systems: Triggers and Rules for Advanced Database Processing*, J. Widom and S. Ceri (editors), Morgan Kaufmann, San Francisco, 151-176.

CHAN, R., DIETRICH, S., AND URBAN, S. 1997. On Control Flow Testing of Active Rules in a Declarative Object-Oriented Framework, *Rules in Database Systems Workshop*, Skovde, Sweden, 1997.

FRATERNALI, P., PARABOSCHI, S., AND TANCA, L. 1992. Automatic rule generation for constraint enforcement in active databases. In *Modelling Database Dynamics*, U. W. Lipeck and B. Thalheim (editors), Springer-Verlag, London, 1993, Selected Papers from the Fourth International Workshop on Foundations of Models and Languages for Data and Objects, (Volkse, Germany, Oct. 19-22), 153-173.

JÄHNE, A., URBAN, S. D., AND DIETRICH, S. W. 1996. PEARD: A Prototype Environment for Active Rule Debugging. *Journal of Intelligent Information Systems 7*, 2 (Oct.), 111-128.

KARADIMCE, A. P. 1997. *Termination and confluence analysis in an active object-oriented database.* Ph.D. Dissertation, Department of Computer Science and Engineering, Arizona State University, Spring 1997.

KARADIMCE, A. P., AND URBAN, S. D. 1996a. Proving termination of active rules in object-oriented databases. In *Proceedings of the International Conference on Data Engineering*, (New Orleans, LA, Feb.), pp. 384-391.

KARADIMCE, A. P., AND URBAN, S. D. 1996b. Refined triggering graphs: A logic-based approach to termination analysis in an active object-oriented database. Submitted for journal publication.

MONTESI, D., AND TORLONE, R. 1995. A transaction transformation approach to active rule processing. In *Proceedings of the Eleventh International Conference on Data Engineering*, (Taipei, Taiwan, Mar. 6-10), 109-116.

ROSENKRANTZ, D., AND HUNT, H. B., III. 1980. Processing conjunctive predicates and queries. In *Proceedings of the Sixth International Conference on Very Large Data Bases*, (Montréal, Canada), 64-72.

TSCHUDI, M. K. 1997. *Static Analysis of Active Database Rules: Evaluating Tools for Termination Analysis*, M.S. Thesis, Department of Computer Science and Engineering, Arizona State University, Spring 1997.

URBAN, S. D., KARADIMCE, A. P., DIETRICH, S. W., BEN ABDELLATIF, T., AND CHAN, H. W. R. 1997. CDOL: A Comprehensive Declarative Object Language, *Data & Knowledge Engineering*, vol. 22, 1997, 67-111.

WEIK, T. AND HEUER, A. 1995. An Algorithm for the Analysis of Termination of Large Trigger Sets in OODBMS, In *Proceedings of the Workshop on Active and Real-Time Databases (ARTDB)*, 170-189.

WIDOM, J. 1996. The Starburst rule system. In *Active Database Systems: Triggers and Rules for Advanced Database Processing*, J. Widom and S. Ceri (editors), Morgan Kaufmann, San Francisco, 87-109.

Appendix: Active Rules in Sample Application

active amphibspeed_restriction
/* Limit The amphibious vehicle's speed to 10 by
resetting the speed if necessary. */
{event   after amphibvehicle:TheAmphib
             [set_speed(integer:New_speed)]
condition   deferred 10 < New_speed
action   deferred
             amphibvehicle:TheAmphib.set_speed(10);
};

active check_engine_rpm_max
/* If the specified rpm range has a maximum value that
exceeds the upper limit for the vehicle, change the
maximum value to the vehicle's upper limit. */
{event   after vehicle:TheVehicle
             [set_rpm_range(integer:Min_rpm,
             integer:Max_rpm)]
condition   immediate
             TheVehicle.max_engine_rating_rpm <
             Max_rpm
action   immediate
             vehicle:TheVehicle.set_rpm_range
             (Min_rpm,
             TheVehicle.max_engine_rating_rpm);};

active check_engine_rpm_range
/* If the rpm range is supplied backwards, reset it with
the values properly ordered. */
{event   after vehicle:TheVehicle
             [set_rpm_range(integer:Min_rpm,
             integer:Max_rpm)]
condition   deferred Min_rpm > Max_rpm
action   immediate
             vehicle:TheVehicle.set_rpm_range
             (Max_rpm, Min_rpm);};

active check_oil_pressure_too_low
/* If the engine is turning quickly and the oil pressure is
below a specified minimum value, immediately shut the
engine down to prevent damage. */
{event   after engine:TheEngine
             [set_speed(integer:New_speed,
             engine_specs:Specs)]
condition   immediate TheEngine.rpm > 60,
             TheEngine.oil_pressure <
             Specs.min_oil_pressure
action   immediate TheEngine.set_speed
             (0, engine_specs:Specs);};

active decr_press_for_low_speed
/* If the vehicle is traveling in the low speed range,
relax the needed oil pressure. */
{event   before vehicle:TheVehicle
             [set_speed(integer:New_speed)]
condition   immediate New_speed <
             TheVehicle.speed_threshold
action   deferred engine:TheEngine =
             TheVehicle.itsEngine,
             TheEngine.set_pressure("low");};

active incr_press_for_high_speed

/* If the vehicle is traveling in the high speed range,
require high oil pressure as well. */
{event   before vehicle:TheVehicle
             [set_speed(integer:New_speed)]
condition   immediate New_speed >=
             TheVehicle.speed_threshold
action   immediate engine:TheEngine =
             TheVehicle.itsEngine,
             TheEngine.set_pressure ("high");};

active incr_speed_with_high_press
/* If the engine's oil pressure is put into the high-
pressure range, speed up the engine to match. Active
rule incr_press_for_high_speed has a higher priority. */
{event   before engine:TheEngine
             [set_pressure(string:New_pressure)]
condition   immediate New_pressure = "high",
             engine:TheEngine[itsVehicle =
             TheVehicle], TheVehicle.speed <
             TheVehicle.speed_threshold
action   immediate vehicle:TheVehicle[
             speed = Desired_speed],
             TheVehicle.set_speed (Desired_speed);
   >   incr_press_for_high_speed};

active landspeed_governor
/* Limit the land vehicle's speed to 15 by resetting the
speed if necessary. */
{event   after landvehicle:TheVehicle
             [set_speed(integer:New_speed)]
condition   deferred 15 < New_speed
action   deferred
             landvehicle:TheVehicle.set_speed(15);};

active landspeed_restriction
/* Limit the vehicle's speed to its stored maximum limit
by resetting the speed if necessary. */
{event   after landvehicle:TheVehicle
             [set_speed(integer:New_speed)]
condition   deferred New_speed >
             TheVehicle.max_speed
action   deferred
landvehicle:TheVehicle.set_speed
             (TheVehicle.max_speed);};

active waterspeed_governor
/* If the water vehicle is traveling faster than "one
third", reduce the speed to "one third". */
{event   after watervehicle:TheVehicle
             [set_speed(string:New_speed)]
condition   deferred New_speed != "stop",
             New_speed != "one third"
action   deferred
             watervehicle:TheVehicle.set_speed
             ("one third");};

Investigating Termination in Active Database Systems with Expressive Rule Languages

Anca Vaduva, Stella Gatziu, Klaus R. Dittrich
Institut für Informatik, Universität Zürich
Email: {vaduva, gatziu, dittrich}@ifi.unizh.ch

Abstract

The powerful functionality that active mechanisms add to database management systems presents, besides many advantages, a number of problems related to the control of their behavior. This paper deals with one of these problems: the termination of rule execution. We explain the termination aspect and the aim of termination analysis. Then, we present our approach to investigating the termination of rule execution. In contrast to others, this approach also addresses expressive rule languages as they have been proposed for various recent active database management system prototypes.

1 Introduction

Many applications from areas like workflow management, network management, finance, and transportation show some sort of active behavior and are thus well-suited for support by active database management systems (*active DBMS*). Accordingly, much research has been done in the area so far, e.g., towards the integration of active mechanisms into relational and object-oriented DBMS, the support of language constructs for the modeling of reactive behavior, the development of concepts for rule execution, or the investigation of architectural issues for the construction of an active DBMS. A number of prototypes have been built, including Starburst [15], POSTGRES [12], REACH [5], Sentinel [6], NAOS [7], Ode [10], Chimera [15], and SAMOS [9].

Although the advantages of active DBMS are nowadays well-known, they are still not widely used in practice. This is even true for simple active mechanisms like triggers in relational systems which have been commercially available for several years. One main problem is that, especially for large rule sets defined by different people at different points in time, rule behavior and potential conflicts and dependencies between rules are hard to predict. A critical aspect is how to guarantee the termination of rule execution, i.e., how to avoid the faulty behavior when rules trigger each other indefinitely (*nontermination*).

There are two ways to approach this problem. A common way is to handle termination only during rule execution. This means that the system would stop rule execution if it assumed that an infinitely cascading triggering was taking place e.g., if a specific upper bound of triggered rules had been reached. The other way to handle termination for a given set of rules is through *termination analysis*, which may be static or dynamic. Dynamic methods [4] examine rule behavior at runtime. The main drawback is that termination cannot be guaranteed before the actual use of active DBMSs. Static analysis investigates rule definitions at compile time in order to determine subsets consisting of rules that may trigger (directly or indirectly) each other. If such a rule subset exists, the rule designer has to modify the specification of some rules and investigate termination again. Otherwise, when no rule subsets are found, termination of rule execution is guaranteed for the given rule set.

Some work on static termination analysis of rule execution has been reported elsewhere [1, 2, 3, 11, 16]. The existing approaches deal, however, only with "simple" rule languages, that is languages supporting only a limited set of constructs for specifying active behavior. Expressive rule languages as supported, for example, in SAMOS [9], REACH [5], Sentinel [6], NAOS [7], and Ode [10] offer more elaborate features (e.g. composite events, time events, complex actions and coupling modes). They generally allow the specification of more application semantics in the form of rules. However, the price to be paid is that rule analysis is more complex. Conflicts between rules are harder to foresee. One of the reasons is that there are far more elements the triggering of a rule depends on. For example, a rule defined on a complex event is triggered only when all component events have occurred. Therefore, compared to a simple rule language, it is more difficult to decide when rules may generate an infinite loop during execution.

The aim of the paper is twofold. First, we clarify the notion of termination of rule execution in active DBMSs and give a definition for it. Second, based on the conclusions from the first part, we present our approach for supporting termination analysis. Our work deals with aspects related to expressive rule languages. The ideas have been implemented in a tool that detects and visualizes potential loops that could occur during the execution of an application. This information helps the rule designer to decide whether the rule set should be improved.

The remainder of this paper is organized as follows. The next section gives an overview of expressive rule languages. Section 3 discusses the exact meaning of termination of rule execution, Section 4 presents our approach for the investigation of termination, Section 5 considers related work, and Section 6 concludes the paper.

2 Expressive Rule Languages

This section introduces the most important concepts of a rule language, and emphasizes the particular elements we would expect to see in an expressive one. A rule definition language is used for the specification of Event/Condition/Action (ECA)-rules [8]. Each rule consists of an event, a condition and an action. If R is the set of defined ECA-rules, we will use the notation $r_i(e_i, c_i, a_i)$ for a rule $r_i \in R$. For the sake of simplicity, if a part of a rule has no relevance in a specific context of discussion, it will be left out in the notation, e.g., $r_i(e_i, a_i)$.

An *event* is an occurrence the active database system must react to. Simple rule languages allow only single events (called *primitive events*) to be specified, whereas expressive rule languages also support the specification of *composite events*. Examples of primitive events are:

- *data modification* (for relational database systems) or *method events* (for object-oriented database systems) occur at the beginning or at the end of a data modification operation or of a method execution
- *transaction events* occur before or after a transaction operation (begin, abort, commit)
- *time events* occur at a specific point in time (absolute time event) or periodically.

Composite events are specified by applying operators to component events which can be primitive or themselves composite events. For example, the *disjunction* is signalled when at least one component event occurs. The *relative time* (<event> ± <time unit>) specifies an event occurring with a certain time distance to another event. The *conjunction* and the *sequence* are signalled when all component events occur, regardless of their order or considering their order, respectively. We distinguish between two groups of operators, depending on the number of event occurrences that the resulting composite event requires in order to occur: (a) "unary" operators (e.g., disjunction, relative time) require only one component event to occur, (b) "binary" operators (e.g., conjunction, sequence) require more than one component event to occur.

For composite events, *event parameter restrictions* may be defined, that establish whether all component events are signalled for the same object, transaction or user, etc.

Primitive events that occur as the direct consequence of the execution of an application program, of an interactive transaction, or that are time events are called *outside events*. A primitive event that occurs as the consequence of a rule execution is called an *inside* or *rule-signalled event*. Moreover, it is possible that, during the execution of an application, the same event definition has occurrences as both inside and outside events.

When an event occurs, all respective rules are *triggered*. If the *condition* of a triggered rule is fulfilled then its *action* is executed. A condition may be a predicate on the database state or a database query. If the result of evaluation is true or non-empty, respectively, the condition is satisfied. The *action* specifies the reactive behavior of the rule. It may contain data modification and retrieval (in relational DBMS), method invocation (in object-oriented DBMS), transaction operations like commit or abort, etc.

The language used for the specification of conditions and actions is called *host* language. It may be anything from a database language (e.g., SQL for Starburst [15], POSTQUEL for POSTGRES [12]) to a general-purpose programming language (e.g., O++ for Ode[10], Smalltalk for HIPAC [15] or a persistent extension of C++ for SAMOS[9]). Obviously, a rule language improves its expressive power if the used host language tends to a general purpose programming language. That means, not only sequence and selection are supported, but also the programming constructs abstraction and iteration. In this case, a condition may be, besides predicate or query, any procedure or method invocation that returns a boolean value. An action may contain any executable program, including any specific database operations, rule operations (like deletion, modification and enabling/disabling of rules), and so on. Therefore, conditions and actions are more complex than those specified using simple rule languages based on database languages.

Some rule languages also allow the specification of execution constraints (like priority and coupling modes). The priority specifies the execution order of a rule related to other rules triggered simultaneously. Coupling modes [8] are pairs of values (x, y) where $x, y \in \{$immediate, deferred, decoupled$\}$. They describe how condition evaluation and action execution are related to the transaction in which the event has occurred. In order to simplify the explanations, we will use the term "immediate execution" when both coupling modes are immediate.

To summarize, the elements that distinguish an expressive rule language from a simple rule language are on the one hand constructs like composite operators, rule execution constraints, event parameter restrictions, rule operations, and on the other hand complex conditions and actions. We will see at the end of Section 3 to which extent these elements influence rule execution and its termination.

3 Termination of Rule Execution

Let R be the set of defined ECA-rules. At runtime, application programs are sequentially executed until an event is signalled[1]. After event signalling, control moves to rule processing. Appropriate rules of R are triggered and inserted into a set, called *conflict set*, containing all triggered and not yet executed rules (see Figure 1, activity ①).

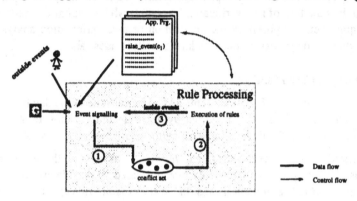

Fig. 1. Rule processing in active database systems

The rule execution component selects one rule at a time from this set in the order required by the *conflict resolution policy* (activity ②). This strategy for solving the conflict depends on the used active DBMS. If the condition of the selected rule is satisfied, its action is executed. If the execution of the action signals further events, these events are inside ones and the execution is *nested* (activity ③). In this case, further rules are inserted into the conflict set. When the set of triggered rules is empty, control moves back to the application program. Note that we refer to sequential execution only, i.e., at any given time only one rule is chosen and executed. We assume also that all participating rules have immediate execution. However, the basic idea also applies for deferred and decoupled execution.

It may happen that the set of triggered rules never empties, for the following reasons:

- Concurrent applications cause the steady arrival of outside events and triggered rules are accumulating in the set because rule processing is not fast enough to keep up with demand.

---

1. For composite event detection several *event consumption modes* are possible. We assume here the most commonly used one, chronicle. In this case, the detector always considers the oldest occurrence for each component description.

- There are rules in R which trigger each other indefinitely and their execution creates an infinite loop (between activities ①, ② and ③).

The aim of termination analysis is precisely to avoid the latter case, i.e., *infinite nested rule execution*, also called *nontermination*. The former case, infinite execution caused by constant occurrence of outside events, is irrelevant for termination analysis because it cannot be considered as faulty rule behavior.

The distinction whether the infinite execution is due to outside events or not underlies our reflections for termination analysis. If a rule subset leads to nontermination then only events raised by the execution of rules in this subset participate in nontermination. This apply also for composite events: all component primitive events have to be raised within the subset. If, on the contrary, one of the primitive events is an outside event which constantly occur, we speak about infinite execution, but not infinite nested execution. It is the task of rule verification to control whether infinite execution matches the requirements imposed by the application or not. Termination analysis detects only infinite nested rule execution, which is (usually) undesirable.

3.1 Definition of Termination

We call a given finite set of outside events and an initial state of the database an *initialization frame*. The rule execution started by a certain initialization frame is called a *rule execution thread*. We then define termination of rule execution as follows:

Definition 1 A rule execution thread *terminates* as soon as the set of triggered rules is either empty or contains only rules triggered by outside events. Generally, *termination of rule execution* means that *every possible* rule execution thread terminates.

Termination of rule execution reached without external intervention is called *normal*. Rule execution can also be enforced to terminate *abnormally*, when the rule execution is explicitly terminated by an application program or by the active DBMS. For example, the active DBMS may support the definition of an upper limit that determines how many (nested) rules are allowed to be executed during rule processing. If during rule execution this limit is reached, rule execution is aborted. However, abnormal termination is only an emergency solution that does not guarantee a correct modeling of the active behavior. In this paper, we focus on termination analysis which must guarantee that rule execution terminates normally.

3.2 Termination Analysis for Expressive Languages

We now summarize to what extent specific features of expressive languages influence termination analysis:

- composite events: termination analysis has to determine whether a rule defined on a composite event may participate in an infinite nested rule execution. In this case, it is important to check whether the composite event is entirely the consequence of the execution of an action, whether it depends on the execution of a certain rule sequence, or whether it depends on one or more occurrences of outside events, etc.

- complex conditions and actions: termination analysis should use information about actions that may trigger events and that may change the evaluation result of conditions. Providing this information for complex actions and conditions is however difficult, because
  - all possible operations that are used within conditions/actions must be taken into account
  - not only actions but also conditions may trigger events
  - methods are invoked not only directly, but by nested calls as well
  - signature of method invocations may not be the same with this of method events
  - actions, conditions and events may refer to different object sets
  - language constructs like conditional statements, loops and late binding make the decision of the triggering of events (respectively the dependence of condition evaluation on action execution) statically undecidable. In order to perform termination analysis hard approximations are required.

Additional problems arise when the host language has no formal specification (like e.g., C++). In this case, the semantic analysis can be done only superficially.

- time events: they cannot be signalled by rules. Thus, they cannot participate in any infinite nested rule execution. The only exception are relative time events. They depend on a basis event which may be signalled by other rules.
- priorities and coupling modes: may be taken into account only if exact information about actions changing the truth value of conditions is available [3,11].

In the following section, we present the underlying concepts of our termination analysis for expressive rule languages. We will focus on how composite events influence the analysis and we will refer only briefly to condition and action analysis.

4 Termination Analysis: Our Approach

Termination analysis determines subsets of R that may lead to potentially nonterminating rule execution, i.e., infinite nested rule execution. To this end, we establish dependencies between rule definitions (called *relationships*) and build a graph that shows possible rule triggering at runtime. Cycles in this graph indicate potentially infinite nested rule execution. In order to make the analysis more precise, we extend it with methods to find out whether each cycle in the graph may lead to nontermination or not.

Our notation uses standard logical connectives ($\wedge$ $\vee$, $\Leftrightarrow$, etc.), universal quantifiers ($\exists$, $\forall$), and set operations ($\in$, $\subset$, $\cup$, etc.) with their standard semantics.

4.1 Relationships Between Rules

Termination analysis strongly relies on the recognition of rule *relationships*. By analyzing rule relationships, we can foresee the termination of rule execution. The accuracy of prediction depends on the granularity of the analysis of rule definitions. For example, the more precisely we can decide when one rule may trigger another, the more accurately we can decide if a nested rule execution will actually occur at runtime. Rule relationships are defined as follows:

Definition 2 $r_i(e_i,c_i,a_i)$ *is related to* $r_j(e_j,c_j,a_j)$ if one of the following cases applies:

(1) **total AC/E-relationship**: The execution of a_i or the evaluation of c_i potentially signal e_j ("r_i *may totally trigger* r_j").

(2) **partial AC/E-relationship**: The execution of a_i or the evaluation of c_i potentially signal at least one, but not all component events of e_j ("r_i *may partially trigger* r_j").

(3) **A/C-relationship**: The execution of a_i potentially modify the truth value of the evaluation result of c_j.

(4) **A/R-relationship**: The execution of a_i enables/disables rule r_j.

The use of "potentially" is necessary because sometimes it is uncertain if an action or a condition signals an event. For example, it is in general statically undecidable if a method executed within an action and an appropriate method event refer to the same object. It is also uncertain whether an event will be signalled if it is raised within a conditional statement.

In order to perform termination analysis, it is necessary to find out which rules may totally or partially trigger other rules, i.e., which rules from the rule set are in AC/E-relationships. For this aim we search information about actions or conditions that may signal primitive events by applying syntax analysis methods to rule definitions. Then we assign to each event e the set $PE(e)=\{pe_k, k=1,\ldots,n\}$ of primitive events that must occur in order to signal e. In this case, $r_i(e_i,a_i)$ may partially trigger $r_j(e_j,a_j)$ if a_i or c_i may signal at least one element of $PE(e_j)$. If all primitive events in the set $PE(e_j)$ may be signalled by a_i or c_i then $r_i(e_i,a_i)$ may totally trigger $r_j(e_j,a_j)$. If e is a primitive event or if it has been built using "unary" composite operators, then $|PE(e_j)|=1$.

If e_j is a composite event, the computation of $PE(e_j)$ depends on the semantics of the composite operators. Transformation rules are provided such that each composite event is rewritten in a disjunctive normal form. Then PE is recursively computed by applying the following two laws:

$$e_j = e_{j1} \wedge e_{j2} \quad \Rightarrow PE(e_j) = PE(e_{j1}) \cup PE(e_{j2})$$
$$e_j = e_{j1} \vee e_{j2} \quad \Rightarrow PE(e_j) = PE(e_{j1}) \vee PE(e_{j2}).$$

How can A/R- and A/C-relationships influence termination? A nested rule execution is terminated, if either a rule has been disabled by the execution of another rule, or a condition is not satisfied any more as a consequence of the execution of a rule. Consider a subset of $R' \subseteq R$, $R' = \{r_1, r_2, r_3\}$ that leads to a nested rule execution:

- assume $\exists\ r_i, r_j \in \{r_1, r_2, r_3\}$ in an A/R-relationship such that r_i disables r_j and no other rule exists which enables r_j. Then the three rules are executed only once. Afterwards, the nested rule execution is terminated because r_j cannot be executed any more.

- assume $\exists\ r_i(c_i,a_i), r_j(c_j,a_j) \in \{r_1, r_2, r_3\}$ in an A/C-relationship such that the execution of action a_i sets the condition c_j to false after the rules have been executed N times. For example, a_i deletes objects from a set with N objects and c_j controls if the set is empty. Then, r_j is triggered but cannot be executed the $(N+1)$-st time because its condition is false and the nested execution is terminated.

An A/C-relationship between two rules r_i and r_j is signalled if a_i includes an operation that may change the value of an attribute appearing in c_j. For example, in object-oriented DBMS this implies the need to examine method implementations in order to find out the ones that change attributes either directly or indirectly by nested method execution. However, this technique for detecting A/C-relationships is based on syntactical methods only and is too weak to determine if the execution of a rule action changes the truth value of another rule condition. The rule designer himself has to decide if A/C-relationships can break a nested rule execution.

4.2 The Relationship Graph

Almost all work on termination analysis [1, 3, 11, 16] approaches the termination problem using a directed *triggering graph* for rules specified using simple rule languages. The nodes of the graph represent rules in the rule set. An edge from rule r_i to rule r_j, denoted (r_i, r_j), exists, if r_i may trigger r_j. If the triggering graph has no cycles, the termination of rule execution is guaranteed [1]. A cycle in the graph means that at least one rule may trigger itself and therefore corresponds to a possible nested rule execution at runtime, which in the worst case, may be infinite. In other words, a cycle in the graph indicates possible nontermination of rule execution.

Our approach refines the concept of a triggering graph with a so-called *relationship graph*, a directed, labelled graph (R, Γ) whose nodes represent the rules and whose edges symbolize the AC/E-relationships between the rules. The relationship graph provides two types of edges, (drawn with solid $(r_i) \longrightarrow (r_j)$ or dashed $(r_i) \dashrightarrow (r_j)$ lines), called total or partial, depending on the sort of relationship they represent. Similar to the classical way to study termination, if the relationship graph has no cycles, the termination of rules in R is *guaranteed*.

We denote with $\Sigma = \{\rho \subseteq (R, \Gamma)$, where $\rho = (r_1, \ldots, r_k, r_1)$ is a cycle$\}$ the set of cycles of a relationship graph. Σ may also contain "false" cycles that must be detected during termination analysis.

Definition 3 A cycle in the relationship graph is called *false* if the subset of rules participating in it can never lead to infinite nested execution.

Recalling the discussion in Section 4.1, a cycle ρ is false if two rules $r_i(e_i, a_i)$, $r_j(e_j, a_j)$ exist such that:

- r_i disables r_j and no other rule in ρ enables r_j again
- r_i is in A/C-relationship with r_j and the rule designer finds arguments to prove that r_i eventually changes the truth value of r_j to false and no other A/C-relationship exists that could again change the truth value of the evaluation of c_j. A/C-relationships are searched not only for rules participating in ρ, but also for rules that may be triggered by the execution of rules from ρ. It depends on priorities whether the execution of these rules outside ρ could change the database state and influence the evaluation of conditions in ρ.

Furthermore, there is another reason why a cycle $\rho \in \Sigma$ may be "false". Let $C \subseteq R$ be a subset of rules that causes infinite nested rule execution:

- If rules in C are defined only on primitive events, nontermination expresses that *each rule* in C triggers (through intermediaries) itself again and again.

- If at least one of the rules in C is specified using a composite event, its triggering depends on the occurrence of several primitive events. These primitive events may be signalled not only by the immediately preceding rule, but also by some other predecessor rules in the nested execution. Thus, each rule in C is triggered as a consequence of the execution of one or more rules in C. Then, we can say that *the subset triggers itself*.

Generalizing, infinite nested rule execution is determined by a rule subset $C \subseteq R$, ($|C|$ may be 1) that triggers itself directly or through intermediaries. In order to detect nontermination, static analysis can only establish when one subset *may* trigger itself.

Definition 4 Let a set $C \subseteq R$ and a rule $r(e,a)$ such that $PE(e) = \{pe_j, j=1,...,k\}$.
- C *may directly trigger* $r(e,a)$ if $\exists \{r_j(e_j, c_j, a_j)\}_{j=1,...,k} \subseteq C$, such that $\forall j$, a_j or c_j may signal pe_j
- C *may indirectly trigger* $r(e,a)$ if $\exists \{r_j(e_j, c_j, a_j)\}_{j=1,...,k} \subseteq R$, such that $\forall j$, C *may trigger* $r_j(e_j, c_j, a_j)$ and a_j or c_j may signal pe_j

Obviously, a set C may also trigger r if a single $r_j(e_j, c_j, a_j) \in C$ exists such that a_j or c_j may signal e.

Definition 5 Let a set $C \subseteq R$ and a rule $r(e,a)$.
- C *may trigger* $r(e,a) \Leftrightarrow$ C *may directly or indirectly trigger* $r(e,a)$
- C *may trigger itself* $\Leftrightarrow \forall r \in C$, C *may trigger* r.

The conclusion for the relationship graph is that a detected cycle ρ is "false" if the set of rules participating in ρ may not trigger itself. Thus, we focus in the following on the detection of such "false" cycles that can never lead to a nested rule execution.

4.3 Detecting a Rule Subset not Triggering Itself

Let $\rho \in \Sigma$ be a cycle in a relationship graph and C the set of rules in ρ. If a rule $r_j \in C$ can be found such that C cannot trigger r_j, then ρ is a false cycle. In order to find such a rule, we investigate the rules in C which are terminal nodes for partial edges. Let $r_j(e_j, a_j)$ be a rule such that (r_{j-1}, r_j) is a partial edge in ρ. This means that the execution of $r_{j-1} \in C$ may only signal one or a few primitive events $(pe_i)_{i=1,...,1} \in PE(e_j)$. We must investigate whether the other primitive events in $PE(e_j) \setminus \{(pe_i)_{i=1,...,1}\}$ can be signalled directly or indirectly by rules of C. This can be done by traversing the relationship graph in a way similar to a "depth-first" search, but against the edges' orientation, beginning with r_j as root. The algorithm terminates when the search reaches either nodes from C, or the event of the last visited rule/node is composed of at least one outside event, i.e an event that cannot be signalled by any other rule. In the latter case, the conclusion is that C cannot trigger the rule r_j; that means C cannot trigger itself and the cycle is proven to be false. If, on the contrary, all rules in C may be triggered by C, then nested execution cannot be precluded.

The Algorithm

In the following we sketch the algorithm for investigating whether a set of rules C may trigger a rule r_j in C.

```
MayTrigger(C, r_j(e_j, c_j, a_j)): BOOLEAN{
result = TRUE
FOREACH pe_i ∈ PE(e_j){
    IF pe_i is outside event THEN RETURN(FALSE)
    FOREACH r_{j-1}(e_{j-1}, c_{j-1}, a_{j-1}) such that a_{j-1} or c_{j-1} may signal pe_i{
        IF r_{j-1} ∈ C THEN flag=TRUE
        ELSE flag=RETURN(MayTrigger(C, r_{j-1}(e_{j-1}, c_{j-1}, a_{j-1})))
        result = result ∧ flag
        }
    }
RETURN(result)}
```

If C may trigger itself and all rules in C are defined for primitive events (i.e., $\forall\, r_j\,(e_j, a_j)$, $|\,PE_{(e_j)}\,| = 1$), then only rules in C determine the nested rule execution. If there are rules in C defined on composite events, then there exist at least another cycle in the graph which has common nodes and edges with C.

4.4 A Tool for Termination Analysis

We are now putting together all pieces introduced so far and summarize our approach to termination analysis (Figure 2). We assume that a set of rules specified using an expressive language is given. We propose a termination analysis tool that investigates rule definitions (at compile time). The rule designer uses the results and decides if the rule set must be changed.

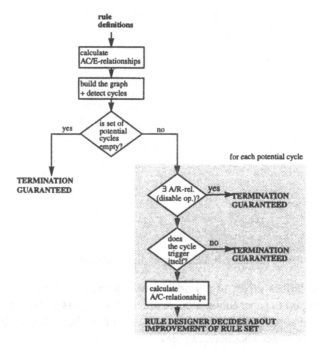

Fig. 2. An overview of the termination analysis

The tool has been implemented for the active database system SAMOS. It works as follows. First of all, the AC/E-relationships are computed. Then, the relationship graph is built. For each detected potential cycle, the tool searches for reasons that could guarantee that the nested rule execution cannot be infinite. Therefore, the cycles are first investigated to determine if they contain rule pairs that can disable each other (A/R-relationships). Then, for each cycle it is investigated if the composite events of the rules in the subset allow the subset to trigger itself. The A/C-relationships between rules are calculated for each of the remaining cycles.

Finally, the tool visualizes potential cycles which could not be proven to be false and displays the A/C-relationships between rules participating in these cycles. Based on this information, the rule designer checks whether eventually the action of one rule in the cycle may change the truth value of the condition of another rule to false. To achieve this, he has to inspect the code and completely understand the semantics of the involved rules. For those cycles that cannot be proven to be false, he must change the definitions of the rules and repeat the termination analysis. This process is iterated until no further cycles are found.

4.5 Example

To illustrate our approach we use the "IFIP case" [14] that deals with the organization of conferences. The purpose is merely to clarify the ideas underlying our approach, rather than to present a full scale application with realistic complexity.

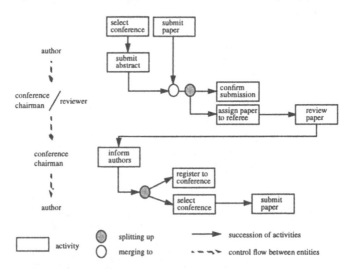

Fig. 3. Workflow of the "IFIP case"

Figure 3 describes a part of a workflow which models administrative tasks performed with regard to paper submission, distribution of papers to the referees, deciding the admission of papers, etc. Some of the operations must be performed by human beings (author, conference chairman, referee).

When authors of a paper select a conference, and its deadline has not already passed, an abstract of the paper is submitted to this conference. Some time later the submission is confirmed. When the abstract and the paper have been submitted, and the topic of the paper matches the topics of the conference, the paper is inserted into the list of submitted papers. Each submitted paper must be assigned to certain referees who must review it. One of the conditions is that no referee is an author of a paper he should review. When all referees of a paper return their review, their responses are evaluated and the authors are informed. If the paper is accepted, its authors may register for the conference. When a paper is rejected, the authors will probably select another conference and send the paper to this new conference.

There are four entities (paper, author, conference chairman, referee) that take part in the workflow. The left side of Figure 3 illustrates which entity performs certain activities. Information about the four entities is stored in a database system. The paper is characterized by a name, topic, a set of authors, a set of assigned_referees that must review the paper and a status (i.e., accepted or rejected). The conference includes as attributes a list of topics, a boolean deadline_occurred, and a list of submitted_papers. The author and the referee are specializations of the type person.

Obviously, if an active database system is used, the workflow activities may be controlled and coordinated using ECA-rules. The actions of the rules contain various operations which may again signal events. For the sake of simplicity, rules are described with an abstract notation that use only instance variable and method names without specifying parameters and objects they are applied on. For the specification of events the composite operator sequence, denoted (e_1 SEQ e_2), is used.

r_1	ON	select_conference		r_5	ON	assign_paper_ref
	IF	¬ deadline_occured			IF	authors ∩ referees = ∅
	DO	submit_abstract			DO	reviewing
r_2	ON	submit_paper		r_6	ON	reviewing
	DO	confirm_submission			IF	reviewready
					DO	inform_authors
r_3	ON	(submit_abstract SEQ submit_paper)				
	IF	PAPER.topic ⊆ CONFERENCE.topics		r_7	ON	inform_authors
	DO	assign_paper_ref			IF	PAPER.rejected
					DO	select_conference
r_4	ON	assign_paper_ref				submit_paper
	IF	authors ∩ referees ≠ ∅				
	DO	assign_paper_ref		r_8	ON	inform_authors
					IF	PAPER.accepted
					DO	register_to_conference

Consider the set of rules R = $\{r_1,..., r_8\}$. Let us see how the termination tool works and where the rule designer must intervene. First of all, the relationship graph (see Figure 4) is built. There are 5 cycles in the relationship graph, caused by the following subsets of rules:

$C_1=\{r_1, r_3, r_4, r_5, r_6, r_7\}$ $C_3=\{r_3, r_4, r_5, r_6, r_7\}$ $C_5=\{r_4\}$
$C_2=\{r_1, r_3, r_5, r_6, r_7\}$ $C_4=\{r_3, r_5, r_6, r_7\}$

In the next step, the termination tool considers each cycle separately. Cycle C_1 does not contain any A/R-relationships. The question is whether the rule subset C_1 may trigger itself. The analysis begins with the terminal node r_3 for the partial edge (r_1, r_3). The set PE(e_3) must be computed, PE(e_3) = {submit_abstract, submit_paper}. All elements of PE(e_3) are determined by the execution of rules in C_1 (r_1 in C_1 may signal submit_abstract and r_7 in C_1 may signal submit_paper). That means, r_3 is triggered by rules in C_1. Because there are no other partial edges in the cycle, it is concluded that C_1 may trigger itself. The cycle could not be proven to be false. The same reasoning is valid for the other cycles, C_2, C_3, C_4. That means, the set $C_1 \cup C_2 \cup C_3 \cup C_4$ may lead to an infinite nested rule execution.

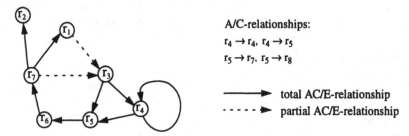

Fig. 4. Relationship Graph

Even if A/C-relationships are signalled by the tool (see Figure 4), we cannot show that nested rule execution does not take place. Therefore, some rule definitions must be changed. One possibility is to change the event that rule r_3 is defined on:

```
ON ((submit_abstract SEQ submit_paper) SEQ deadline)
```

The new semantics of e_3 requires another primitive event, deadline to occur in order to trigger r_3. After this modification the analysis is started again. Deadline is an outside event. Applying again the algorithm for determining if C_1 (respectively C_2, C_3, C_4) may trigger itself, the answer is negative. Not all events in $PE(e_3) = \{$submit_abstract, submit_paper, deadline$\}$ are signalled by rules in C_1. Therefore, a nested execution will never take place. The execution may be infinite but, because it is not nested, does not necessary imply a wrong rule behavior. Therefore, nontermination, as defined in Section 3, has been avoided.

Let us now discuss the cycle determined by r_4. The rule designer considers the A/C-relationships signalled by the tool that include r_4. r_4 is in A/C-relationship with itself. r_4 imposes that each referee of a paper is not among the authors of this paper. The execution of the rule should be repeated as long as its condition is fulfilled. The rule designer then has to decide whether the self-triggering of r_4 will eventually terminate when the condition is not fulfilled anymore. For example, if there are enough referees then it is sure that the operation assign_paper_ref will find a set of assigned_referees for each paper such that authors $\cap$ assigned_referees = 0.

5 Related work

Much work has been done in the area of termination investigation, covering static methods analyzing the specification of rules [1, 2, 3, 11, 16] (at compile time) and dynamic methods analyzing rule execution [4] (at runtime). However, no method handle termination analysis for rules specified using composite events, although nowadays most advanced active database systems [5, 6, 7, 9, 10, 15] support an event algebra. Our approach considers composite events as well. The basic idea of using a graph for termination analysis with rules as nodes is the same as in [1, 2, 3, 11, 16]. We have extended it to make it applicable for rules defined for composite events as well. Our method is complementary to other approaches [3, 11, 16] that refine the triggering graph in order to improve the accuracy of analysis. For example:

- [3] builds an activation graph that reflects the semantic information contained in the actions and conditions (i.e., special A/C-relationships). In this case, a more powerful termination investigation may be performed. However, the requirements are quite strong. This method can be applied only if the accurate detection that actions may change the truth value of conditions from false to true is possible. If no rule may falsify its own condition after execution, the activation graph does not provide any additional information with respect to the triggering graph. Note that the building of activation graph requires A/C-relationships to be computed for all rules in the rule set. Our approach compute them only for some rules (for each cycle in the triggering graph it is sufficient to consider only the rules belonging to the same connected component as the cycle).

- [11] uses logical formalism and efficiently applies unification methods to prune the triggering graph. For each edge (r_i, r_j) the satisfiability of the corresponding so called triggering formula is checked. If it is not satisfiable, the edge may be erased from the triggering graph. In particular, the evaluation of triggering formula checks if methods called in a_i and the event definition e_j unify and if constraints identified in a_i and c_i are compatible with constraints imposed by e_j and c_j. The implementation is described in [13].

All known static methods are conservative, i.e., they aim at fulfilling sufficient (but not necessary) conditions. Approximations are performed. However, the precision of termination analysis directly depends on the host DML used for the specification of actions and conditions:

- If the host language supports conditional statements and while statements, AC/E-relationships cannot be accurately provided because it cannot be definitely decided if an event appearing within such a statement will be raised at runtime. Additional problems occur in systems where the host language supports late binding and pointers. We encountered these problems in our implementation for SAMOS which has as host language a persistent C++.

- If the host language supports the explicit specification of the type of operations that are used (e.g., insert, delete, increase, decrease, retrieve, update), computing A/C-relationships is more precise. This applies for [16]. Due to the language of the OS-CAR Trigger System, the analysis can detect cases when incremental (decremental) updates reach the upper (lower) bound and the potential loop stops.

- We used in our implementation a coarse syntactical method for computing A/C-relationships. If, on the contrary, a formal language definition is provided, it may be more precisely established whether an action may change the truth value of a condition. For example, [2] assumes that conditions and actions are both represented by relational algebra expressions. In this case, formal considerations are applied and the approach may accurately detect A/C-relationships. Unfortunately, these ideas cannot be directly used for non declarative host languages that are not based on relational algebra or relational calculus. Furthermore, the argumentation of [2] is valid only for CA-rules, which have different execution semantics than rules supporting explicit events.

For runtime analysis, [4] proposes a technique to recognize that a given situation (i.e., a database state and the rule selected for execution) has already occurred and therefore will occur an infinite number of times in the future. However, for general rule sets, if the rule execution does not terminate, this does not necessarily mean that situations should repeat. Therefore, this method works only for rule sets which do not generate new values in the database or which do not include rules that are nondeterministically selected by the rule processing.

6 Summary

This paper introduces concepts needed for a better understanding of the problem of rule termination in active DBMS, and describes our approach for handling termination analysis for expressive rule languages. The expressiveness of a rule language depends on:

1. the number of constructs provided by the rule language (composite operators, coupling modes, etc.), and
2. the host language used for the specification of actions and conditions. If the host language tends to a general-purpose language, the flexibility of specification increases.

We referred in this paper mainly to the aspect of composite operators and proposed a solution for deciding if rules defined for composite events may lead to nontermination. Termination of rule execution is guaranteed if *no rule subset* may trigger itself directly or indirectly. A rule subset may trigger itself if *all* the primitive component events of the rules may be triggered by the execution of other rules in the subset. Using these ideas, we extended classical approaches [1, 3, 11] to be applicable also for the termination analysis of expressive rule languages.

We also discussed problems raised by host languages that tend to provide the same expressive power as general-purpose languages. They are hard to analyze statically and the rule analysis lacks precision.

Summarizing, more expressiveness for rule specification must be paid for with a more conservative termination analysis. However, if the rule designer chooses the use of an expressive language, the basic idea of our approach regarding composite events is indispensable for the investigation of termination. To the best of our knowledge, it is the only approach so far that eliminates the signalling of "false" cases of nonterminating rule execution due to composite events.

Acknowledgments
We thank Andreas Geppert and Dirk Jonscher for helpful comments on an initial draft, Michelle Hoyle and Birgitte Krogh for carefully reading the paper and anonymous reviewers for their constructive criticism.

7 References

1   Aiken A., Widom J., Hellerstein J.M.; Behaviour of Database Production Rules: Termination, Confluence and Observable Determinism; *Proc. of the ACM SIGMOD Intl. Conf. on Management of Data*, San Diego, June 92.

2   Baralis E., Widom J.; An Algebraic Approach to Rule Analysis in Expert Database Systems; *Proc. of the 20th VLDB Conf.*, Santiago, Chile 94.

3   Baralis E., Ceri S., Paraboschi S.; Improved Rule Analysis by Means of Triggering and Activation Graphs; *Proc. of 2nd Intl. Workshop on Rules in Database Systems*, RIDS '95, Athens, Greece, September 95.

4   Baralis E., Ceri S., Paraboschi S.; Run-Time Detection of Non-Terminating Active Rule Systems; *Proc. of the 4th Intl. Conf. on Deductive and Object-Oriented Databases*, DOOD'95, Singapore, December 95.

5   Buchmann A.P., Blakeley J., Zimmermann J.A., Wells D.L.: Building an Integrated Active OODBMS: Requirements, Architecture, and Design Decisions; *Proc. of the 11th Intl. Conf. on Data Engineering*, Taipei, Taiwan, March 95.

6   Chakravarthy S., Krishnaprasad V., Tamizuddin Z., Badani R.H.; ECA Rule Integration into an OODBMS: Architecture and Implementation; *Proc. of the 11th Intl. Conf. on Data Engineering*, Taipei, Taiwan, March 95.

7   Collet C., Coupaye T., Svensen T.; NAOS: Efficient and Modular Reactive Capabilities in an Object-Oriented Database System; *Proc. of the 20th VLDB Conf.*, Santiago, Chile, September 94.

8   Dayal U.; Active Database Management Systems; *Proc. of the 3rd Intl. Conf. on Data and Knowledge Bases*, Jerusalem, 88.

9   Gatziu S., Dittrich K.R; Events in an Active Object-Oriented Database System; *Proc. of the 1st Intl. Workshop on Rules in Database Systems*, Edinburgh, 93.

10   Gehani N.H., Jagadish H.V.; Ode as an Active Database: Constraints and Triggers; *Proc. 17th Intl. Conf. on Very Large Data Bases*, Barcelona, September 91.

11   Karadimce A.P., Urban S.D.; Refined Triggering Graphs: A Logic Based Approach to Termination Analysis in an Active Object-Oriented Database; *Proc. of the 12th Intl. Conf. on Data Engineering, ICDE 96*, New Orleans, Louisiana, February 96.

12   Stonebraker M.L., Kemnithz G.; The POSTGRES Next-Generation Database Management System; *Communications of the ACM*, 34(10), October 91.

13   Tschudi M., Urban S., Dietrich S., Karadimce A.; An Implementation and Evaluation of the Refined Triggering Graph Method for Active Rule Termination Analysis; *Proc. of the 3rd Intl. Workshop on Rules in Database Systems*, Skoevde, Sweden, June 97.

14   Van Assche F., Moulin B., Rolland C.; Object Oriented Approach in Information Systems; *Proc. of the IFIP TC8/WG8.1 Conf. on the Object Oriented Approach in Information Systems*, Quebec City, Canada, October 91.

15   Widom J., Ceri S.; *Active Database Systems: Triggers and Rules for Advanced Database Processing*, Morgan-Kaufmann, San Francisco, California, 96.

16   Weik, T., Heuer, A.; An Algorithm for the Analysis of Termination of Large Trigger Sets in an OODBMS; *Proc. of the 1st Intl. Workshop on Active and Real-Time Database Systems*, Skoevde, Sweden, June 95.

On Control Flow Testing of Active Rules in a Declarative Object-Oriented Framework*

Hon Wai Rene Chan, Suzanne W. Dietrich, and Susan D. Urban

Department of Computer Science and Engineering,
Arizona State University, Tempe, AZ 85287, U.S.A.
{rene.chan|s.dietrich|s.urban}@asu.edu

Abstract. Advances in active database technology offer more powerful systems than conventional passive databases. However, the introduction of production rules and autonomous reactive responses in active databases also adds complexity to such systems. To assure the quality of active database systems, a testing methodology has to be developed. In this paper, we describe the architecture of an active rule testing tool set and the implementation of the control flow test data generator, which generates the constraints on test data in the form of test scripts. The work, which is adapted from the testing theory and test data generation techniques for control flow testing of imperative programs, represents the first step in the development of an effective active database testing framework.

1 Introduction

Active databases have been explored for several years now as an alternative to conventional passive databases. By introducing production rules into a database environment, events and conditions of interest can be monitored and actions can be automatically invoked within the database. Active rules have been used to enforce general integrity constraints [2,8,15] and to send notifications to users of special database conditions. More recently, active rules have been investigated as a technology in support of workflow control [7]. The additional advantages of active databases, however, are attained at the cost of additional complexity resulting from the intricate interactions between autonomous active rule executions and user-submitted data manipulations. As Widom and Ceri pointed out in [27], "Even small numbers of active rules can be quite complex to understand and manage." With a more complex system, testing becomes even more important to active databases for their users' acceptance. Although there are several active database prototypes [1,9,12,14,23] (and others) and implementations of debugging environments [4,9,10,13,17], we are not familiar with any literature on the testing of active database rules.

---
* This research is supported by NSF Grant No. IRI-9410983

Software testing is a very expensive process and it typically accounts for a significant factor in the cost of software development. Yet, a well-designed test suite is essential to a piece of software for acceptance by users. Throughout the history of different programming paradigms, programs are first created and perhaps randomly tested for initial uses. As the programming paradigm matures, the growth of program complexity posts confidence issues. Users then call for more formal testing considerations and random testing is replaced by planned testing activities. Active databases have introduced active rules as a new programming paradigm within database applications. With the proliferation of active database prototypes, the active rule programming paradigm is becoming more mature. Given the complexity of active rule programming, however, the research community has not yet developed effective testing methodologies to support the testing of active database applications. The goal of our work is to address the testing issues of active rules in an active, declarative, object-oriented framework.

In pursuit of our goal, we are adapting existing software testing techniques for testing active database applications. Testing techniques can be broadly classified into structural and functional approaches. Structural techniques derive test data solely from program code whereas functional techniques derive test data solely from functional specifications [3,18]. The two classes of testing techniques are designed for different purposes. Structural techniques are used to test the execution coverage of certain program structural elements. Functional techniques are, instead, used to verify functional conformance to the specification. It is generally recognized that no single testing technique is superior to others and that a suite of complementary testing techniques is needed for testing to be effective.

In this paper, we describe some of the results from our work on the adaptation of existing software testing techniques to active databases [11]. Specifically, we describe a technique adapted from the well-known structural, control flow testing approach for exercising every alternative flow of control in a program. The control flow testing approach analyzes the control flow of active rules and utilizes the decision-to-decision graph (*ddgraph*) technique [6] to automatically generate the constraints on test data in the form of test scripts. Control flow testing is applied to active rules written in the CDOL (Comprehensive Declarative Object Language)[26] language, which is based on an active, deductive, and object-oriented framework. This paper also reports on the experimental control flow test data generator as part of the work in progress of the ADOOD RANCH active database project (URL http://www.eas.asu.edu/~adood) in developing an integrated development environment for active database applications [25].

One contribution of this research is found in the study of control flow for declarative active rules and its utilization in test data generation. Specifically, the study includes an examination of the intra-rule and inter-rule control flow characteristics of declarative CDOL active rules. This research has also contributed to a better understanding of the architecture of an active rule testing environment. Automating test data generation and test execution is identified as a major challenge in developing such an environment. An implementation of a control flow test data generator is provided as a partial solution to the problem. While this research is based on active rules written in CDOL, we believe that the technique described in this paper is also applicable to other active database systems. As a result of this work, we have taken the first steps towards achieving software quality for active applications. We have done so through the exploration of testing techniques that are typically used in the software engineering domain and through the application of such techniques to active database technology.

The remainder of this paper is structured as follows. Section 2 discusses related work in software testing both in general and with respect to active databases. Section 3 gives an overview of control flow testing and the issues in testing control flow of declarative CDOL active rules. In Sect. 4, we present the details of the prototype control flow test data generator in the context of an example. The paper concludes in Sect. 5 with a summary and discussion of future research directions.

2 Related Work

Software testing is a generic term, referring to the process of exercising a software system with input that resembles actual processing data. Software testing is still the dominant technique for software verification and validation (V&V) [22]. According to the IEEE Standard Glossary of Software Engineering Terminology [19], verification involves checking a software system against the specification established during the previous development phase, and validation involves evaluating a software system in meeting its requirements at the end of the development process. Many of the widely used software testing techniques are documented in [3] and [18]. Control flow testing is one of the most popular structural testing techniques in which the program's code is used to derived test data to exercise all control flow structures. In [5,6], Bertolino and Marré describe a technique for automatic test data generation for control flow testing. Sections 3 and 4 of this paper give more details on control flow testing as well as Bertolino and Marré's test data generation technique.

At the time of the writing of this paper, there is no literature devoted to testing of active rules in database systems. There are research literatures describing active rule debugging and prototype implementations of debugging environments [4,10,13,17]. Many of these debugging environments support tracing executions of active rules [4,10,13,17], visualizing active rule firing [4,10,13,17], and detecting possible infinite rule cycles [17]. Although testing and debugging are often referred to in the same context, the objectives of testing and debugging are, however, fundamentally different. The objective of testing is to discover program errors through a planned process that is automatable, whereas the objective of debugging is to locate and correct program errors knowing that they already exist [3]. In other words, debugging usually follows tests that discover failures. While the aforementioned active rule debuggers may offer support for tracing and profiling during manual test execution, they lack support in test design and automatic test execution. As test design is crucial to the test effectiveness, the lack of support in this area makes these debugging tools alone inadequate for testing purposes.

3 Control Flow Testing of Active Rules

In this section, we reveal the application of control flow testing to CDOL active rules. We begin with an overview of the general control flow testing methodology, followed by a discussion on issues in testing CDOL active rules. Finally, we describe control flow testing for CDOL active rules.

3.1 Control Flow Testing Methodology

Control flow testing is also referred to as a form of path testing in [3] and [18], since control flow forms paths through a program. Control flow testing is one of the oldest structural test techniques and it is motivated by the intuition of executing every branch and statement in a program at least once in some test path. Being a structural test, it is based solely on the program's source code, and not on its definition. Thus, the method is "very amenable to rigorous definitions, mathematic analysis, and precise measurement" [18].

To apply the technique, a program is first analyzed to identify its control flow structure. Then, the control flow information is used to derive test inputs that will direct the program to traverse the structure in different paths. The control flow structure identified in the first step is usually represented in some form of a directed graph, generally referred to as a program flow-graph. There are various specializations of flow-graphs with different notations. However, we can understand most of them by treating a node either as a statement or as part of a statement and a directed edge as an alternative flow of control. When a node has two or more edges coming out of it, a branch structure exists.

There are different criteria for selecting test paths with varying degrees of coverage [3,18]. The weakest metric is the 100% *statement* coverage, which requires that every statement has to be executed at least once. Statement coverage corresponds to path selection covering every node in a flow-graph at least once. The strongest metric is the 100% *path* coverage, which requires that every possible path through the program structure has to be executed at least once. Path coverage corresponds to path selection covering every possible sequence of edges from the entry to the exit node in a program flow-graph. Since the statement coverage metric is too weak in the sense that covering one branch alternative in a branch statement is said to have satisfied the requirement and the path coverage metric is both expensive and, in general, unachievable, intermediate metrics, such as *branch* coverage, have been adopted by many organizations as the mandatory minimum criteria. Branch coverage corresponds to requiring that every possible branch alternative has been executed at least once, and thus corresponds to path selection covering every edge in a flow-graph at least once. The technique described in Sect. 4.2 is an example of a branch coverage approach.

3.2 Issues in Testing CDOL Active Rules

We have just given a general overview of control flow testing. There are special considerations that we need to take into account when applying the technique to CDOL active rules. CDOL is a rule-based, active, declarative, and object-oriented database language. It consists of several sublanguages for the expression of active behaviors, declarative updates, derived data, and constraints. The language supports an object-oriented type system in which user-defined types are organized into class hierarchies and class instances are manipulated using methods. In the following paragraphs, we will introduce the CDOL active rule sublanguage and discuss some of the related testing issues. Readers are referred to [26] for a complete description of CDOL.

The CDOL active rule sublanguage supports the Event-Condition-Action (ECA) rule model for active behavior specifications. Events in CDOL are method and transaction invocations, which can be further refined to trigger before or after the invocations. Conditions are queries against the database specified as conjunctions of subgoals using CDOL's rule query language. Finally, actions in CDOL are sequences of update rules. Each update rule in an active rule action has a head and a body. An update rule can be mostly understood like a horn rule where the rule body, specified as conjunctions of subgoals using CDOL's rule query language, produces the bindings for the data manipulation operation specified in the rule head. The declarative CDOL active rule also supports the immediate, deferred, and decoupled *coupling modes*, as well as relative rule priority.

To illustrate CDOL's active rule specifications, consider the Horse Racing Database (HRDB) application shown in Fig. 1. The HRDB stores information about horse race events, participating horses, and related personnel. The application defines nine classes indicated by boxes in Fig. 1. Class relationships and attributes are shown by thin arrows and inheritance relationships are shown by bold arrows. The complete CDOL definition of the HRDB can be found in [26] or at URL http://www.eas.asu.edu/~adood. Suppose that in the HRDB application, winning the first place in any race wins 3/5 of the total purse for the race, and if the amount won is greater than 10% of the horse's price, the horse's price will increase by 5%. Furthermore, suppose that we want to enforce these semantics whenever the finish_position of the entries class is updated. We can define the finish_first_win and performance_price rules as shown in Fig. 2 for this purpose. The finish_first_win rule specifies that after the finish_position attribute of the entries class is updated to one and if the amount won is not equal to 3/5 of the purse, the amount_won attribute will be updated to the correct value. The performance_price rule specifies that after the amount_won attribute of the entries class is updated, if the update value is greater than 10% of the horse's price, the price of the horse will be increased by 5%. Additionally, the performance_price rule specified that it has a lower priority than the finish_first_win rule and therefore it will execute after the finish_first_win finishes execution.

The rule-based nature of CDOL introduces issues in control flow testing that need to be explored. One issue is related to the global nature of rules and the

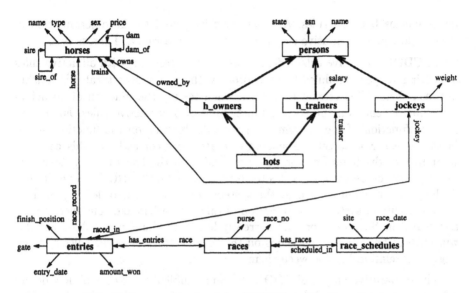

Fig. 1. Horse racing database (HRDB) application schema

```
active finish_first_win
{
    event       after       entries:Entry[update_finish_position(New_Pos)]
    condition deferred       New_Pos=1, entries:Entry,
                             Entry.amount_won <> Entry.race.purse * 0.6
    action      deferred     entries:Entry[update_amount_won(Amt*0.6)]
                                 <- entries:Entry[race.purse=Amt];
};

active performance_price
{
    event       after       entries:Entry[update_amount_won(Amt_Won)]
    condition deferred       entries:Entry,
                             Amt_Won > Entry.horse.price * 0.1
    action      deferred     horses:Horse[update_price(New_Price)]
                                 <- entries:Entry[horse=Horse],
                                    New_Price = Horse.price * 1.05;

    > finish_first_win
};
```

Fig. 2. Active rules finish_first_win and performance_price

dependencies between rules. Another issue is related to the determination of control flow in a declarative language, both within a rule and across rules.

In CDOL, an active rule is defined as a global concept, with all active rules appearing as peer modules to each other without any structural relationship between them. This creates a problem when testing the function of an active rule that depends on the correct functioning of other active rules. For example, the function of the performance_price rule depends on the function of the finish_first_win rule to set the amount_won attribute correctly. In this case, we want to test the finish_first_win rule first and then the two rules together, but the dependency between the rules to correctly enforce the HRDB semantics described earlier is not known to the system. This lack of knowledge precludes the possibility of system determination of rule test orders and rule selections to test together. Such decisions are currently left to the human test designer who will have to base his/her decisions on the specifications of active rules and the triggering relationships between them.

The declarative nature of CDOL presents a difficulty for control flow determination. In a traditional declarative system, programs define what the results should be, and leave how to find the result to the system discretion. Consequently, there are no control flow constructs in a declarative language and the control within an active rule appears to flow from event to condition and then to action. However, there are more control flow details within the condition part and within the rule body in the update rules of the action part. Theoretically, the order of subgoals in a rule language does not change the meaning of a rule. For example in the condition part of the finish_first_win rule, whether we specify to test the new finish position first before testing the amount won as shown in Fig. 2, or to specify them in the reverse order shall mean the same. However, to determine the control flow in CDOL, we must take into account the evaluation scheme of the language, specifically understanding its subgoal evaluation order. For testing CDOL active rules, we have defined a normalization requirement in which subgoals of a normalized rule are evaluated with a left to right order. With the normalization requirement, we can view every subgoal of a rule as a branching construct such that the satisfaction of a subgoal will continue the evaluation process to the next subgoal, but the failure of a subgoal will end the evaluation of the current rule. This scheme determines the intra-rule control flow.

Finally, there are difficulties in identifying inter-rule control flow due to the active rule execution nature. Control flows between active rules when the execution of one active rule triggers and switches control to another active rule. The important point to note here is that inter-rule control flow is not solely defined by the triggering relationships between them. The fact that one rule triggers another merely indicates that there is a possible flow of control from the former to the latter. Recall that active rules in CDOL are prioritized. If another active rule with an intermediate priority between the triggering and the triggered rule is already triggered when the triggering occurs, the control will flow to the intermediate priority rule first before flowing to the triggered rule. For example, if there is another active rule with priority between the finish_first_win and the performance_price rules that is already triggered and ready to execute at the moment the former triggers the latter, the control will flow from the finish_first_win rule to the other active rule before flowing into the performance_price rule. There are further complications when multiple rules with the same priority are triggered simultaneously. In the CDOL execution model, such a situation is handled by processing each active rule in an arbitrary order. In general, it is impossible to predict what other active rules are already triggered when another triggering occurs. Furthermore, it is impossible to predict the execution order of simultaneously triggered rules with the same priority. Trying to design test cases to account for the effect of already triggered rules or to test all different execution order combinations for simultaneously triggered rules is similar to trying to achieve 100% path coverage. It is generally unachievable in practice. For our test analysis, we consider each triggering and triggered rule pair separately and we assume that there is an actual flow of control from the triggering rule to the triggered rule. When we execute the test, we may need to disable any intermediate priority rules and also verify that an actual control flow from the triggering rule to the triggered rule is exercised at least once in some test.

3.3 Control Flow Test for CDOL Active Rules

In order to explain control flow tests for active rules, we must first describe what are control flow alternatives through a single active rule in CDOL. Recall that CDOL is a declarative object-oriented language and no control flow language construct, such as the if-then-else statement, is provided. What, instead, amount to control flow alternatives within an active rule is the satisfaction or failure of the subgoals in the condition part and the rule body of the action update rules. For the condition part, if the subgoal is satisfied, active rule processing continues, and if the subgoal fails, the processing of that active rule ends. In other words, every subgoal represents a *potential* point of alternatives to either continue or to end the processing of the active rule. The reason why we said each subgoal is a *potential* alternative is because certain subgoals, such as an equality between an expression and a free variable, can never fail by nature. Note also that the active rules we referred to in this section are the *normalized* active rule definitions generated by compiling the user's original rule definitions. Normalized rules guarantee the left-to-right subgoal evaluation order for control flow to make sense in a declarative environment. The normalization process also breaks compound predicates in each subgoal into simple predicates in multiple subgoals resulting in more control flow alternatives and paths to cover. This produced a higher degree of coverage referred to as multiple condition coverage in [18].

The generalized control flow of a normalized active rule is shown in Fig. 3. In the figure, execution begins after the event occurs. The evaluation of the condition proceeds from left to right. When a subgoal is evaluated to satisfactory, the evaluation continues to the next subgoal to the right. If, however, a subgoal fails, control of the active rule flows down and ends the processing of the rule. Recall that certain subgoals can never fail and therefore branches occur between grouping of subgoals in general. This is depicted in Fig. 3 by arrows coming out of subgoal groups indicated by boxes drawn in dotted lines. When all condition subgoals are satisfied, update rules in the action part are scheduled for execution before the processing of the active rule completes. Each update rule in the action part is executed in turn. If the body of an update rule is satisfied, then the action in the head of the update rule is executed. If the body of an update rule fails, control flows to the next update rule. With the above definition of active rule control flow, the application of control flow testing is reduced to the problem of carefully crafting a series of events in conjunction with the condition and action update rule subgoals to cover each arrow in the control flow diagram.

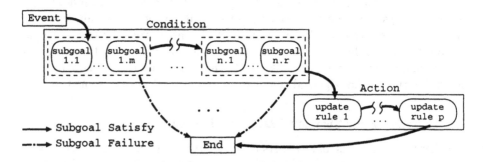

Fig. 3. Generalized control flow within a normalized CDOL active rule

4 Prototype Test Data Generator for CDOL

In this section, we describe the prototype control flow test data generator for CDOL. The control flow test data generator is part of the active rule testing tool set, which in turn is part of the active database development environment for CDOL applications. Section 4.1 describes the architecture of the testing tool set, indicating where the control flow test data generator fits in the overall testing process, it input and expected output. Section 4.2 details the prototype implementation of the test data generator, explaining the adaptation and implementation of Bertolino and Marré's control flow testing technique and its application on an example CDOL active rule.

4.1 Functional Architecture of CDOL Control Flow Testing Tools

Figure 4 gives the functional architecture of the CDOL control flow testing tool. To test active rules, they are first selected by the test engineer. Then the control flow test data generator retrieves the definitions of the selected active rules together with the triggering information between them to produce the requirements on the test data. The test data generator also collects expected results from the test engineer and they are consolidated with the test data generated to produce a test script. Unlike the test data generator described in [21], which generates a textual guideline of what the tester should test, our test data generator generates a test script that will be fed into an automatic test execution manager.

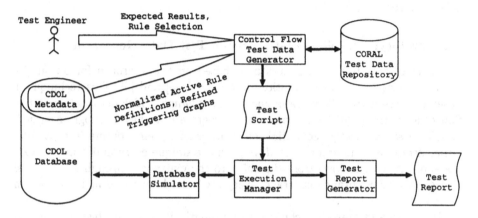

Fig. 4. Functional architecture of CDOL control flow testing tools

Our experience with testing database applications reveals that a substantial amount of time is spent on creating the initial database state for running each test. In fact, the need to recreate an initial database state for each test is not only time consuming, but if the test fails, it is often useful to debug the application by tracing the execution against the database state that produced the original failure. Therefore, instead of allowing the test runs to directly manipulate objects in the database, the test execution manager runs the tests against a database simulator. From the viewpoint of the test execution manager, the database simulator appears as a real CDOL database and any operations allowable on the CDOL database are also allowed by the database simulator. However, database state changes applied to the database simulator are not applied to the actual database. So, when the test execution manager needs to run a new test or re-run the same test with the original database state, it only has to instruct the database simulator to reset the simulated database state. There is no need for explicit state recreation. Note also that in addition to time saved in recreating database states, the database simulator allows active rule testing on the actual database data without interruption to the application's normal services and without the risk of tests tampering with the actual database.

During test execution, the test execution manager sends the test results to a test report generator. The report generator then consolidates the test results into test reports. Upon completion of the test execution, one iteration of the testing process is completed and the test report can be used for debugging or for revising the test plan.

Among the tool modules shown in Fig. 4, the control flow test data generator has been implemented with CORAL [20] and C++. This implementation is described in detail in the next subsection. We are currently investigating the implementation of the database simulator using the technique of object deltas [16,24]. We will begin the design and implementation of the test execution manager and the test report generator when the design of the execution engine has been finalized.

4.2 Prototype Implementation of the Test Data Generator

The control flow test data generator is based on the approach for automatic branch testing test data generation described in [5] and [6]. This technique is based on a specialized flow-graph known as a *ddgraph*, which depicts the control flow of a program with arcs representing program branches. A program branch is defined as "a strictly sequential set of program statements uninterrupted by either decisions or junctions". A *ddgraph* has a unique entry and a unique exit node and execution flows from the entry to the exit node through the internal nodes. To achieve branch coverage, every arc must be covered at least once in some test.

Bertolino and Marré's technique to automatically generate test data is formally defined in [5] and an imperative algorithm to implement the test data generation process is provided in [6]. The implementation of the prototype test data generator for CDOL active rules uses a mixture of declarative and imperative approaches to implement a variation of the Bertolino and Marré algorithm described in [6]. Since the ddgraph and the concepts defined over the ddgraph rely heavily on graph theoretic principles, we chose to implement this part of the algorithm declaratively using CORAL [20]. This declarative implementation is interfaced with various C++ modules for retrieving rule definitions and triggering information from the metadata, and for generating the output test scripts. We will use the CORAL implementation, shown in Fig. 5, to guide the reader through the technique of Bertolino and Marré on the finish_first_win active rule in the HRDB application introduced earlier in the paper.

Recall that each subgoal in the condition part and the rule body of action update rule amount to a potential point of control flow alternatives. Generating the ddgraph is the first step in the automatic test data generation process. Using the normalized definition of finish_first_win rule shown in Fig. 6, a C++ module of the test data generator produces the *ddgraph* shown in Fig. 7 and populates the corresponding *ddgraph* extensional relations in the CORAL module. In Fig. 7, the numbers beside each path show the subgoals associated with the path, and they correspond to the numbers beside the subgoals shown in Fig. 6.

In the CORAL implementation, a ddgraph is represented by a collection of tuples in the extensional relation ddEdge of arity 4, which identifies the Graph of interest, the starting node, the destination node and the name of the edge. Each node in the *ddgraph* is also represented in a ddNode extensional relation. The unique entry and exit node of a *ddgraph* are identified by the extensional relation ddEntry and ddExit, respectively. The intensional relation ddPath defines

```
module ddGraph.
export ddPath(bbbf).
export dominates(bfb, bbb, bbf, bff).
export implies(bfb, bbb, bbf, bff).
export unconstrained_edge(bb, bf).
export pathCover(bf).
export minimalPathCover(bf).

ddPath(Graph, StartEdge, DestEdge, PathEdgeList) :-
    ddEdge(Graph, _, InterNode, StartEdge),
    ddEdge(Graph, InterNode, _, DestEdge),
    not StartEdge = DestEdge,
    PathEdgeList = [StartEdge|[DestEdge]].

ddPath(Graph, StartEdge, DestEdge, PathEdgeList) :-
    ddEdge(Graph, _, InterNode, StartEdge),
    ddEdge(Graph, InterNode, _, InterEdge),
    ddPath(Graph, InterEdge, DestEdge, SubPathList),
    not list_member(SubPathList, StartEdge),
    PathEdgeList = [StartEdge|SubPathList].

exist_path_from_Edge1_to_Edge2_not_containing_Edge3(
        Graph, Edge1, Edge2, Edge3) :-
    ddPath(Graph, Edge1, Edge2, Path),
    not list_member(Path, Edge3).

dominates(Graph, DominateEdge, DominateOveredEdge) :-
    ddEntry(Graph, EntryNode),
    ddEdge(Graph, EntryNode, _, EntryEdge),
    ddEdge(Graph, _, _, DominateOveredEdge),
    ddEdge(Graph, _, _, DominateEdge),
    not DominateOveredEdge = EntryEdge,
    not DominateOveredEdge = DominateOveredEdge,
    not exist_path_from_Edge1_to_Edge2_not_containing_Edge3(
        Graph, EntryEdge, DominateOveredEdge, DominateEdge).

implies(Graph, ImplyingEdge, ImpliedEdge) :-
    ddExit(Graph, ExitNode),
    ddEdge(Graph, _, ExitNode, ExitEdge),
    ddEdge(Graph, _, _, ImpliedEdge),
    ddEdge(Graph, _, _, ImplyingEdge),
    not ImplyingEdge = ExitEdge,
    not ImplyingEdge = ImpliedEdge,
    not exist_path_from_Edge1_to_Edge2_not_containing_Edge3(
        Graph, ImplyingEdge, ExitEdge, ImpliedEdge).

unconstrained_edge(Graph, Edge) :-
    ddEdge(Graph, _, _, Edge),
    not dominates(Graph, Edge, _),
    not implies(Graph, _, Edge).

pathCover(Graph, OnePath) :-
    unconstrained_edge(Graph, UnconstrainedEdge),
    ddEntry(Graph, EntryNode),
    ddEdge(Graph, EntryNode, _, EntryEdge),
    ddExit(Graph, ExitNode),
    ddEdge(Graph, _, ExitNode, ExitEdge),
    any_ddPath(Graph, EntryEdge, UnconstrainedEdge, SubPath1),
    any_ddPath(Graph, UnconstrainedEdge, ExitEdge, SubPath2),
    SubPath2 = [SubPath2Head|SubPath2Tail],
    list_append(SubPath1, SubPath2Tail, OnePath).

end_module.

module any_ddPath.
export any_ddPath(bbbf).

%% Set aggregate_selection to return an arbitrary path
%% in AnyPath.
@aggregate_selection any_ddPath(Graph, StartEdge, DestEdge,
        AnyPath) (Graph, StartEdge, DestEdge) any(AnyPath).

any_ddPath(Graph, StartEdge, DestEdge, AnyPath) :-
    ddPath(Graph, StartEdge, DestEdge, AnyPath).

end_module.
```

Fig. 5. CORAL implementation of path cover algorithm

```
active finish_first_win
{
    event    after    entries:Entry[update_finish_position(New_Pos)]
    condition deferred New_Pos=1,                                          (1)
                       entries:Entry,                                      (2)
                       Entry.amount_won=V1,                               (3)
                       Entry.race=V2,                                      (4)
                       V2.purse=V3,                                        (5)
                       V3*0.6=V4,                                          (6)
                       V1<>V4                                              (7)
    action deferred    entries:Entry[update_amount_won(Amt*0.6)]          (8)
                       <- entries:Entry,                                   (9)
                          Entry.race=V5,                                  (10)
                          V5.purse=Amt;                                   (11)
};
```

Fig. 6. Normalized definition of finish_first_win rule

a path in the **Graph** of interest from a starting edge to a destination edge that returns the list of edges on the path.

The **dominates** intensional relation defines the *dominance* relationship between edges in a *ddgraph* such that DominateEdge dominates DominateOveredEdge if and only if every path from the unique entry node of the *ddgraph* to DominateOveredEdge contains DominateEdge. For instance, in the *ddgraph* shown in Fig. 7, the edge b dominates the edges c and d. On the other hand, the **implies** intensional relation defines a 'symmetric' *implication* relationship between edges in a *ddgraph* such that ImplyingEdge implies ImpliedEdge if and only if every path from ImplyingEdge to the unique exit node of the *ddgraph* contains ImpliedEdge. For instance, in the *ddgraph* shown in Fig. 7, the edge a implies the edge f.

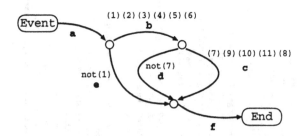

Fig. 7. ddgraph of normalized finish_first_win rule

The **unconstrained_edge** intensional relation defines the unconstrained edges as edges that cannot be guaranteed to be covered by any other edge in the *ddgraph* but covering them will guarantee the coverage of every other edge. In other words, *unconstrained edges* are edges that neither dominate nor are implied by any edge in a *ddgraph*. For the example in Fig. 7, edges c, d, and e are unconstrained.

The pathCover intensional relation defines paths that cover the unconstrained edges in the *ddgraph*. It is based on arbitrarily finding paths from the unique entry node to the unique exit node through each *unconstrained edge*. By proof [6], the set of paths in the pathCover relation guarantees to cover every edge in the *ddgraph*. For the example, the test data generator generates the path cover with the conditions corresponding to each path as shown in Table 1.

Table 1. Path cover and the path conditions for testing finish_first_win rule

Path	Path Condition
a, b, c, f	New_Pos=1, entries:Entry, Entry.amount_won=V1, Entry.race=V2, V2.purse=V3, V3*0.6=V4, V1<>V4, Entry.race=V5, V5.purse=Amt
a, b, d, f	New_Pos=1, entries:Entry, Entry.amount_won=V1, Entry.race=V2, V2.purse=V3, V3*0.6=V4, V1=V4
a, e, f	New_Pos<>1

Finally a C++ module in the test data generator uses the information in Table 1 and the test engineer's input queries to verify expected rule processing output to generate the test script, which is then given to the test execution manager to run the tests. Fig. 8 shows a portion of the test script generated to cover the path (a,b,d,f) in Table 1. The test script asserts that the database instance under test satisfies the conditions to execute that path. Then an object satisfying the condition is selected and the method is invoked to test that path.

```
// path a, b, d, f
BEGIN_TEST
BEGIN_TRANSACTION

ASSERT "entries:Entry, Entry.amount_won=V1, Entry.race=V2, V2.purse=V3, V3*0.6=V4, V1=V4"
    ON_FAIL CONT_WITH_NEXT_TEST

SELECT_ANY Entry FROM "entries:Entry, Entry.amount_won=V1, Entry.race=V2,
    V2.purse=V3, V3*0.6=V4, V1=V4"  INTO E_Subject

INVOKE_METHOD E_Subject update_finish_position 1

COMMIT_TRANSACTION
END_TEST
```

Fig. 8. Test script section for the path a, b, d, f in Fig. 7

To summarize, Bertolino and Marré's technique works by first finding all the *unconstrained edges* in a *ddgraph* that are potentially more difficult to cover than the other edges. Then test data requirements are derived to cover all the *unconstrained edges*. By proof, such a set of test data will automatically cover every edge in the *ddgraph*, and thus provide a branch cover for the program. Our approach follows the same theory and has been generalized to handle multiple active rule triggerings in a declarative environment.

5 Summary and Future Work

In this paper, we presented an approach for testing active rules by exploring the application of accepted control flow testing techniques, typically used in the software engineering domain, to the domain of active database rules. This study required an examination of the intra-rule and inter-rule control flow of active rules. We also described a tool set architecture for automating the entire testing process. An implementation of the control flow test data generator, which automatically generates test scripts that guarantee 100% multiple condition branch coverage, was described on an example. While this research is based on active rules written in CDOL, we believe that the technique is also applicable to other active database systems.

An important idea in testing is that no single technique is sufficient. Instead, we need a suite of complementary techniques for testing to become an effective means of active rule verification. We, therefore, are currently investigating other structural and functional testing techniques for testing CDOL active rules. In particular, we are investigating data flow tests, input domain tests, and boundary value tests [3,18]. In addition, we are also investigating the use of object deltas [16,24] to implement the test database simulator, which is an essential component for efficient test execution. As a long term goal, we would like to study the effectiveness of our testing techniques in finding errors in active rules and estimating their reliabilities.

References

1. Anwar, E., Maugis, L, Chakravarthy, S.: A new perspective on rule suport for object-oriented databases. Proc. of the ACM SIGMOD International Conf. on Management of Data, Washingtion, D.C. (May 1993) 99–108
2. Baralis, E., Ceri, S., Paraboschi, S.: Declarative specification of constraint maintenance. Proc. of the 13th International Conf. on the Entity-Relationship Approach, Manchester, UK (Dec. 1994) 205–222
3. Beizer, B.: Software Testing Techniques, 2nd ed. Van Nostrand Reinhold (1990)
4. Benazet, E., Guehl, H., Bouzeghoub, M.: VITAL: a visual tool for analysis of rules behaviour in active databases. Proc. of the 2nd International Workshop on Rules in Database Systems (RIDS'95), Glyfada, Athens, Greece (Sep. 1995) 182–196
5. Bertolino, A.: Unconstrained edges and their application to branch testing of programs. Journal of Systems Software 20 (1993) 125–133
6. Bertolino, A., Marré, M.: Automatic generation of path covers based on the control flow analysis of computer programs. IEEE Transactions on Software Engineering 20(12) (Dec. 1994) 885–899
7. Bussler, C., Jablonski, S.: Implementing agent coordination for workflow management systems using active database systems. Proc. of the 4th International Workshop on Research Issues in Data Engineering (RIDE-ADS '94), Houston, Texas (Feb. 1994) 53–59
8. Ceri, S., Fraternali, P., Paraboschi, S., Tanca, L.: Automatic generation of production rules for integrity maintenance. ACM Transactions on Database Systems 19(3) (Sep. 1994) 367–422

9. Ceri, S., Manthey, R.: Consolidated specification of Chimera (CM and CL). Technical report, Dipartimento di Elettronica e Informazione, Politecnico di Milano, Piazza L. Da Vinci, 32, 20133 Milano, Italy (Nov. 1993)

10. Chakravathy, S., Tamizuddin, Z., Zhou, J.: A visualization and explanation tool for debugging ECA rules in active databases. Proc. of the 2nd International Workshop on Rules in Database Systems (RIDS'95), Glyfada, Athens, Greece (Sep. 1995) 197–209

11. Chan, H.W.R.: Active rule testing: A case study of structural and functional testing for the Comprehensive Declarative Object Language (CDOL). Master's thesis, Arizona State University. Document under preparation.

12. Dayal, U.: Active database management systems. Proc. of the 3rd International Conf. on Data and Knowledge Bases, Jerusalem (Jun. 1988) 150–170

13. Díaz, O., Jaime, A., Paton, N.: DEAR: A DEbugger for Active Rules in an object-oriented context. Proc. of the 1st International Workshop on Rules in Database Systems (RIDS '93), Edinburgh, Scotland (Aug.–Sep. 1993) 180–193

14. Gehani, N., Jagadish, H.V.: Ode as an active database: Constraints and triggers. Proc. of the 17th International Conf. on Very Large Data Bases, Barcelona, Spain (Sep. 1991) 327–336

15. Gertz, M.: Specifying reactive integrity control for active databases. Proc. of the 4th International Workshop on Research Issues in Data Engineering (RIDE-ADS '94), Houston, Texas (Feb. 1994) 2–9

16. Ghandeharizadeh, S., Hull, R., Jacobs, D.: Heraclitus: Elevating deltas to be first-class citizens in a database programming language. ACM Transactions on Database Systems $21(3)$ (Sep. 1996) 370–426

17. Jähne, A., Urban, S.,Dietrich, S.: PEARD: A prototype environment for active rule debugging. Journal of Intelligent Information Systems $7(2)$ (Oct. 1996) 111–128

18. Jorgensen, P.: Software Testing: A Craftman's Approach. CRC Press, Inc. (1995)

19. Institute of Electrical and Electronics Engineers: Software Engineering Standards, ANSI/IEEE Std 729-1983, Glossary of Software Engineering Terminology (1984)

20. Ramakrishnan, R., Srivastava, D., Sudarshan, S.: CORAL: Control, Relations and Logic. Proc. of the 18th International Conf. on Very Large Data Bases, Vancouver, British Columbia, Canada (1992) 238–250

21. Robbert, M., Maryanski, F.: Automated test plan generator for database application systems. SIGSMALL/PC Notes $17(3)$ (Fall 1991) 29–35

22. Sommerville, I.: Software Engineering, 4th ed. Addison Wesley Publishing Company (1992)

23. Stonebraker, M., Hanson, E.N., Potamianos, S.: The POSTGRES rule manager. IEEE Transactions on Software Engineering $14(7)$ (Jul. 1988) 897–907

24. Sundermier, A.: Condition monitoring in an active, deductive, object-oriented database. Master's thesis proposal, Arizona State University. Document under preparation.

25. Urban, S., Dietrich, S.: A development environment for active database systems: Testing and analysis of active database rule. National Science Foundation grant no. IRI-9410983 (1994)

26. Urban, S., Karadimce, A., Dietrich, S., Ben Abdellatif, T., Chan, H.W.R.: CDOL: A Comprehensive Declarative Object Language. Data & Knowledge Engineering 22 (1997) 67–111

27. Widom, J., Ceri, S., editors: Active Database Systems: Triggers and Rules for Advanced Database Processing. Morgan Kaufmann Publishers, Inc. (1996)

Validating Active Rules by Planning

Piero Fraternali †, Ernest Teniente ‡, Toni Urpí ‡

†Dipartimento di Elettronica e Informazione, Politecnico di Milano
P.zza L. da Vinci, 32, Milano, Italy - e-mail: fraterna@elet.polimi.it

‡Universitat Politècnica de Catalunya, LSI Department
Jordi Girona Salgado 1-3, Barcelona, Catalonia -
e-mail [teniente|urpi]@lsi.upc.es

1. Introduction

Active rules are a widely diffused extension of modern database technology, presently available on most commercial DBMS platforms and research prototypes.

Recently, the role of active rules in the design of Information Systems has received great attention [LTP91,PL94,Ros94,CF97], due to the perception that active rules can offer an important aid in capturing the most challenging aspect of Information Systems: the so called *business rules*, i.e., those enterprise-wide policies that must be enforced across all applications.

However, developing active rules is commonly perceived as a difficult task, for a variety of reasons. Active rules are low-level, they have a procedural semantics which is hard to master. Rules available in existing systems have no standard syntax nor semantics, which makes rule porting problematic. Large rule sets are difficult to design, understand, and evolve, due to the lack of modularization and analysis techniques. CASE tools supporting rule design "in-the-large" are not available.

Various solutions to these problems have been proposed, going from automatic generation of active rules from higher-level specification (e.g. [CW90), to manual or automatic support to the analysis of different active rule properties [CTZ95,DJ93,Etz95,KU96].

In this paper, we face the general problem of *active rule validation*, by which we denote a phase of the development of a rule-based application in which the design of an active rule set is evaluated to verify the presence of useful properties and the absence of undesired behaviour.

The novel contribution of this paper is the use of *planning* as a unifying framework for the validation of rules with respect to a wide variety of properties. Planning is a general-purpose technique by which an initial goal is established (e.g., the positioning of an object by a robot in a certain location in a room), and a suitable sequence of actions (called a *plan*) is determined, which ensures the fulfilment of the goal (e.g., a sequence of movements of the robot's arm that ends up with the object in the desired position). The actions constituting the plan are chosen among the possible actions defined in the planning mini-world. Typically, planning proceeds backwards: the prerequisites for the initial goal are identified and established as subgoals, on which planning is recursively applied.

In our approach to validation, the desired rule properties are described as first-order goals, and the actions that the planner can exploit are those available in the "active database mini-world", namely: *operations* and *active rules*. A typical validation session not only permits the designer to verify that a certain property of active rules holds (by checking that a plan exists), but also outputs the plan, which acts as an explanation tool showing one of the possible sequences of actions leading to a state in which the property is satisfied.

As a first result of the application of planning to active rule validation, we have collected and formally expressed as declarative goals a set of interesting properties of active rules, which we expect to extend in the future work.

For making the proposed approach to validation applicable to a wide range of systems in spite of the lack of standardization of active rule features, we have adopted an existing abstract model of active rules and database updates [FT95], which captures the semantics of most commercial and prototype implementations of active rules. We use this model to describe the actions (operations and active rules) available to the planner.

The rest of the paper is organized as follows: Section 2 shortly presents the model of active rules and operations, and introduces a running case study used throughout the paper; Section 3 summarizes the major issues concerning planning; Section 4 presents various properties of active rules that can be validated by means of the proposed technique and shows examples of plans generated from the validation of these properties in the context of the running case study; Section 5 discusses the requirements posed to the planner by the different active rule properties that can be validated; Section 6 compares our approach to the related work; finally, Section 7 contains the conclusions and an outlook on the future work.

2. Framework of updates & active rule semantics

Active rule semantics is the result of the interplay of two different aspects: how rules are evaluated and executed, and how rule processing relates to "normal" transaction processing.

In this section we outline a framework accommodating both aspects of active rules semantics. We assume the usual *ECA model* [WC96] of active rules, whereby an active rule consists of three parts: *event, condition*, and *action*, normally written as: WHEN *event* IF *condition* THEN *action*.

2.1 Dimensions of rule semantics

Active rules of different systems, either commercial products or research prototypes, exhibit many differences both in their syntax and semantics. These differences can be classified along a number of dimensions that can be used to qualify the behaviour of rules of any system. To capture such a diversity, we adopt a model of active rule semantics called the *core model*, first proposed in [FT95].

The basic idea of the core model is to capture active rule semantics by first extending the notion of database with auxiliary data structures that record information about the reactive processing, and then by expressing active rules and updates in a logical language with fixpoint semantics, taking advantage of the auxiliary data structures to express the important aspects of rule processing.

2.2 The event base

In the core model, an active database consists of a repository of data (the *passive database*) augmented with data structures representing occurred events, the triggering relationships between events and active rules, and logged past values. These additional data structures are collectively known as the *eventbase*.

The minimal information needed to represent reactive processing is encoded in two relations: called *event* and *active*.

Relation *event* is a container of all the events occurred since the start of a transaction. Its schema is: *event(EID,TYPE,DATA,TS)*, where:

- EID is a numerical identifier, distinct for each occurred event;
- TYPE is the symbolic name of the event type;
- DATA contains a reference to the data item(s) affected by the event;
- TS is a numerical attribute denoting the occurrence timestamp of the event.

Relation *active* associates occurred events appearing in relation *event* to the rules they are triggering; its schema is: *active(EID,RID)*, where:

- EID is a numerical identifier, distinct for each occurred event;
- RID is the identifier of an active rule.

A tuple *event[e,t,d,ts]* means that an event with identifier e of type t has occurred at timestamp ts of the current transaction, involving the data object(s) d. A tuple *active[e,r]* denotes that event e is still triggering rule r.

A quiescent state is an eventbase state where no rule is triggered; for convenience we introduce an ad hoc intensional predicate **quiescent**, to identify such states:

quiescent $\leftarrow \neg$some-triggered;   some-triggered$\leftarrow$active(x,y);

2.3 Atomic updates and operations

Atomic updates are the elementary units of change that can be applied to the database. As usual, we postulate the following atomic updates:

1. *ins <literal>*: inserts the fact denoted by <literal> into the database, if this does not exist; <literal> must be ground by the evaluation.
2. *del <literal>*: deletes the fact denoted by <literal> from the database, if this exists; <literal> may be ground or contain universally quantified variables, denoted by a dash.
3. Fact modification is achieved by removing the old version of the fact and inserting the new instance.

Atomic updates are clustered to form operations and active rules.

Operations are update units defined in the universe of discourse, used to write data manipulation transactions. They consist of a *precondition* and an *action*. The precondition is a declarative formula used to guard the operation application and to retrieve values from the database, which can be used in the action to operate on data. The action is a set of atomic updates.

The general form of an operation is: *opname*(x) *if* C(y) *then* A(z), where x is a vector of input parameters; C is a range restricted first order formula with free variables y and A is set of atomic updates, with input variables $z \subseteq x \cup y$.

When an operation is invoked, the condition is evaluated with respect to the variable substitution determined by the actual parameters supplied by the caller; if the condition is satisfied, the action is executed, with respect to the variable substitution determined by the actual parameters and by the evaluation of the condition.

The proper semantics of operations with respect to reactive processing is established by:

1. including suitable eventbase updates into the action part of operations, which explicitly dictate which events are produced and made active for which rules.
2. conjoining the literal *quiescent* to the precondition, to ensure that operations are only applicable to quiescent states.[1]

---

[1] Since the *quiescent* literal appears identically in the condition of all operations, we assume it is implicitly present and omit it from the examples.

For example, assume a database containing a relation *empsal(employee,salary)*, the operation:

```
newemp (X)
if not empsal(X,-)
then
ins empsal(X,0)
```

is used to insert a new employee with a default initial salary; since the action does not produce any event the operation will not trigger any active rule.

2.4 Core rules

Core rules are reactive programs executed by a fixpoint algorithm, embedded in the database management system, at specific points during transaction processing called rule starting points; in the simplest case, there is a rule starting point after each operation execution.

Differently from operations, core rules cannot be invoked directly from user transactions; are executed on non-quiescent states; and have a precondition that includes a test on the eventbase, to ensure that a rule is applicable only when its triggering events have occurred.

The syntax of core rules can be better understood if compared with the usual ECA syntax, which can be viewed as a high level specification of rule behaviour; ECA-syntax can be translated into the lower-level core syntax to make the semantic options of rule behaviour visible.

An ECA rule *R: WHEN e IF c THEN a* is mapped into a pair of core rules (r and $\neg r$) with the following form:

```
r: event(E,e,TS,X) and active(E,r) and c →
   a, a', del active(E,r), del active(E,¬r)
¬r: event(E,e,TS,X) and active(E,r) and ¬c →
   del active(E,r), del active(E,¬r)
```

Both rules have a similar structure, consisting of a condition (before the → symbol) and an action (after the → symbol).

The core condition consists of two parts: the *core event part,* denoted by $EBQ(y_1)$, and *the core condition part,* denoted by $DB\text{-}EBQ(x_2,y_2)$, where the x and y are arrays of logical variables, and $x_2 \subseteq y_1$. $EBQ(y_1)$, is a conjunction of literals on the event base structures that is satisfied only if the active rule is triggered, in which case variables y are bound by the evaluation to the identifiers of triggering events to be used in other parts of the rule. In the simplest case shown above, the core event part $EBQ(y_1)$ conjoins two literals on eventbase relations *event* and *active*, and it is satisfied iff the eventbase contains at least one event of the proper type (e), active for the core rule (r or $\neg r$).

The core condition part $DB\text{-}EBQ(x_2,y_2)$ is either the ECA condition c (for rule r) or its negation $\neg c$ (for rule $\neg r$); the x are variables bound in the core event part and used in the core condition part, and the y are variables whose bindings are computed in the condition part and transferred to the action.

The core action part is different for rule r and $\neg r$. In rule r it extends the ECA action part (a) by adding:

1. suitable insertions into relations *event* and *active* (a'), expressing in the core model the events produced by the execution of the ECA rule action part (a);
2. two fixed eventbase updates which delete the tuples of relation *active* representing the triggering of rules r and $\neg r$ by event E. These updates model detriggering, the fact that after a rule is considered, its activating event is no longer triggering.

In rule ¬r, the action has a simpler structure including only the eventbase updates for detriggering described at point 2.

Note that the production of a new event, described in point 1, requires the invention of an event identifier and a timestamp. This can be easily done by means of two dedicated relations holding two counters. For simplicity, we omit to show in the condition and action part of core rules how new identifiers and timestamps are computed and prefix invented values with a $ to recall this syntactic simplification. Moreover, we assume that the events produced in the action part of rules and operations share the same timestamp, because the action is a *set* of updates whose sequence is irrelevant, and which can be considered simultaneous.

The splitting of a single ECA rule R into two core rules r and ¬r is needed to model detriggering also when consideration fails: if a triggered rule is considered on a state where its condition does not hold, still its triggering event must be deactivated; this task is accomplished by evaluating rule ¬r, which is applicable exactly in those eventbase states in which its sibling rule r is triggered but not executable.

For simplicity, the examples of core rules illustrated in this paper will always refer to ECA rules with instance-oriented granularity, immediate EC and CA coupling, non interruptable actions, belonging to a unique transaction, with serial nondeterministic conflict resolution strategy, and without composite events [FT95].

2.5 A complete example

We now introduce a small scale example illustrating the usage of eventbase updates, operations, and core rules.

2.5.1 Schema

The schema contains three relations: `empsal(employee,salary)` describes employees and their salary, `empdept(employee,department)` assigns employees to departments, and `deptbudget(department,budget)` specifies the budget of departments.

2.5.2 Operations

```
newemp(X,D)
    if not empsal(X,-) and deptbutget(D,B)and
       not empdept(X,D)
    then
    ins empsal(X,0)
    ins empdept(X,D)

newsal(X,S)
    if empsal(X,-) and not empsal(X,S) and S<10,000
    then
    del empsal(X,-),
    ins empsal(X,S),
    ins event($E1, modify-salary, $TS1, X),
    ins active($E1, r1), -trigger rules
    ins active($E1, ¬r1),
    ins active($E1, r2),
    ins active($E1, ¬r2)

newdept(D)
    if not deptbudget(D,B)
    then
    ins deptbudget(D,0)
```

Three operations are provided: operation *newemp* creates a new employee with a default salary value and assign this employee to an existing department; since in this example we don't want to monitor the creation of employees neither the assignments to a department, we define operation *newemp* so that it does not produce events.

Operation *newsal* modifies the salary of an employee to a value less than 10,000 and produces an event of type *modify-salary*, which triggers rules r1, ¬r1, r2, and ¬r2. Finally, operation *newdept* introduces a new department without producing any event.

2.5.3 Rules

Rule 1: informal description in ECA format
   WHEN the salary of an employee is modified
   IF the new value is less than 1.000
   THEN set the value to 1.1 times the current value

Core version of R1
```
r1:
event(E, modify-salary, TS, X) and
active(E, r1) and empsal(X,I) and I<1.000
->
del empsal(X,I),
ins empsal(X,I*1.1),
ins event($E1, modify-salary, $TS1, X),
ins active($E1, r1), ins active($E1, ¬r1),--trigger rules
ins active($E1, r2), ins active($E1, ¬r2),
del active(E, r1),del active(E, ¬r1)--detrigger r1 and ¬r1 wrt E

¬r1:
event(E, modify-salary, TS, X) and active(E, r1) and
not (empsal(X,I) and I<1.000)
->
del active(E, r1), --detrigger r1 and ¬r1 wrt E
del active(E, ¬r1)
```

ECA rule R1 is split into the two core rules r1 and ¬r1; r1's condition contains a core event part satisfied whenever an event of type *modify-salary* is present in relation *event* and associated to rule r1 by relation *active*; this guarantees that rule r1 is triggered after operation *newsal* is executed. The condition part is simply the test required by the ECA rule, performed with the help of variable X, which gets bound to the object affected by the triggering event E. The action part contains the production of an event of type *modify-salary*, which recursively triggers r1 and activates all the other rules, and the deletion of the tuples of relation *active* associating event E to rules r1 and ¬r1, which models detriggering. Rule ¬r1 is simpler: it is triggered whenever r1 is triggered and tests for the negated ECA condition; if ¬r1 is satisfied, it detriggers both itself and its sibling rule r1.

Rule 2: informal description in ECA format
   WHEN the salary of an employee is modified
   IF the employee belongs to department D
   THEN increase the value of D's salary budget of 1000 units

Core version of R2
```
r2:
event(E, modify-salary, TS, X) and active(E, r2) and
empdept(X,D) and deptbudget(D,I)
->
del deptbudget(D,I),
ins deptbudget(D,I+1.000),
ins event($E1, modify-salbudget, $TS1, D),
del active(E, r2), --detrigger r1 and ¬r1 for E
del active(E, ¬r2)
```

¬r2:
```
event(E, modify-salary, TS, X) and active(E, r2) and
not (empdept(X,D) and deptbudget(D,I))
->
del active(E, r2),   --detrigger r1 and ¬r1 for E
del active(E, ¬r2)
```

3. Planning

A typical planning problem can be stated as follows: given a description of the world or domain of the problem; an initial state of that world and a goal to accomplish at a final state; obtain one or several plans able to perform the transition from the initial state to a final state in which the desired goal holds. The obtained plans have to be consistent with respect to the world description.

A planning method has to provide both a way to *represent* a planning problem and a mechanism to *generate* plans for the planning problems it is able to represent.

The representation used by a planning method is important because it characterizes the planning problems the method is able to handle. For a planning method to be usable for the validation of the design of an active database modelled as described in Section 2, the representation of a planning problem must support the concepts of the active database core model.

Using this representation the planning problem can be formulated more concretely as: given an active database schema, including a set of operations and active rules; an initial state of the database expressed as a set of base tuples;[2] and a goal expressed as a range-restricted first order formula to be accomplished at a final state of the database; obtain one or several valid sequences of operation and active rule executions able to perform the transition from the initial state of the database to a final state of the database where the desired goal holds.

For example, given the planning domain described by the database schema, rules and operations of Section 2; the initial state: {deptbudget(Marketing, 1000)};the goal: $\exists$ e empdept(e,Marketing) $\wedge$ empsal(e,550); a possible plan is the sequence: newemp(John,Marketing), newsal(John,500), Rule 1.

We have also a requirement on the plan generation mechanism: it must obtain at least a solution plan for a given planning problem, if any solution plan for the planning problem exists. The need of this requirement will become clear in section 4 when defining the properties to validate in terms of planning.

In planning, we are only interested in the generation of *reachable* states. A database state is reachable only if it can be obtained by a valid sequence of operations and active rules. The state {deptbutget(Marketing,1000), empdept(John,Marketing), empsal(John,550)} is reachable in the database defined in our example (section 2.5) since it can be obtained by the sequence newdept(Marketing), newemp(John,Marketing), newsal(John,500), Rule 1.

Note that a reachable state may not be quiescent, since some triggered active rules may still remain for consideration.

---

[2] Note that we only need the base facts of the database to describe the initial state because the derived tuples may be computed using the intensional rules. In particular, the set of base tuples may be empty, and we will call *empty initial state* the corresponding initial state.

4. Active rule properties and their validation

In this section we define a set of desirable properties that an active database should satisfy or that a designer would like to evaluate, and we show how the validation of these properties can be handled by using planning. The main idea is to define for each property an initial state and a goal to accomplish at a final state, such that if there exists a sequence of operations and rules able to achieve the goal departing from the initial state, the active database satisfies this property. If a property is not satisfied, it may be the case that the active database is ill-specified and its design should be revised. In general, this may be due to the specification of active rules, operations, or both.

The set of properties we define in this paper refers only to active rules. In our previous work [DTU96, CTUF96] we used a similar approach for validating the schema and the operations.

4.1 Applicability

The first property that an active rule should satisfy is its applicability. An active rule is applicable if it may be triggered and its condition may hold. However, since it could be the case that whenever a rule is triggered its condition does not hold, we distinguish two different kinds of applicability of an active rule: *triggerability* and *condition satisfaction*.

4.1.1 Triggerability

Intuitively, an active rule is triggerable if an occurrence of its relevant events is produced by the execution of a sequence of operations and active rules. If an active rule is not triggerable, it may never be executed. Therefore, this is an useless rule and probably the active database in which it is defined is ill-specified.

Example 4.1: Consider again our example database of section 2.5 Triggerability of r1 requires an event that modifies the salary of an employee, which can be obtained as a result of the execution of the operation newsal(E,S). However, to execute this operation its precondition must be true which implies a previous execution of operation newemp(E,D). In a similar way, executing newemp(E,D) requires a previous execution of newdept(D). Thus, the sequence {newdept(D), newemp(E,D), newsal(E,S)} shows the triggerability of r1.

Example 4.2: We assume now that operation newdept(D) is not defined. Then, r1 would not be triggerable since no sequence that modifies an employee's salary would exist. Note that, even though newsal(E,S) modifies the salary of an employee, it would never be executed since it would not be possible to add departments nor employees to the database.

In the core model, information about the occurrence of events is stored in the eventbase. Thus, an active rule is triggerable if it is possible to reach a state such that the eventbase contains at least one occurrence of its activating event. Therefore, the problem of finding out whether an active rule R, with core event part EBQ(y1), is triggerable is equivalent to the planning problem of finding a plan for the goal $\exists y1\ EBQ(y1)$, where the description of the world is given by the active database and the initial state is empty. If there exists at least a plan for such a goal, then the plan will contain a valid sequence of operations and active rules that leads to a reachable state in which EBQ is true and thus rule R is triggerable. Otherwise, R is not triggerable.

In our example, checking for triggerability of r1 is performed by considering the goal: $\exists E,\ TS,\ X$ (event(E, modify-salary, TS, X) $\land$ active(E,r1)). A possible plan for this goal is {newdept(Sales), newemp(John,Sales), newsal(John, 100)}, which shows that rule r1 is triggerable.

It could be argued that triggerability can also be validated by means of a syntactic check between the event part of rules and the action of rules and operations. However, a syntactic check can only determine potential triggerability, in the sense that it does not ensure that at execution time the rule can be actually triggered. On the contrary, our results obtained when validating triggerability by planning are more precise due to the *simulation* of the execution of active rules. For instance, in example 4.2, a simple syntactic check would determine that rule r1 is triggerable; while it is not.

4.1.2 Condition satisfiability

Triggerability of a rule does not ensure that when the rule is considered after being triggered, its condition part may hold. Then, another desirable property of active rules validation is *condition satisfiability*. The condition of an active rule is satisfiable if there exists a state in which the rule is triggered and its condition part holds. If an active rule is not condition satisfiable, it may never be executed.

Example 4.2: Consider again our example database of section 2.5, and assume that it contains the following additional active rule:

     r3:   WHEN the salary of an employee X is modified

              IF empsal(X,S) $\land$ S > 10,000

              THEN assign the employee to department "Rich Department"

R3 is triggerable. However, when it is triggered its condition never holds. The reason is that to satisfy the condition part of r3, there must exist an employee with a salary greater than 10,000. In our sample database, assignment of salaries to employees can be performed only by means of the operation newsal(E,S), with S ranging between 1,000 and 10,000, or by assigning a salary less than 1,000 and executing rule r1 a certain number of times until the salary reaches 1,000. In both cases, the maximum salary is strictly less than 10,000.

Formally, the problem of finding out whether an active rule R, with core event part EBQ(y_1) and core condition part DB-EBQ(x_1,y_2), is condition satisfiable is equivalent to the planning problem of finding a plan for the goal $\exists x_1,y_1,y_2$ EBQ(y_1) $\land$ DB-EBQ(x_1,y_2) where the description of the world is given by the active database and the initial state is empty. If there exists at least a plan for such a goal, then rule R is condition satisfiable. Otherwise it is not.

In our example, the corresponding goal is $\exists$E, TS, X, S, (event(E, modify-salary, TS, X) $\land$ active(E,r3) $\land$ empsal(X,S) $\land$ S > 10.000) and, since no possible plan for this goal exists, r3 is not condition satisfiable.

Note that condition satisfiability always implies the executability of the rule if the CA coupling mode is immediate and conflict resolution is done nondeterministically. Indeed, only a priority assignment such that another rule, say r4, is always executed before r3 and makes r3's condition false may prevent r3 form being executed.

4.2 Joint Applicability

In the previous section, we have validated the applicability property for a single active rule. However, we can also be interested in evaluating whether there exists a state in which two different active rules are applicable at the same time. The same distinction between triggerability and condition satisfiability is pertinent in this case. We call the corresponding properties *joint triggerability* and *joint condition satisfiability*. Joint applicability is useful for identifying rules that may compete for execution in the conflict set and for assessing whether two rules are mutually exclusive.

Joint triggerability: Two active rules r1 and r2 are jointly triggerable if it is possible to find an state in which both r1 and r2 are triggered.

More precisely, two active rules will be jointly triggerable if it is possible to reach a state such that the eventbase contains at least one occurrence of the relevant events of each rule.

In terms of planning, the problem of finding out whether two active rules r1 and r2, with core event parts $EBQ_1(y_1)$ and $EBQ_2(y_2)$, are jointly triggerable is equivalent to the problem of finding a plan for the goal $\exists y_1\ EBQ_1(y_1) \wedge \exists y_2\ EBQ_2(y_2)$, where the description of the world is given by the active database and the initial state is empty. If there exists at least a plan for such a goal, then the plan will contain a valid sequence of operations and active rules that leads to a reachable state in which both $EBQ_1(y_1)$ and $EBQ_2(y_2)$ are true and thus rules r1 and r2 are jointly triggerable. Otherwise they are not.

Joint condition satisfiability: Two active rules r1 and r2 are jointly condition satisfiable if it is possible to find an state in which r1 and r2 are triggerable and such that the condition part of both rules is satisfied.

Similarly to the previous case, the problem of finding out whether two active rules r1 and r2, with core event and condition parts $EBQ_1(y_1)$, $DB\text{-}EBQ_1(x_1,y_2)$, $EBQ_2(z_1)$ and $DB\text{-}EBQ_2(x_2,z_2)$ are jointly condition-satisfiable is equivalent to the problem of finding a plan for the goal $\exists x_1,y_1,y_2\ (EBQ_1(y_1) \wedge DB\text{-}EBQ_1(x_1,y_2)) \wedge \exists x_2,z_1,z_2\ (EBQ_2(z_1) \wedge DB\text{-}EBQ_2(x_2,z_2))$, where the description of the world is given by the active database and the initial state is empty. If there exists at least a plan for such a goal, rules r1 and r2 are jointly condition-satisfiable.

4.3 Rule coverage

Another interesting property to validate is whether two active rules are mutually covered. We will start by defining when an active rule r1 is covered by another rule r2. Intuitively, r1 is covered by r2 if every time r1 is triggered and its condition is satisfied, then also r2 is triggered and its condition is satisfied. This occurrence is shown in the following example.

Example 4.3: Consider again our example database of section 2.5. Triggerability of r1 requires an event that modifies the salary of an employee, which can only be obtained as a result of the execution of the operation newsal(E,S). Newsal requires in turn the previous execution of operation newemp(E,D), which also assigns employees to departments. On the other hand, r2 is always triggered by a modification of an employee's salary and its condition is satisfied when this employee belongs to some department. Thus, r1 is covered by r2, because it is not possible to assign salaries to employees that do not belong to any department.

On the contrary, r2 is not covered by r1 since, even though they are triggered by the same event, it is possible to modify the salary of an employee to a value greater than 1,000. Then, r2 may be triggered and its condition part may be satisfied, whereas the condition part of r1 may not hold.

Previous properties (triggerability, condition satisfiability and the joint properties) are checked by showing the existence of some reachable state that satisfies a condition. As opposed to that, the definition of rule coverage requires something for *each* state. Hence, rule coverage is best checked by verifying or falsifying the lack of coverage, which can be done by attempting to construct *one* state in which one rule is triggered and its condition part is satisfied while the other rule is not.

Thus, the property that rule r1 is not covered by rule r2 is checked by showing the existence of a plan for the goal $\exists x_1, y_1, y_2$ (EBQ$_1$(y$_1$) $\wedge$ DB-EBQ$_1$(x$_1$,y$_2$)) $\wedge$ $\forall x_2, z_1, z_2$ $\neg$(EBQ$_2$(z$_1$) $\wedge$ DB-EBQ$_2$(x$_2$,z$_2$)) where the description of the world is given by the active database and the initial state is empty. If *no plan* exists for this goal, then rule r1 is covered by rule r2.

In our example, checking that rule r2 is not covered by rule r1 is performed by considering the goal:

$$\exists E, TS, X, S, D, B \text{ (event(E, modify-salary, TS, X)} \wedge \text{active(E,r2)} \wedge$$
$$\text{empdept(X,D)} \wedge \text{deptbudget(D,B))} \wedge$$
$$\forall E', TS', X', S' \neg(\text{event(E', modify-salary, TS', X')} \wedge \text{active(E',r1)} \wedge$$
$$\text{empsal(X',S')} \wedge S' < 1000)$$

Since the plan: {newdept(Promotions), newemp(Susan,Promotions), newsal(Susan, 5,000)}, is a possible plan for the above goal then rule r2 is not covered by rule r1. On the contrary, no plan exists for the goal that validates "r1 is not covered by r2". Then, r1 is covered by r2.

Two active rules r1 and r2 are mutually covered if r1 is covered by r2 and r2 is covered by r1. The interest of this property relies on the fact that whenever two rules are mutually covered, they may be combined into a single rule by merging their action parts.

4.4 Rule cascading

The designer may also be interested on validating whether the execution of a rule r2 *always* follows the execution of another rule r1. In this case, we speak of rule cascading. Two variants can be considered: *strict cascading*, if r2 always executes *immediately* after r1; *weak cascading (of order N)*, if r2 is always executed within the next N rule executions after r1 is executed (with N≥1). Clearly, strict cascading is an instance of weak cascading, with N=1.

Example 4.4: Consider again our example database of section 2.5, and assume that it contains the following additional active rule:

r3: WHEN the budget of a department is modified
IF deptbudget(D,B) $\wedge$ B>1000
THEN insert D in the departments with a non-empty budget

This example illustrates both weak and strict cascading. On one side, r3 is always executed after the execution of r2 because r2 is the only possible means to increase the budget of a department. Thus, there is weak cascading between r2 and r3. On the other hand, it is possible to execute r1 between the execution of r2 and r3. Thus, there is not strict cascading between r2 and r3.

Example 4.5: A simple modification of the previous example, in which r1 is not defined, results in a relation of strict cascading between r2 and r3, because whenever r2 is executed in this new example, r3 is executed immediately after.

Similarly to rule coverage, the definition of strict rule cascading requires something for *each* execution of a rule. Hence, strict rule cascading is best checked by verifying the lack of cascading. This can be done by attempting to construct *one* plan showing that rule r1 is executed and that a rule different from r2 or an operation is executed immediately after r1. To be able to obtain such a plan, we extend the core model in a simple way: for each core rule r$_i$ (operation op$_i$) an eventbase update which produces an event of type "executed-r$_i$" ("executed-op$_i$") is added at the end of the action part, so to record in the eventbase the execution of the rule or operation.

For convenience in distinguishing events caused by rule and operation executions from ordinary events, we introduce predicates named *rule-execution, operation-execution,* and *execution,* which range over event type names:

rule-execution(X) ← X = executed-r1 ∨ X=executed-r2 ... ∨ X= executed-rn
operation-execution(X) ← X = executed-op1 ∨ X=executed-op2 ...∨ X= executed-opn
execution(X) ← rule-execution(X) ∨ operation-execution(X)

With these assumptions, we may check for the *lack* of strict rule cascading between rule r1 and r2 by evaluating a goal of the form ∃ TS (∃ E, X (event(E, executed-r1,TS,X)) ∧ ∃ E',Z,X' (event(E',Z,TS+1,Xi) ∧ execution(Z) ∧ Z ≠ executed-r2)).

The goal simply states that there is an eventbase state which records the occurrence of two events E and E' such that E' immediately follows E (it has the next timestamp) and is caused by the execution of an operation or a rule different from r2. If this goal is provably impossible to achieve (for example because there are no rules other that r1 and r2, and r1 always causes r2 to be executed), then r2 strictly cascades after r1.

Weak cascading of order N can be investigated in a analogous way, by formulating a goal that requires:
1) that the next N execution events are produced by rules different from r2; OR
2) that at least one of the next N execution events is caused by an operation.

∃ TS (∃ E, X (event(E, executed-r1,TS,X)) ∧
1) ∃ E1,Z1,X1 (event(E1,Z1,TS+1,X1)∧rule-execution(Z1) ∧ Z1≠executed-r2) ∧
... ∃ En,Zn,Xn (event(En,Zn,TS+N,Xn) ∧ rule-execution(Zn) ∧ Zn ≠ executed-r2) ∨
2) ∃ E',Z,TS',X' (event(E',Z,TS',Xi) ∧ operation–execution(Z) ∧ TS' <= TS+N).

As an example, consider the sequence {newdept(Finances), newemp(Peter,Finances), newsal(Peter, 500), r2, r1}; this is an admissible plan for the goal showing that there is no strict rule cascading between r2 and r3, because r2 is executed and produces an event *executed-r2* with timestamp k, and then r1 is executed producing an event *executed-r1* (different from type *executed-r3*) with timestamp k+1.

Note that cascading of r1 and r2 does not imply a causal dependency between the execution of r1 and r2. In other terms, the execution of r1 is a sufficient, not necessary, condition for the execution of r2. Other properties could be defined, along the way illustrated for rule cascading, to evaluate more in detail the interaction of two rules: for example, whether r2's execution is triggered by an event produced by r1, or whether the execution of r1 is a necessary prerequisite for r2's execution.

4.5 Postcondition satisfaction

Even if a rule is applicable, its definition may not describe the designer's intended needs. For instance, it may turn out that a certain undesirable postcondition is always reached as a consequence of the execution of that rule. Mechanisms for checking whether a postcondition is satisfied immediately after the execution of an active rule help avoid such ill-defined specifications at schema validation time.

Example 4.6: Consider again our example database of section 2.5. Assume now that when defining r1 the designer had in mind that a single execution of this rule would be enough to raise the salary of an employee to more than 1,000. This is equivalent to require a postcondition stating that an employee has a salary greater than 1,000 after each execution of r1. However, this postcondition does not always hold, as shown by the following sequence: {newdept(Marketing), newemp(Mary,

Marketing), newsal(Mary,300), r1}, which results in Mary having a salary lower than 1,000.

Similarly to the previous property, the definition of postcondition satisfaction requires something for *each* execution of r1. Hence, it is easier to check whether a postcondition is not satisfied. This can be done by attempting to construct *one* plan showing that rule r1 is executed and that the postcondition is not satisfied immediately after.

In most cases, the postcondition P need to refer to the same database item whose modification triggered the rule; for generality, we write P(X) instead of P to show that the binding of variable X to the item affected by the triggering event is used in the postcondition.

Then, the fact that a certain postcondition P(X) *does not hold* after every execution of r1 is checked by showing the existence of a valid plan for the goal $\exists$ TS ($\exists$ E ,X (event(E, executed-r1,TS,X) $\wedge \neg$P(X)) $\wedge \forall$ E',Z,X' ($\neg$event(E', Z,TS+1,X'))).

The above goal simply states that the condition P(X) does not hold in the database state which is the direct result of executing r1; the fact that P(X) is checked on the correct state is ensured by the second subformula, which imposes that the goal be evaluated in a state where no event is recorded after *executed-r1*.

If some plan exists for the goal, then P does not hold after *each* execution of r1; otherwise it does.

In the previous example, validating that an employee may have a salary less than 1,000 after an execution of r1 is checked by showing the existence of a valid plan for the goal $\exists$ TS ($\exists$ E ,X (event(E, executed-r1,TS,X) $\wedge$ empsal(X,S) $\wedge$ S<1,000)) $\wedge \forall$ E',Z,X' ($\neg$event(E', Z,TS+1,X'))).

A possible plan for this goal is: {newdept(Marketing), newemp(Mary,Marketing), newsal(Mary, 300), r1}. Indeed, at the end of this sequence, *executed-r1* is the last recorded event and Mary has a salary of 330.

5. Requirements for Planning

The generality of our approach allows us to be independent of the concrete planning method considered for validating the properties defined in Section 4. This facilitates the application of improvements in the planning research area to our validation technique. However, not all planning methods can be considered for validating arbitrary rule properties, because the structure of the applicable planning actions and of the goals to be satisfied imposes requirements on the capabilities of the planning method to adopt.

First, a planning method must support the representation of the planning problem required by our semantic framework for updates and active rules. In practice, the planner must accept the definition of actions as the ones used in this paper to model active rules and operations, and must also be able to handle intensional predicates, as the *quiescent* predicate defined in Section 2, and the execution, *rule-execution* and *operation-execution* predicates defined in Section 4.

Second, the chosen method must allow first-order goals as the ones used to define the properties illustrated in Section 4.

Third, if solutions for the input goal do exist, then the planner must be able to output at least one such solution (but not necessarily all of them). This is a requirement on the plan generation mechanism, and it is needed to guarantee that when the planning method fails to prove a certain property, this property does not actually hold.

These three requirements are sufficient for validating all the properties discussed on Section 4. CDP [DMM91] and Costal and Olivé's method [CO97] are two of the current planning tools that satisfy these requirements. In the first case, the representation required to express the core operations and rules is directly provided, whereas in the second a transformation from the core syntax to planner's syntax is needed, which can be done automatically [CTUF96].

6. Related Work

Validation has been widely investigated in the field of information systems engineering, in particular with respect to conceptual models of information systems. Since the validation task is not fully formalizable and it is based on intuition, it is desirable to provide the designer with the widest set of tools that assist him in the validation process [Bub86]. Among the support capabilities that have been proposed there are: infological simulation [Kun85, VF85], paraphrasing specifications [JC92], animation and symbolic execution [LL93], explanation generation [GW93, OS95], and semantic prototyping [LK93].

Planning has also been used for validation purposes in the field of information systems. Furtado et al. [VF85] proposed a concrete planning method for reasoning about conceptual models. In their approach, the designer is provided with a tool that obtains a sequence of operations able to perform the transition between a given initial state and a target final state. Therefore, the success of validation relies only on the designer's intuition and experience when defining the initial and target states.

Recently, Feenstra and Wieringa [FW95] have also outlined a method for reasoning about conceptual models. They propose a system able to answer reachability queries which permit the designer to express some properties. In addition to the contrast due to the different area of interest, the main drawback of this proposal is that its method is based on extending planning techniques with a satisfiability tester [BDM88], while reachability query properties can be directly checked by using some of the current planning methods.

Validation has also been investigated in the field of passive databases (e.g., [BDM88, IKH92, CDM93, GSUW94]). These proposal handle different schema validation tasks by means of different techniques.

The approach proposed in this paper extends our previous work in the context of passive databases [DTU96], which focused on the use of view updating for validating a database schema without taking into account predefined transactions (operations) nor active rules. It also extends our work reported in [CTUF96], which showed the of planning for validating a database schema with a set of predefined transaction.

The model of active rules employed in the paper is a modification of the core model described in [FT95]. Core rule syntax has been simplified to fit into the description capabilities of current planning methods, without reducing the expressiveness of the core model. Also, the set of semantic dimensions treated in this paper is a subset of those classified in [FT95]; further dimensions could be introduced, by varying the translation of active rules from ECA format into core format.

Another model of active rules suitable to be adopted for validating active rule properties is described in [Zan95]. In this proposal, the basic features of ECA rules are describes as Datalog1S deductive rules, and a variety of extensions to the basic model permit the representation of sophisticated rule features.

7. Conclusions and future work

In this paper we have presented a technique for active rule validation based on planning. Desired rule properties (like triggerability, condition satisfiability, joint applicability, rule coverage, rule cascading, postcondition satisfaction) are identified, and expressed as declarative, first order goals. These goals, together with an abstract description of the semantics of the active database, can be submitted to a planner: if a plan is found for the input goal, then the property under investigation is satisfied (in some cases we submit a goal that demonstrates that a property *does not* hold). In addition, the planner outputs an example of database transaction leading from the empty database state to a state where the property holds. Such example constitutes an explanation by which the designer may obtain a deeper insight into the behaviour of his rules.

Compared to syntactic techniques for rule analysis, this approach to validation incorporates a larger fraction of the database semantics, due to the possibility of exploiting the structure of the database and of update operations in the generation of the plan.

Presently we have investigated very simple, although useful, rule properties, which are handled by at least two implemented planning methods. As soon as the planning technology improves, we will be able to experiment with more sophisticated properties, requiring complex goals involving several planning states. A future direction is to incorporate into our validation framework classical aspects of rule behaviour like confluence, termination, and observable determinism.

Ernest Teniente and Toni Urpí have been partially supported by PRONTIC CICYT program projects TIC94-0512.

References

[BDM88] Bry, F; Decker, H; Manthey, R. "A Uniform Approach to Constraint Satisfaction and Constraint Satisfiabilityin Deductive Databases", in J, Schmidt et al. (Eds.): Proc. EDBT, pp.488-505, Springer LNCS 303, 1988

[Bub86] Bubenko, J. A. "Information System Methodologies - A research Review", in Olle T. W., Sol H. G., Verrijn-Stuart A. A. (Eds.) Information Sytems Design Methodologies: Improving the Practice, pp. 289-318, North Holland, 1986.

[BCP96] Baralis, E.; Ceri, S.; Paraboschi, S. "Compile-time and Run-time Analysis of Active Behaviours", *Internal Report of the Politecnico di Milano,*1996.

[CF97] Ceri, S.; Fraternali, P. "Designing Applications with Objects and Rules: the IDEA Methodology", International Series on Database Systems and Applications, Addison-Wesley Longman, 1997.

[CMD93] Casamayor, J. C.; Decker, H: Marques F. "A mechanism for verification of knowledge base schema specification", in Meseguer P. (Ed.) Proc. *European Symp. Validation and Verification of KBSystems*, pp. 103-155, 1993

[CO97] Costal D.; Olivé A. 'Planning based on View Updating in Deductive Databases' to appear in the Proc. of the Tenth Inter. Symposium on Methodologies for Intelligent Systems (ISMIS'97), USA, October 1997.

[CTFU96] Costal D.; Teniente E.; Urpi T.; Farré C. "Handling Conceptual Model Validation by planning", *Proc. CAiSE-96* Greeca 1996, pp. 255-271

[CTZ95] Chakravartht, S.; Tamizuddin, Z.; Zhou, J. "A Visualization and Explabnation Tool for Debugging ECA Rules in Active Databases", *RIDS'95*, Springer-Verlag, LNCS 985, Athens (Greece), 1995, pp. 197-209.

[CW90]   Ceri S.; Widom J. Deriving Production Rules for Constraint Maintainance. *VLDB'90*, Brisbane (Australia), 1990, pp. 566-577

[Dal92]   Dalianis, H. "A Method for Validating a Conceptual Model by Natural Language Discourse and Generation",*CAiSE'92*, Manchester, 1992, pp. 425-444

[DJ93]   Díaz, O; Jaime, A. "DEAR: a DEbugger for Active Rules in an object-oriented context", *RIDS'93*, Edinburgh, 1993, pp. 180-193.

[DMMP91]Decker M.; Moerkotte G.; Muller H.; Possega J. "Consistency Driven Planning", *Proc.5th Portuguese Conf. on AI*, Albufeira , 1991, pp. 195-209

[DTU96]   Decker H.; Teniente E.; Urpi T. "How to Tackle Schema Validation by View Updating", *Proc. EDBT96*, Avignon, 1996, pp. 535-549

[Etz95]   Etzion, O. "Reasoning About the Behaviour of Active Database Applications", *RIDS'95,*, Athens (Greece), 1995, pp. 86-100.

[FT95]   Fraternali, P.; Tanca, L. "A Structured Approach for the Definition of the Semantics of Active Databases", *ACM TODS*, 20(4), 1995, pp. 414-471.

[FW95]   Feenstra R.; Wieringa R. "Validating Database Constraints and Updates Using Automated Reasoning Techniques", *Proc. of the Workshop on Semantics in Databases*,Cottbus (Germany), 1995, pp24-32

[GSUW94] Gupta, A; Sagiv Y.; Ullman J. D.; Widom J. "Constraint Checking with Partial Information", Proc. 13th PODS, ACM Press, 1994, pp.45-55

[GW93]   Gulla J. A.; Willumsen G. "Using Explanations to Improve the Validation of Executable Models", *CAiSE'93 Conf.*, Paris (France), 1993, pp.118-142

[IKH92]   Inoue K.; Koshimura M., Hasegawa R. "Embedding Negation as Failure into a Model Generation Theorem Prover" *Proc. 11th CADE*, 1992

[KU96]   Karadimce A. P.; Urban S. D. "Refined Triggering Graphs: A Logic-Based Approach to Termination Analysis in an Active Object-oriented Database", ICDE'96, New Orleans (Louisiana), 1996, pp. 384-391

[Kun85]   Kung C. H. "A Tableaux Approach for Consistency Checking", *Inf. Systems: Theoretical and Formal Aspects*, Elsevier Science, 1985, pp. 191-207

[LK93]   Lindland O. I.; Krogstie J. "Validating Conceptual Models by Transformational Prototyping" *CAISE'93*, Paris (France), 1993, pp. 165-183

[LL93]   Lalioti V.; Loucopoulos P. "Visualisation for Validation", *Proc. of the CAise93 Conf.*, Paris (France), 1993, pp.143-164

[OS95]   Olive A.; Sancho M. R.; "A Method for Explaining the Behaviour of Conceptual Models", *Proc. of the CAiSE95 Conf.* Jyvaskyla, 1995, pp. 12-25

[PL94]   Petrounias I., Loucopoulos P. "A Rule-Based Approach for the Design and Implementation of Information Systems ", EDBT'94, Cambridge (UK), 1994, pp. 159-172

[Ros94]   Ross R. G. "The Business Rule Book: Classifying, Defining and Modelling Rules", Database research Group Inc., 1994

[VF85]   Veloso P. A. S.; Furtado A. L. "Toward Simpler and yet Complete Formal Specification", *Proc. IFIP Working Conf. on the TFAIS* 1985, pp. 175-189

[WC96]   Widom, J; Ceri, S. *Active Database Systems: Triggers and Rules for Advanced Applications*, Morgan-Kaufmann, 1996.

[Zan95]   Carlo Zaniolo: The Dynamics of Active Database Rules: Models and Refinements. *NGITS '95*, Naharia, Israel. 1995

Active-Design:
A Generic Toolkit for Deriving Specific Rule Execution Models

Mokrane Bouzeghoub[1] and Françoise Fabret[2] and François Llirbat[2] and Maja Matulovic[2] and Eric Simon[2]

[1] University of Versailles, 78035 France,
Mokrane.Bouzeghoub@prism.uvsq.fr
[2] INRIA, Rocquencourt,78153 France,
FirstName.LastName@inria.fr

Abstract. Active rules or triggers are widely accepted as powerful mechanisms to implement applications or systems behaviour. Several rule execution models were proposed as extended functionalities for different database systems. However, these models lack in flexibility and adaptability to specific database systems or specific application requirements. In this paper, we propose a generic framework which provides a set of basic functions which can be used to implement any execution model. This framework, called Active-Design toolkit, can be exploited in many situations where applications need specific model or different models for different subsets of rules.

1 Introduction

Active systems extend traditional database systems by enabling the automatic execution of rules when certain events occur. This mechanism is widely accepted as a uniform and powerful way to implement general system extensions (e.g., integrity checking, maintenance of materialized views, management of replicated data, etc.), and business rules in a wide variety of applications. An active database system is generally considered as a passive database system with three extra components (see e.g., the Manifesto in [DGG95]):

- A rule specification language - Rules are specified as an ECA triple: an event expression (E) that triggers the rule, a condition (C) to be evaluated if the rule is triggered, and an action (A) to execute if the condition evaluates to true.
- An event detector - It detects the occurrences of events and signal them, together with possible parameters, to a rule execution engine.
- A rule execution engine - It invokes and synchronizes the execution of rule conditions and actions with respect to the events that have been signaled.

The execution model underneath an active database system depends on many parameters (also called dimensions), which describe the operational semantics of rule execution (see e.g., [WC96, FT95]). These parameters specify for instance how the events that have occured are used to determine if a rule is triggered, at which point in time a triggered rule should be executed, or how a rule should be selected among several other conflicting rules.

Usually, an active application makes particular assumptions on the dimensions of the execution model which seem the most appropriate for the active rules it intends to use. The problem that sometimes arises in practice is that these assumptions are not consistent with the execution model supported by the active database system on which the application has to be developed [KDS97]. To illustrate this, consider a relational active database system that provides SQL triggers[3]. Suppose that your application needs to use active rules that (i) are triggered at the end of transactions, (ii) consider globally all the events that have occurred since the beginning of the transaction, and (iii) schedule the rules according to some priority-based policy. Unfortunately, these dimensions are not compatible with the restricted SQL triggers currently implemented by existing products. The application developer will be forced to implement an active rule monitoring layer, let us call it Active Monitor, on top of the database system. The SQL triggers provided by the active database system will merely be used to interrupt the execution of user transactions after each SQL statement, and pass the control to the Active Monitor. In particular, at each interruption, the Active Monitor will have to record the event that has just occurred into specific database relations.

Several examples of similar situations are described in [KDS97], concerning experiences of development of active database applications that implement ad-hoc system extensions or business rules. Usually, the major drawback for application developers is that developing and maintaining an Active Monitor is a quite difficult task that requires a lot of skill and training.

1.1 Related work

The usual answer given to this problem in the research literature is to design an active database system that offers a powerful parametrized rule execution model, which can presumably accommodate the requirements of a large class of application's semantics. This approach, is emphasized by the Chimera environment [WC96], Acto [MFLS96], and Naos [Cou96]. In these systems, the user specifying the rules can choose the appropriate values of the execution model's parameters that correspond to the desired excution semantics for the rules. In NAOS, the parametrized execution model is implemented within the O2 database system. Thus, every application pays the price for active functionalities that are implemented by the database system in order to support the parametrized execution model, but that will possibly be bypassed, and hence not used by the application. On the positive side, the implementation of the execution model can a priori be better optimized because it makes use of the database system internals. On the

---

[3] By SQL triggers, we refer to the kind of SQL3-like triggers, which are supported by most today relational products.

contrary, Chimera and ACTO follow an approach whereby the target database system is a "light-weight" active database system, which, for instance, only supports SQL triggers. The Chimera and ACTO systems behave more like "active application generators" for the target database system. More concretely, the user defines rules through a specific language or interface and then the system (that is, Chimera or ACTO) generate the appropriate code, including the definition of triggers in the target database system, that is needed to monitor the execution of the user-defined rules.

However, the three above approaches still suffer from the following drawbacks. First, it is not possible for the application developer to accomodate other parameters values than the ones hard-wired in those systems. For instance, if one desires that the action of a rule be executed as an independant transaction, then if the system does not incorporate this possibility, the application developer will not be able to add it. Second, the user cannot customize, for optimization purposes, the implementation of the rules she defined. For instance, all these systems make use of so-called "delta structures" that are used to manage the history of events that occured within a transaction. However, the application developer is not able to modify the format and the implementation of these delta structures. Last, for the above "application generator" approaches, the code that is generated always incoporate a fixed engine that is not minimal with respect to the application needs.

1.2 A Toolkit Approach

In this paper, we propose an alternative approach, whereby the implementation of an active application follows three distinct phases.

The first phase consists of using an extensible Toolbox to build an Active Monitor, on top of a DBMS. Like with Chimera and ACTO, this DBMS is supposed to be a "light-weight" active system. The minimal requirements to this system are to support the detection of primitive database events (e.g., as modern relational systems do), and enable a trigger's action to execute an arbitrary user-defined program in a given language. The Toolbox is specific to the target DBMS because: (i) it makes use of the capabilities of the target DBMS (detection of events, management of temporary relations, creation of stored procedures, etc), and (ii) it must be implemented in a language that can be invoked from within the action of the trigger supported by the DBMS. The Toolbox consists of a set of reusable building blocks that can be combined to implement a specific rule execution model. The design of the Toolbox is the major contribution of this paper.

During the second phase, the user defines the active rules. Each rule definition entails the specification of an event part that can be recognized by the Active Monitor, a condition consisting of a query executable by the DBMS, and an action that contains statements executable by the DBMS. The condition and action of a rule may also include and possible specific events that can be recognized by the Active Monitor.

Finally, during the third phase, the user-defined rules lead to the generation of several components. DBMS triggers are generated to detect the events that contribute to the triggering of the user-defined rules, and invoke the Active Monitor. Specific procedures that implement the conditions and actions of rules are generated. They will be directly invoked by the Active Monitor. Finally, the necessary information about the user-defined rules is loaded into the internal data structures of the Active Monitor.

In this paper, we focus on the design of the Toolkit used to produce the code of an Active Monitor. Apart from this introduction, this paper is structured as follows. In Section 2, we give a formal model of a generic Active Monitor, which can describe the execution of rules under any execution model. In Section 3, we derive a generic functional architecture for an Active Monitor, and show how to design the building blocks that are necessary to generate such a functional architecture. We also detail the interfaces of the building blocks. Section 4 concludes.

2 Modeling a Generic Active Monitor

2.1 Preliminaries

An event is described by its name and a sequence of parameters. In this paper, we consider primitive and complex events: A primitive event may be a user's notification (explicit event) or a database operation i.e., an insertion, deletion, updating, selection on a relational table, or any method invocation in an object database system. A complex event is a combination of primitive events (using logical, arithmetic and/or temporal operators) An event whose parameters are instantiated is an event instance. An active rule r is defined by a triggering event, r_e, a condition and an action programs. A rule instance of r results from the triggering of r due to an occurrence of an instance of r_e: it is represented by a triple $<r, r\_i, e\_i>$ where e_i denotes the instance of r_e that triggered r and r_i is the instance identifier. Executing a rule instance $<r, r\_i, e\_i>$ consists in computing its condition and performing its action when the condition is evaluated to true. Condition and action programs may use the e_i value as input parameter.

Throughout this paper, we assume that the rules are triggered by events occurring during the execution of a user program which may be an application program or a flat transaction. The execution of this program may be interrupted for executing the rules. We also assume that there is no external event, i.e., the occurrences of triggering events are due to the execution of the operations occurring in the user program or in the corresponding triggered rules.

2.2 The model

We represent the execution of a set of rules by means of the notions of tasks, task synchronizer, event history and task history. Communications beetwen the

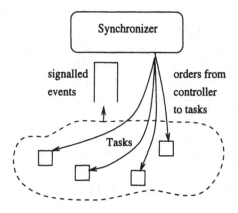

Fig. 1. Execution system

tasks and the synchronizer are represented by messages. There is no inter-task communication. Every time a task sends a message, it is inactive until the synchronizer sends a response. The synchronizer handles the messages in the order in which they were sent by the tasks, in response to the messages, it may create tasks or send commands to the waiting tasks. A task represents a rule instance or an initial program triggering the rules. At every step in the execution process, the current set of tasks consists of the active tasks plus the tasks waiting for a command from the synchronizer. The event history and the task history respectively contain all the messages sent by the tasks and the commands sent by the synchronizer from the beginning of the transaction.

2.3 Tasks : State diagram and messages

We describe a rule instance task by the state transition diagram depicted in Figure 2 with labelled transitions. Grey ovals, dashed ovals, and white ovals respectively represent inactive states (i.e. states where T is waiting for a command sent by the synchronizer), final states of T, and active states (i.e. states where T performs computations and, possibly, send messages to the synchronizer). There are four inactive states : *triggered, evaluated, interrupted,* and *wait*. A transition from state S to state S', noted (S, S'), with a label of the form "R:m" has the following meaning: "on receive command m from synchronizer" T executes command m and enters in state S' (remark that such situation occurs only if S is an inactive state). On the opposite, a label of the form "S:m" may only occur if S is an active state, the meaning is: T sends message m to the synchronizer and enters in state S' (remark that S' is necessarily an inactive state).

State *triggered* is the initial state of T where the task is waiting for the command begin_rule. On receive this command, T enters in active state *evaluating* where it computes the condition, sends the message cond_eval including the reporting of the result of the computation, then T enters in the inactive state *wait* where

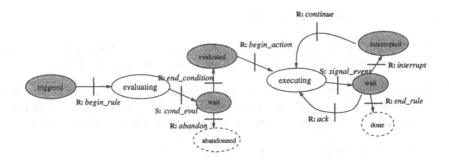

Fig. 2. Rule instance execution state diagram

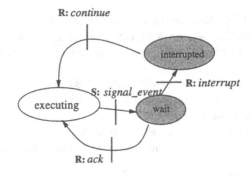

Fig. 3. transaction execution state diagram

it does nothing. At this state, the command received by T depends on the result of the condition evaluation: if the condition has the value false, T receives the command abandon and enters in state *abandon* where it, possibly, executes protocols ending the task. On the opposite, if the condition holds, T enters into the *evaluated* state, and waits for the begin_action command. On receive this command, T enters in the *executing* state where it executes the action program. During this execution, T may send messages to the synchronizer (for example to signal database operations occurred during the execution). After each message, T enters in the inactive state *wait* where it does nothing. In response to these messages, the synchronizer may send an interrupt command that leads T in the inactive state *interrupted* or an ack command (for acknowledgement) that leads T to continue the program, or an end_rule command. This last command responds to a message signalling the end of the program execution; it leads T in the final state *done*.

The state transition diagram of the task representing the initial program is given in Figure 3. This task may be *executing*, signalling events, or be *interrupted* for executing rules.

2.4 Event and Task Histories

The execution of an initial program that triggers active rules can be traced using two histories: The *Event History (EH)* and the *Task History (TH)*.

The *Event History (EH)* contains the messages sent by the tasks, that is the event instances that occur during the execution of the initial program and of the rules. Each event instance is described by a triplet $<E, args, ts>$ where:

1. E is the name of the associated event,
2. *args* contains the event parameter values associated with the event,
3. *ts* is a timestamp that indicates the time when the event occured (i.e. the message is sent).

The *Task history (TH)* records the scheduling of rule instances during the program execution. It is a sequence of tuples $<r, ri, O, ts>$ that reflects the commands sent to the tasks during execution of the transaction.

1. r is either a rule identifier, or the initial program,
2. ri is an identifier of an instance of r (i.e. a task),
3. O is a command name,
4. *ts* is a timestamp that indicates the time when the command is taken into account by the task (i.e. the time when the task changes its state).

Moreover, TH contains a tuple of the form $<r, ri, init, ts>$ per rule instance ri, where *ts* indicates the time when the task was created.

2.5 Synchronizer: Built-in functions

The synchronizer may be seen as a process which is awaken by the messages sent by the tasks. It is in charge of two works: creating new tasks, and sending commands to the inactive tasks. Creating new tasks raises several problems: when creating new tasks? what rules are triggered at a certain point in the time? what instance(s) have to be created for each triggered rule? Sending commands to the inactive tasks requires to select the task(s) to activate: what are the selection criteria? Answering these questions fully determines the semantics of the rule execution.

When creating new tasks? : function check_synchro
Function check_synchro checks the histories and derives a *synchronization point* that may be a *processing* point, a *scheduling* point or a *null* point. This function may be specified by using two boolean functions Processing and Scheduling:

$$check\_synchro() = \text{processing point iff Processing(HT, HE)}$$
$$check\_synchro() = \text{scheduling point iff Scheduling(HT, HE)}$$
$$check\_synchro() = \text{null point} \quad \text{iff } \neg(\text{Processing(HT, HE)}$$
$$\lor \text{Scheduling(HT, HE))}$$

The synchronizer uses the *synchronization* point returned by check_synchro to take the following decision: it creates new tasks if the point is a *processing* point, it sends an ack to the task having sent the last message if the point is a *null* point, and otherwise it sends a command to an inactive task.

What are the triggered rules, and the new instances?: function trigger
Function *trigger* computes a set of rule instances: It checks the histories in order to compute the triggered rules. Then it computes the instance(s) associated with each triggered rule. To do that, function *trigger*, uses three functions: *is_triggered*, *synthesis*, and *compute_interval*.

1. *compute_interval* specifies what subset of elements contained in the histories must be considered for computing the triggered rules, *compute_interval* may be specified by means of a formula over the histories.

$$compute\_interval : \quad () \longrightarrow \quad \text{set of event instances}$$

2. *synthesis* takes a set of event instances and derives a set of event instances, it may be specified by a formula over *compute_interval*.

3. *is_triggered* takes a rule r, tests if r is triggered with respect to the set of event instances returned by functions *compute_interval* and *synthesis*, and returns the set of rule instances for r.

$$< r, r\_i, e\_i > \in is\_triggered \text{ iff } \exists e = < E, args > \quad s.t$$
$$(r \text{ is set\_oriented and } args = \{a \,|< E, a> \in synthesis(compute\_interval)\})$$
$$or$$
$$(r \text{ is instance\_oriented and } < E, a > \in synthesis(compute\_interval))$$

Finally, function *trigger* is specified as :

$$< r, r\_i, e\_i > \in \quad trigger() \quad \Rightarrow \quad < r, r\_i, e\_i > \in \quad is\_triggered$$

Example 1. In Starburst, the rules are set-oriented, *compute_interval* contains all the event occurrences that have arisen since the last time r was executed and *synthesis* specifies the standard *net-effect*. A possible specification of *compute_interval* could be:

$$compute\_interval = \{< e, args, ts > \in EH \,|\, \forall < r', r'\_id, begin\_rule, ts' > \in TH$$
$$(r = r' \text{ and } command = begin\_action) \Rightarrow ts > ts'\}$$

What tasks to activate?: function choose Function choose takes a set of inactive tasks and selects a set of tasks to activate. It may be specified by a logical formula over the task history. For example, the SQL triggers are executed in depth first search. Every time an event arises, the rules triggered by this event are executed. The specification of the function *choose* may be :

$$< r, r\_i, e\_i > \in \quad choose() \text{ iff } < r, r\_id, init, ts > \in \quad HT \text{ and}$$
$$\forall < r', r'\_id, any, ts' > \in TH, \ (ts' < ts) \text{ or}$$
$$(ts' = ts \text{ `and } (r = r' \text{ or } r \text{ has priority over r'}))$$

2.6 Synchronizer algorithm

Every time the synchronizer receives message e from task t, it uses function check_synchro to compute the associated synchronization point. If this point is a *null* point the synchronizer sends an *ack* command to t, else the procedure synchro_point implements the actions of the synchronizer.

```
On receive message e from t:
    let p = check_synchro();
    if p is not null
        then synchro_point(p, t, e);
        else send back ack to t
```

Fig. 4. Synchronization point computation

```
synchro_point algorithm
input: a synchronization point p, a task t and a message e
    case e is
        cond_eval: let v denote the result of the condition evaluation reported in e
            if v = true then send end_condition to t;
            else send abandon to t;
        signal_event: let v denote the event signalled in the message;
            if v = end_action then send end_rule to t;
            else send interrupt to t;
    end case;
    if p is a processing point
        then for rt in trigger() do create_task(rt); end do
    end if
    let selectedSet = choose();
    for rs in selectedSet do
        case current state of rs is
            "triggered" : send begin_rule to rs;
            "evaluated": send begin_action to rs;
            "interrupted": send continue to rs;
        end case;
    end do
```

Fig. 5. Synchro-point algorithm

3 Active-design Toolkit

Our toolkit is based on a generic functional decomposition of an active monitor. Before describing the toolkit architecture we first present our functional view of an active monitor.

3.1 Functional decomposition of an Active Monitor

The functional organization of an Active Monitor is shown in Figure 6. It consists of a DBMS, an event manager, a task executor and an execution controller.

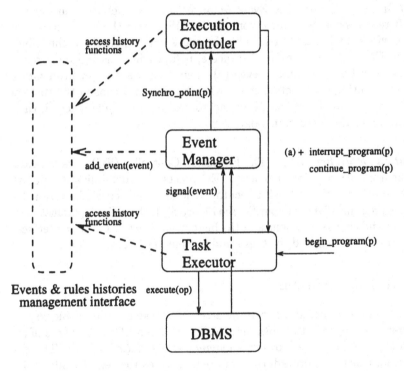

Events & rules histories management interface

$(a) =$ begin_rule(r), abandon(r), evaluated(r), begin_action(r), interrupt(r), continue(r), done(r)

⟶ procedure call — – –> call to the history mangement interface

Fig. 6. Functional decomposition of an active application

The DBMS: It executes the database operations occurring in the initial program and the rule condition and action programs. The DBMS may also provide a detection output interface which computes the event instances (if any) produced by the operations and signals them to the event manager.

The Task executor (TE): In particular, it enforces execution commands sent by the execution controller. For this purpose, it uses the DBMS to perform database operations such as queries, update operations and transactional commands. It provides to the execution controller an input interface which consists of the transition functions of the task state transition diagram (see Figures 2 and 3).

The Task Executor also provides a detection output interface. Indeed, it may detect some specific events during the execution of rules and programs that cannot be detected by the DBMS. It signals them to the Event Manager. For example it may signal the end of a condition evaluation and/or the end of an action execution.

The Event Manager (EM): The Event Manager is called each time an event is detected. It receives events coming from the DBMS and/or the TE. It follows a generic behavior that is parametrized by the add_event and check_synchro functions: When EM receives an event instance e, it first adds this instance to the history by calling the function add_event(e), then it checks if a synchronization point is reached, using the function check_synchro which may consult the History by using various access functions. If a synchronization point p is reached, then EM transmits p to the Execution Controller.

The Execution Controller (EC): The Execution Controller (EC) is called each time a synchronization point is reached. EC reacts to synchronization points by sending commands to the Task Executor. It follows the generic behavior described in the procedure Synchro_point() (see Figure 5). Its behavior is parametrized by the trigger and choose functions and the history management access interface. It may use several Is_triggered, synthesis and compute-interval functions.

3.2 The toolkit architecture

The Active-design toolkit consists in a set of reusable building blocks, or modules that are combined to implement the RE, EM and EC components of an active monitor. Each module provides a *dynamic* and a *static* interface. The *dynamic* interface consists in procedures that are invoked by the generic code of the active monitor components during the execution of the rules. The *static* interface consists in procedures that are called when new rules are defined. They generate code and/or static information that will be used during the execution. Figure 7 shows the dependencies between the modules: Each module uses the interfaces provided by the module(s) right bellow. Other components of our toolkit architecture (not shown in Figure 7) are libraries of module implementations. There is one library per module. The designer defines the execution model semantics by selecting one module implementation from each library. For example, the library associated with the *choose* module may provide implementations of various rule execution policies (depth-first, iterative with priority, $\cdots$). The toolkit is extensible by adding new implementations to the libraries. In the following, we briefly describe the interfaces of each module.

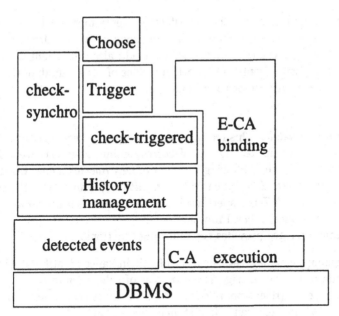

Fig. 7. Toolkit architecture

C-A execution module This module ensures the execution of the condition and action parts of rules. It implements coupling modes between condition and action. The static interface consists of two functions add_condition(rulename, CDesc) and add_action(rulename, Adesc) that respectively allow to define a rule condition and a rule action. The type of the input parameters Cdesc and Adesc may vary according to the module implementations that are available in the library. The dynamic interface consists in procedures that execute the condition and/or action parts of the rules.

detected events module: This block is responsible for the detection of events. Its implementation depends on the active capabilities of the underlying DBMS and the implementation of the C-A execution module. Indeed, an event can be detected by using triggers or by rewriting the code of the programs and/or rule action parts. The static interface consists of the new_event(D-E-D, S-E-D) procedure. The D-E-D parameter gives the description of the event that must be detected. The S-E-D parameter indicates the format in which the event must be transmitted to the history management module. There is no dynamic interface.

History management module: This module is responsible for building the event history. Its dynamic interface contains (i) the add_event(event) procedure that is used to store events in the history and, (ii)various history access functions. There is a huge variety of possible implementations. The simplest implementation stores the history in a simple sequential log of events and provides functions that allow to consult this log. More complicated implementations store events in delta relations and compute the net-effect of events incrementally. Such implementations enrich their interface with operations between deltas and functions that allow to select and consult deltas. We could also implement a module that constructs composite events. The static interface of such a module would consist in a composite event specification language.

Check_triggered module: This module has in charge to check if a rule is triggered. In which case, it computes the set of corresponding rule instances. The static interface consists in the following procedure: new_rule(rulename, EG, SYNT, Interval) The parameter EG indicates the execution granularity of the rule (tuple or set oriented), $SYNT$ is a specification of the synthesis function and *Intervall* specifies the compute_interval function.

The dynamic interface provides the following functions:

- Is_triggered(rulename) returns a set of rule instance identifiers. This set corresponds to the set of triggered instances of rule *rulename*.
- Triggering_event(rulename, rule-instance-id) returns the value of the event associated to the triggered rule instance *rule-instance-id*.

E-C-A binding module: This module is responsible for the execution of rule instances. The static interface consists in the procedure new_rule(rulename, EP, CM). EP indicates if and how the triggering event has to be passed as input parameter to condition and/or action of the rule. CM indicates the transactional coupling mode. Several implementations of transactional coupling modes are feasible depending on the capabilities of the underlying DBMS.

The dynamic interface provides the following procedures:

1. begin_rule(rulename, r) where r is a rule instance identifier. This procedure prepares the condition evaluation context of the rule instance and starts its execution. Such context preparation may consist in creating a new process, initiating some variables and/or sending transactional commands to the DBMS (such as `start transaction` or `start sub-transaction`[4]).
2. end_condition((rulename, r) ends the condition evaluation context and prepares the action execution context. For example, it may enforce parameter passing between condition and action and/or execute transactional commands.
3. begin_action(rulename, r) starts the execution of the rule action. It may also first execute some transactional commands depending on transactional coupling modes.
4. interrupt(rulename, r) stops the execution of r action.
5. continue (rulename, r) continues the execution of r action.
6. abandon(rulename, r) and end_rule(rulename, r) close the execution context of r. For example, they may send some transactional commands depending on the transactional coupling modes.

---

[4] If the targeted system provides the nested transactions model

Let us note that some interface functions may be not provided by some E-C-A binding modules implementations. For example, the *end_condition* and *begin_action* functions are not provided by implementations that only ensure the immediate C-A coupling mode.

Check-synchro module : This module has in charge to check if there is a synchronization point. The static interface consists in the new_synchropoint(ST,SDesc) procedure where ST indicates if the synchronization point is a rule processing or a rule scheduling point. The parameter $SDesc$ describes the function that has to be checked on the history in order to detect a synchronization point. The dynamic interface consists in the checksynchro() function that returns a synchropoint or the value NULL if no synchropoint is detected. the synchropoint.

Trigger module : The trigger module computes a set of triggered rule instances. Various implementations are possible. The usual implementation computes all the triggered rule instances. Another implementation may select specific rule instances. The static interface consists in the add_rule(rulename, AUX) function where AUX is auxilliary informations that are used to select rule instances (e.g., order priority). The definition of the AUX parameter may vary according to the module implementations. The dynamic interface is the trigger() function that returns a set of rule instances identifiers.

Choose module : The choose module computes a set of rule instances to be executed. Various implementations are possible according to the rule execution policies. The static interface consists in the add_rule(rulename, AUX) function where AUX is auxilliary informations that is used to select rule instances. The definition of the AUX parameter may vary according to the module implementations. For example, if the module implementation enforces an iterative execution with priority, the AUX information provides the priority of the rule. The dynamic interface is the choose() function that returns a set of rule instances identifiers.

4   Conclusion and future work

This paper has addressed the problem of engineering active applications by using a generic toolkit. The idea is to provide a set of basic functions which can be used to implement any of the semantic parameters which characterize a rule execution model. We have defined these functions and demonstrated their capability to implement known execution models. The main features of the toolkit based on these basic building blocks are (i) its *genericity* which allows to implement any rule execution model, (ii) its *flexibility* which allows its adaptation to specific application requirements, and (iii) its *extensibility* which allows addition of hight level components to facilitate application development.

Future work wil concern an effective implementation of the toolkit libraries and the organization of these libraries. We also envision the definition of some hight level components which allow the toolkit to be inserted in the context of middleware tools which facilitate rapid development.

To validate the Active-Design toolkit, we envision to use it for developping update propagation techniques within a datawarehouse architecture.

References

[Cou96]   T. Coupaye. *Un Modèle d'exécution paramétrique pour base de données active*. Ph.d. thesis, Université Joseph Fourier - Grenoble 1, 1996.

[DGG95]   K. R. Dittrich, S. Gatziu, and A. Geppert. The Active Databse Management System Manifesto : A Rulebase of ADBMS Features. In *Proc. 2-th International Workshop on Rules in Database Systems, RIDS'95*, volume 985, Athens, Greece, 1995. Lecture in Computer Science, Springer-Verlag.

[FT95]   P. Fraternali and L. Tanca. A Structured Approach for the Definition of the Semantics of Active Databases. *ACM Transactions On Database Systems*, December 1995.

[KDS97]   A. Kotz-Dittrich and E. Simon. Active database systems: Expectations, experiences, and beyond. In N. Paton and O. Diaz, editors, *Active Rules in Databases*. Springer Verlag, 1997.

[MFLS96] M. Matulovic, F. Fabret, F. Llirbat, and E. Simon. Un Système de Règles à la Sémantique Paramétrable. In *BDA'96*, pages 291–311. INRIA, 1996. Proc. 12-emes Journées Bases de Données Avancées, Geneve.

[WC96]   J. Widom and S. Ceri. *Active Database Systems: Triggers and Rules for Advanced Database Processing*. Morgan-Kaufmann, San Francisco, California, 1996.

Author Index

Lecture Notes in Computer Science

For information about Vols. 1–1229

please contact your bookseller or Springer-Verlag